Where on Earth

Where on Earth

**A Guide to Specialty Nurseries
and Other Resources
for California Gardeners**

Barbara Stevens
Nancy Conner

Heyday Books
Berkeley, California

Orders, inquiries, and correspondence should be addressed to Heyday Books, P. O. Box 9145, Berkeley, CA 94709. (510) 549-3564; Fax (510) 549-1889. heyday@heydaybooks.com

Library of Congress Cataloging-in-Publication Data:

Stevens, Barbara.
  Where on earth : a guide to specialty nurseries and other resources for California gardeners / Barbara Stevens, Nancy Conner.
  — 4th ed.
      p.   cm.
  Includes indexes.
  ISBN 1-890771-17-1 (paperback)
  1. Nurseries (Horticulture)—California—Directories.
  2. Ornamental plant industry—California—Directories.
  3. Gardens—California—Directories. 4. Horticulture—California—Directories.
  I. Conner, Nancy. II. Title.
  SB118.487.C2S74   1999
  635'.025'794—dc21   98-45913
                                                  CIP

Editing, interior design, and production by Wendy Low
Editing and production, 4th edition, by Simone Scott
Cover design by Tracy Dean, Design Site, Berkeley
Printing by Publishers Press, Salt Lake City

Printed in the United States of America

10 9 8 7 6 5 4 3 2 1

CONTENTS

INTRODUCTION

This book is a guide to California's horticultural resources—to the growers, the plant societies, the splendid public gardens and arboreta, the state-supported schools and public service organizations, and all the fascinating and curious individuals who take part in these endeavors. This book is as much about people as it is about plants.

Where on Earth features specialty growers—small and large—whose passion for plants is infectious. Their discoveries stretch the concept of California-grown and make gardening here a lot more interesting. Some growers have decided to commit their life's work to the propagation of geraniums. Some to the collection of every known species of Acacia. Some to growing revegetation material for such specific areas as a storm-torn coast in Santa Cruz County. We think the people who make these decisions are worth knowing. They have freed California's horticulture from its lingering homage to culturally impossible East Coast gardening. They have combed the world to discover what works best here.

"Here," of course, covers a wide range of climatic considerations. The *Sunset Western Garden Book* awards California with 24 separate climate zones. The good news is that in each area plant specialists are dedicated to developing appropriate plant material by propagating successful native plants and tracking down plants from similar climates throughout the world.

Because this book is about growers, we do not list garden centers unless they grow at least half of what they sell. Because this book is intended to be used by the gardening public as well as by landscape professionals, we include both wholesale and retail growers, though not the giant growers who sell entirely to retail nurseries. Within these bounds, we tried to be as inclusive as possible and hope that this does not create problems. Many wholesale operations welcome plant connoisseurs, but are not set up to provide retail services. Some are in residential areas which prohibit retail business. Readers are asked not to visit inappropriate locations.

This book is divided into geographical regions to help you find plants suited to your area and to help you plan a horticulturally enlightening driving trip throughout California. Sized to fit in your pocket or glove compartment, *Where on Earth* makes driving in California a low-speed adventure.

Some caveats. We have visited almost all of the nurseries listed. All have been recommended to us by respected professional horticulturists, but there are no guarantees that you will find each entry enchanting. Also, though accurate as of November 1998, the factual information of any listing is subject to change; it is always best to call before visiting.

Our profits from the sale of this book directly benefit Friends of Recreation and Parks and their efforts to restore The Conservation of Flowers and revitalize neighborhood parks in San Francisco. For more information about how you can help, call (415) 750-5105.

You remain our greatest resource for future editions of *Where on Earth*. Let us know about the horticultural treasures in your area. Contact us by mail: 2698 Vallejo Street, San Francisco 94123, fax: (415) 346-0510, or e-mail: conner5@earthlink.net.

Barbara Stevens
Nancy Conner

Where on Earth

North Coast

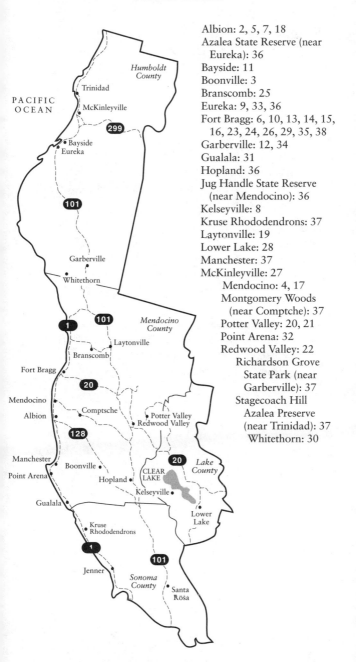

Albion: 2, 5, 7, 18
Azalea State Reserve (near Eureka): 36
Bayside: 11
Boonville: 3
Branscomb: 25
Eureka: 9, 33, 36
Fort Bragg: 6, 10, 13, 14, 15, 16, 23, 24, 26, 29, 35, 38
Garberville: 12, 34
Gualala: 31
Hopland: 36
Jug Handle State Reserve (near Mendocino): 36
Kelseyville: 8
Kruse Rhododendrons: 37
Laytonville: 19
Lower Lake: 28
Manchester: 37
McKinleyville: 27
Mendocino: 4, 17
Montgomery Woods (near Comptche): 37
Potter Valley: 20, 21
Point Arena: 32
Redwood Valley: 22
Richardson Grove State Park (near Garberville): 37
Stagecoach Hill Azalea Preserve (near Trinidad): 37
Whitethorn: 30

Albion Ridge Nursery
30901 Albion Ridge Road, Albion 95410
(707) 937-1835
Greg Ross
Retail and Wholesale

Plant specialties: Bonsai starters, California native plants suited to coastal region, dwarf conifers, deer-resistant plants, Mediterranean plants, perennials, roses (50 varieties of old ramblers), Rhododendron species (and selected connoisseur hybrids), Acer (40 kinds of maples).

History/description: Greg Ross is a guy who grew up in the farmland of Orange County raising Toggenburg goats while his father bred orchids in a nearby greenhouse—perfect preparation for a life on the land. After a stint as an English teacher, he started a landscape business in 1981 and quickly saw the need to supply essential plants for his projects. Today, the 1-acre nursery and its thematic display gardens (deer-resistant, alpine rockery, among others) capture his primary attention.

How to get there: From Highway 1, go east on Albion Ridge Road in Albion for 3 miles.

General information: Open Saturday and Sunday, 9:00 am–4:00 pm, or by appointment. Plant list and site-specific consultations are available.

Anderson Valley Nursery

18151 Mountain View Road, Boonville 95415
(707) 895-3853, fax (707) 895-2850
Kenneth R. Montgomery, M.S.
Retail and Wholesale

Plant specialties: California native plants (especially of the North Coast) and Mediterranean plants, including Cistus (over 40 species and hybrids), rosemary, Lavandula, Helianthemum. Also, many herbs and drought-tolerant plants.

History/description: In 1978 Ken Montgomery gave up a career in research and education, figuring it was time to practice what he had been teaching. The result was a splendid 4-acre farm in the beauty and tranquility of Mendocino County. This self-described "micro-business" aims to grow the highest quality plant material in an environmentally sound, low-tech way. It obviously works. Over the years Ken has introduced seven varieties of Cistus, Lavandula 'Lisa Marie', and native selections including Mimulus aurantiacus 'Dark Gulch'. The nursery and nearby Andersen Valley High School recently teamed up to form Mendocino Natives Nursery, a nonprofit business employing students to collect and grow site-specific native plants for local watershed restoration projects.

How to get there: From Highway 101 in Cloverdale (30 miles north of Santa Rosa), take Highway 128 through the mountains about 30 miles northwest to Boonville. Continue through Boonville and make a left turn onto Mountain View Road. Nursery is on the left.

General information: Open for retail Saturday and Sunday, 10:00 am–4:00 pm and for wholesale by appointment. Wholesale orders shipped from the Bay Area to Eureka and from the Central Valley to the Coast.

Big River Nursery
at the Stanford Inn by the Sea
P. O. Box 487, Mendocino 95460
(707) 937-5026, fax (707) 937-0305
Joan and Jeff Stanford; Dana Williams, manager
Retail and Wholesale

Plant specialties: Ornamental and edible herbs,
old-fashioned and non-hybridized perennials suited
to coastal climates, deer-resistant plants, especially
Digitalis, Verbascum, Campanula.

History/description: This certified organic nursery
is the result of much searching for hard-to-come-by,
dependable, and deer-resistant plants. Big River has
reintroduced several old-fashioned plants having
discovered that these really do work best. The
nursery covers an acre, part of a 10-acre garden site
which includes a market garden brimming with
vegetables and herbs. The produce is not for sale but
individual plants and seeds are. The nursery offers
workshops in pruning fruit trees, care of coastal
native plants, and natural healing remedies.

How to get there: The nursery is located 1/4 mile
south of Mendocino where the Comptche-Ukiah
Road joins Highway 1.

General information: Open from April through
November every day, 10:00 am–4:00 pm, by
appointment only. A plant list is available for SASE.
Workshops available.

Cottage Farm Nursery

30300 Navarro Ridge Road, Albion 95410
P. O. Box 27, Albion 95410 (mailing address)
(707) 937-1337
Laurie Hartzie
Retail and Wholesale

Plant specialties: Rhododendron hybrids, varieties, and species.

History/description: Cottage Farm Nursery comes from venerable lineage, dating back to the old Drucker's Nursery which flourished from the 1930s to 1960s. It was renamed Fee's and bought by the present owner's father in 1991. Taking early retirement, he was able to devote his full energies to raising rhododendrons, a hobby of his for 30 years. Cottage Farm's rhododendron collection got a big boost from their recent buy out of Noyo Hill Nursery. Now owned by his daughter, this 2-acre enterprise remains family run.

How to get there: Navarro Ridge Road is off Highway 1, 1-1/2 miles north of the intersection of Highway 1 and Highway 128. The nursery is 3-1/2 miles down Navarro Ridge Road.

General information: Open every day, February through October. Wholesale catalogue and plant list available for SASE. Wholesale deliveries possible.

Descanso Nurseries
20100 Hanson Road, Fort Bragg 95437
(707) 964-5397, fax (707) 964-3879
Robert Boddy
Wholesale

Plant specialties: Rhododendron, Pieris japonica
and P. forrestii (15 hybrids), heathers, Hydrangea
macrophylla (16 cultivars), Leucodendron, Daphne,
Sarcococca, Boronia, Viburnum (double). A host of
enticing shrubs.

History/description: Robert Boddy had the great
good fortune to grow up at Descanso Gardens in
Southern California, and the even better fortune of
being related to its founder. His father was a well-
known camellia grower who started Descanso
Nursery on the family property in 1946. The
nursery moved north to Fort Bragg when Los
Angeles County took over the estate in 1969. This
family's horticultural enthusiasm and knowledge
remains firmly intact through this generation and no
doubt for many more to come.

How to get there: Call ahead for directions.

General information: Not open to the public.
Open six days a week to landscape professionals, by
appointment only. Plant availability list. Deliveries
on orders over $250 throughout Northern California.

Digging Dog Nursery

P. O. Box 471, Albion 95410
(707) 937-1130, fax (707) 937-2480
Gary Ratway, Deborah Whigham
Retail, Mail Order, and limited Wholesale

Plant specialties: Top select perennials (especially late-summer and fall bloomers), shrubs, trees, ground covers, ornamental grasses, and deer-resistant and drought-tolerant plants. Significant collections of heaths and heathers (Erica, Calluna), Lavandula, Campanula, Aster, Cimicifuga, Geranium, Helleborus, Euphorbia, Kniphofia, Dierama, Rodgersia, Miscanthus, and Viburnum.

History/description: A founding member of Mendocino Coast Botanical Gardens, Gary Ratway acquired an interest in native and Mediterranean plants from his days as a landscape architecture student at UC Davis. Originally next door to the Botanical Gardens, the nursery moved to its present 1-acre location in 1988 and is credited with the introduction of Heuchera x brizoides 'Weston Pink' and Cistus 'John Catterson'. An on-site display garden features strong garden performers which offer year-round interest. Annually they propagate and grow about 20,000 lavender plants for people interested in planting fields of lavender for commercial production. Their first field at Matanzas Creek Winery in Santa Rosa is well worth a visit.

How to get there: Directions given when appointment is made.

General information: Open by appointment only, Tuesday through Saturday, 9:30 am–4:00 pm. Though business is primarily mail order, retail customers may visit with appointment. Catalogue available for $3.50. Bay Area deliveries occasionally on retail orders over $250. Garden talks for groups by arrangement. Design services available.

Evergreen Gardenworks

P. O. Box 537, Kelseyville 95451
e-mail: bonsai@pacific.net
website: www.EvergreenGardenworks.com
Brent Walston, Susan Meier
Mail Order

Plant specialties: Bonsai, alpines, rock garden
plants, dwarf conifers, trees, and shrubs mostly for
bonsai use, including collections of Acer, Carpinus,
Cedrus, Chaenomeles, Chamaecyparis, Cotoneaster,
Cryptomeria, Malus, Ulmus. Introductions by
Evergreen include Acer buergeranum 'Evergreen's
Rough Bark', Chaenomeles 'Not Minerva' and
'Contorted Salmon Pink'.

History/description: This nursery started in 1987
to provide plants for Brent Walston's landscape
maintenance, construction, and design business.
Gradually, growing plants suitable for bonsai
became the main thrust of their business. In 1989,
the nursery moved to its present 10-acre location in
Lake County. Future plans include a retail store, but
for now the nursery is mail order only. There are
also plans for creating a small botanical garden
showcasing plant material appropriate for hot, dry
inland California valleys. Brent does all the propagating and growing, occasionally offers classes in
bonsai design, and regularly contributes articles to
the Internet Bonsai Club. Susie hopes to expand the
rock garden and Mediterranean plant business for
the new store. Their website is full of good information about horticulture and growing bonsai.

How to get there: The nursery is scheduled to open
in 2001.

General information: On-line catalogue and
ordering at website. Print catalogue $2. Questions
answered by e-mail. Year-round shipping to the
continental US. Phone orders difficult at present.

Freshwater Farms

5851 Myrtle Avenue, Eureka 95503
(707) 444-8261, (800) 200-8969, fax (707) 442-2490
e-mail: r.storre@worldnet.att.net
website: www.FreshwaterFarms.com
Rick Storre
Retail, Wholesale, Mail Order

Plant specialties: Site-specific wetland and riparian plants. California native plants and seeds, including rushes, sedges, trillium, ferns, riparian trees—Pacific dogwood, western azalea, bigleaf maple, redwood.

History/description: Rick Storre's devotion to native plants stems from his admiration for their toughness and suitability, especially after the big freeze in the mid-1980s. His brother alerted him to the growing demand for wetland plants as communities responded to environmental interest and federal regulations about water quality. Sitting on 74 acres of tidal land in Humboldt Bay, he found himself in a perfect place to grow wetland natives. All propagation is done by seed to avoid destroying old habitats and to maintain genetic diversity. Seed is collected by an army of 200 well-trained collectors, from Boy Scout troops to engineers on holiday. The nursery opened in 1990 in a group of rustic barns and sheds of a former a Class A dairy. He plans to establish a wetland education center here as a venue for ecotourists and the mildly curious.

How to get there: From Highway 101 between Eureka and Arcata, take the Indianola Road cutoff up and over a hill. Go right on Myrtle Avenue for 1.8 miles. The nursery is on the south bank of Freshwater Creek.

General information: Open Monday through Friday, 9:00 am–5:00 pm and on Saturday, 10:00 am–5:00 pm. Catalogue, seed list, and plant list available. Orders by mail, fax, or e-mail.

Fuchsiarama

23201 North Highway One, Fort Bragg 95437
(707) 964-0429, fax same
Howard Berry
Retail

Plant specialties: Fuchsias (40 species, 600 varieties). All plants rated for tolerance to hot, cold, and
dry conditions. Other nursery stock is variable.

History/description: This retired meteorologist
bought his wife one fuchsia plant in 1980 and
became an overnight hobbyist. He has transferred
his years of expertise as a weatherman to the
scientific monitoring of the hardiness of fuchsia
varieties. He bought a struggling fuchsia business in
1985 and has given it a new life—to say nothing of his
own. He oversees a 10,000-square-foot greenhouse
profusely planted with rare fuchsias and a waterfall
in a 5-acre picnic ground open to the public. The
gift shop is unique to say the least, selling anything
emblazoned with a fuchsia—medieval armor,
dragons, gargoyles, and a collection of lighthouses.
The whole enterprise is staffed by self-described
friendly, slightly unbalanced, wonderful people.

How to get there: The nursery is located 2 miles
north of Fort Bragg on Highway 1.

General information: Open every day including
holidays. Winter hours: 9:00 am–5:00 pm. Summer
hours: 9:00 am–6:00 pm. Plant demonstrations on-
site in the nursery's education booth.

Glenmar Heather Nursery, Inc.

P. O. Box 479, Bayside 95524-0479 (mailing address)
(707) 268-5560, fax (707) 822-8247
e-mail: glenmar@humboldt1.com
Glennda Couch-Carlberg and Carl Carlberg, Maria and
Tom Krenek
Retail and Wholesale

Plant specialties: Heaths and heathers (Calluna,
Daboecia, Erica primarily). Over 400 varieties with
additions all the time.

History/description: Inspired by the Jim and Bev
Thompson Garden in Manchester, and aided and
abetted by the Heather Enthusiasts of the Redwood
Empire (the local chapter of the North American
Heather Society), the Carlbergs and Kreneks banded
together to start a nursery at the Krenek home.
Named after both wives and sounding suitably
Scottish, the nursery is sited next to a nearly 100-
year-old redwood barn (a remnant of the dairy farm
built there a couple of generations past) with
redwoods on the fringe and the ocean just west.
Heathers thrive here with the occasional mist,
coastal temperatures, and bountiful rain.

How to get there: Call for directions. Just one mile
off Highway 101 north of Eureka.

General information: Open by appointment only.
Glenmar also sells plants at the Arcata Farmers'
Market Saturday mornings from mid-April to mid-
November. Display garden in progress. Plant list
available after March 1999. Call for information
about membership in the North American Heather
Society and its affiliated chapters.

Greenmantle Nursery
3010 Ettersburg Road, Garberville 95542
(707) 986-7504
Marissa and Ram Fishman
Retail and Mail Order

Plant specialties: Over 300 old and rare roses, species Iris collection, and many other unusual landscape plants. Fruit trees, including 130 varieties of apples, featuring pink-fleshed apples and sweet-meat crabapples bred by Albert Etter (1872–1950).

History/description: Homesteaded in 1895, Ettersburg was Albert Etter's private experiment station, renowned for the apple, strawberry, and chestnut varieties he developed here. The local apple industry long ago fell victim to codling moth and competition from eastern Washington. In the 1970s the area was re-inhabited by a new generation of homesteaders whose interest in the history of the area sparked a renaissance in fruit production. The Fishmans are involved in the task of retrieving the best of the Etter fruit varieties. In addition, Marissa has assembled a large collection of rose varieties and species in her hillside garden. Primarily a catalogue business since 1983, this garden nursery can accommodate a limited number of visitors when time and bloom are felicitous (late May to early June), by appointment only.

How to get there: Off the beaten track and normally closed to the public. Call well in advance for appointment and directions.

General information: Open by appointment only. Bare-root shipping season from January into April. Container stock available at Benbow Summer Arts Festival in June. Catalogue of fruit trees is $4 pre-paid. Separate rose list available for business-size SASE.

Heartwood Nursery

525 South Franklin, Fort Bragg 95437
(707) 964-3555
Dan Charvet, Patty Leahy
Retail

Plant specialties: Perennials, hardy geraniums, heathers, ornamental grasses, alstroemerias, phormiums, a fine collection of cryptomeria and sequoia varieties, camellia species, Camellia reticulata and non-retic hybrids, recently introducing plants resulting from 25 years of camellia hybridizing. Also, trees, shrubs, and vines.

History/description: After college both partners worked at Berkeley Horticultural Nursery in Berkeley, gaining familiarity with Berkeley Hort's broad selection of plant material. They bought an existing nursery business in 1983 and have been expanding it ever since, introducing many unique plants to fit the needs and interests of the community. All propagation is done on a 2-1/2-acre growing ground, which will open to the public in the Spring of 1999.

How to get there: From Highway 101 north in Fort Bragg, go right on Chestnut Street. After a block, go right on Franklin Street.

General information: Open Monday through Saturday, 10:00 am–5:00 pm and March through August, also open Sunday, noon–4:00 pm.

Heritage Roses of Tanglewood Farms
16831 Mitchell Creek Drive, Fort Bragg 95437
(707) 964-3748
Joyce Demits
Retail and Mail Order

Plant specialties: Well over 150 varieties of antique roses, grown on their own rootstock. The nursery maintains an index of roses which are virus-free for six years. All field grown, sold two to three years old. Specializing in Victorian ramblers and the re-establishment of "lost" roses. Rosa noisette, R. gallica, R. damascena, and hybrid China roses.

History/description: Joyce Demits grew roses as a hobby, encouraged by the Heritage Rose Group. She went into business with her sister in 1981 in a collaborative venture combining both of their personal collections. Now each has her own nursery. Joyce has become increasingly interested in the romance and history of old roses. This indefatigable rosarian tends an informal garden of antique roses and perennials on her 1-1/2-acre site, as well as all the nursery operations. Primarily a mail-order business, the nursery does some selling on-site. Joyce recommends you take the walking tour of Mendocino during rose season and visit the Mendocino Coast Botanical Garden and the Jughandle Creek State Reserve.

How to get there: Be sure to call first. From Highway 1, 1/4 mile north of the Botanical Garden, go right on Simpson Lane. Right on Mitchell Creek after 2.2 miles. They are the fourth house on the left. Pull rings of deer gate towards you.

General information: Open by appointment only. Plant list available for $1. Mail orders for bare-root stock shipped January through March. Tours of the garden nursery can be arranged.

Hortus Botanicus
20103 Hanson Road, Fort Bragg 95437
(707) 964-4786, fax (707) 962-0616
Retail, Mail Order, and limited Wholesale

Plant specialties: Annuals, perennials, succulents, roses (including a wide selection of Austin's), orchids, clematis, trees, shrubs, and tuberous begonias in season.

History/description: Another plantsman with solid horticultural roots, Robert Goleman started collecting orchids and unusual plants as a child, inspired by his nursery-owning great-aunt and -uncle. He had plenty of room for his early collections, growing up on historic Bolden's dairy farm in what is now downtown Fort Bragg. He worked for many years at an orchid nursery before opening his own in 1995. Several test gardens enable customers to see mature plants in a landscape setting. In the evenings, he sings and performs magic with a touring show.

How to get there: From Highway 1, go east on Highway 20 for 1.7 miles. Go left (north) at Benson Lane. It curves to the left. Take a right at Hanson Road. Hortus Botanicus is opposite Descanso Nursery.

General information: Open Thursday through Monday, 10:00 am–5:00 pm. Robert Goleman hosts an annual open house on Mother's Day weekend, arranges orchid workshops, and will make arrangements of cut flowers in customer-provided containers. A plant list of their rose and clematis offerings is available in the spring. Send $1 for catalogue.

The Iris Gallery
33450 Little Valley Road, Fort Bragg 95437
(707) 964-3907, fax same
e-mail: irishud@mcn.org
Jay and Terri Hudson
Retail, Wholesale, and Mail Order

Plant specialties: Iris—several hundred varieties of
bearded iris, Siberian, Spuria, Japanese, Species and
Pacific Coast hybrids.

History/description: When Jay Hudson retired in
the mid-1980s, the Hudsons started gardening with
a vengeance. They began to collect irises in 1988
from around the world and acquired the consider-
able Pacific Coast and species Iris collection of Colin
Rigby's Portable Acres in Penngrove. The Hudsons
are very active with the American Iris Society, Jay
being the current President of the Society of Pacific
Coast Iris. They have a large collection of water iris
for pond enthusiasts.

How to get there: Little Valley Road is 5 miles
north of Fort Bragg on Highway 1. Traveling north,
go right on Little Valley Road. The nursery is 1/2
mile on the left.

General information: Open every day, except
Tuesday, during the bloom season of tall bearded
iris, usually May 1 to June 15, 10:00 am–6:00 pm,
or by appointment. Catalogue available for $2.

Mendocino Maples

41569 Little Lake Road, Mendocino 95460
(707) 937-2534
Robert Jamgochian and family
Retail and Wholesale

Plant specialties: Maples—35 Acer species, 110 cultivars of those species, including 80 varieties of Acer palmatum.

History/description: Robert Jamgochian was introduced to Japanese maples by his father-in-law's collection, but it was his fascination with experimentation as a biology teacher that made a passing fancy an enduring fixation. He continues to collect and test maple species and varieties that prosper along the North Coast. With seed from the International Maple Society, this zealous scientist grows and grafts an ever-increasing supply of interesting maples. The half-acre nursery features a small koi pond surrounded by a lovely tableau of maples.

How to get there: From Highway 1 in Mendocino, go right (east) at the stoplight onto Little Lake Road. Continue for 3-1/2 miles.

General information: Open by appointment only. Plant list available for SASE. Owner will custom-propagate any maple in his collection.

Moon River Nursery

32033 Middle Ridge Road, Albion 95410
(707) 937-1314, fax (707) 937-1340
Jackie Clark
Wholesale, but public welcome

Plant specialties: Perennials (Anemone, Campanula, hardy Geranium, Helleborus, Penstemon, Salvia), Mediterranean plants (Lavandula, rosemary), Euphorbia, vines, and ground covers. Shade, deer-resistant, and scented plants.

History/description: Established in 1988 by Sharon Hansen and Tom Wodetzky, Moon River quickly became known for its unusual and climate-appropriate plants. In 1997 they sold it to Jackie Clark, a long-time employee, who has made the nursery business a family affair. Son Jackson, a horticulture student at Mendocino College, and daughter Sky are there full-time, and two other children are also involved. Moon River mostly wholesales perennials to Northern California retail nurseries like Smith & Hawken, Berkeley Hort, and Filoli. The nursery staff encourages visitors to its 1-acre-plus site in the coastal redwoods. Albion is becoming a nursery mecca with several other notable plant purveyors in the area.

How to get there: Call for directions.

General information: Open Monday through Friday, 9:00 am–4:00 pm, and always by appointment. Please call before coming. Plant list is available. Deliveries from Bay Area up North Coast to McKinleyville on minimum orders of $250.

Mountain Maples

54561 Registered Guest Road, Laytonville 95454
P. O. Box 1329, Laytonville 95454 (mailing address)
(707) 984-6522, fax (707) 984-7433
e-mail: mtmaple@mcn.org
website: www.mountainmaples.com
Don and Nancy Fiers
Retail and Mail Order

Plant specialties: Japanese maples (one-, two-,
three-year-old, bench-grafted Acer palmatum for
bonsai and for landscape use; more than 200
cultivars). Twelve other Acer species. Fagus sylvatica
(European beech—25 cultivars).

History/description: The Fiers live on a 4,000-foot
ridge top in northern Mendocino County, with
distant views of the ocean 20 miles away over
upland meadows of wildflowers. Quite naturally,
they wanted to work at home. Under the aegis of
J. D. Vertrees, author of a well-known book on the
genus Acer, they started a nursery specializing in
Japanese maples, all propagated and grown on the
property. They now have eight large shade houses,
thousands of trees, and rock and shade gardens.
They recommend a visit to Richardson Grove State
Park and the Nature Conservancy walk on
Branscomb Road toward the coast from Laytonville.

How to get there: From Highway 101 travel 10
miles north of Laytonville. Go right on Spy Rock
Road for 7-1/2 miles to Registered Guest Road, a left-
hand fork. The nursery is in 1/2 mile, on the right.

General information: Open by appointment only.
Catalogue is available for $2. Mail orders sent
during dormant season (preferably) by UPS Second
Day delivery. Workshops offered. Nursery tours may
be arranged.

Rare Conifer Nursery
P. O. Box 100, Dept. H, Potter Valley 95469
(707) 463-1245
John Mayginnes
Retail, Wholesale, and Mail Order

Plant specialties: Rare, endangered, and threatened
conifer species, including Larix, Abies, Picea.
Ungrafted whenever possible. Seeds and seedlings to
30-inch boxes.

History/description: Resourceful businessman John
Mayginnes has combined his love of conifers with
an investment banking career on and off Wall Street.
Relocating to Ukiah in 1972 to start a chemical
company, he bought a piece of land in the nearby,
remote mountainous area near the Mendocino
National Forest and founded the nursery. Since 1989
he has been hard at work developing an 80-acre
arboretum of conifer species, called Garden of
Kirpal (meaning "compassion" in Hindi). He is also
founder and director of the Rare Conifer Foundation, a nonprofit, global seed bank, dedicated to
protecting conifers from extinction in their native
habitats. Funds raised help defray the cost of
worldwide, plant-collecting expeditions.

How to get there: Directions given when appointment is made.

General information: Open by appointment only.
Be patient. He is not always home and may be on
expedition in search of new seeds. Catalogue and seed
list available. Plants and seeds may be mail ordered.

Red Tail Farms

Potter Valley 95469
(707) 743-2734, fax (707) 743-2735
Tom and Alison Gervase
Wholesale

Plant specialties: California native plants for coastal and foothill regions, perennials, deer-resistant plants, drought-tolerant plants, vines.

History/description: Tom Gervase worked as a grower at Boething Nurseries in the Bay Area where he met his wife, who was in horticultural sales. Just the right combination to start their own business, which they did in 1989.

How to get there: Call for directions.

General information: Open to landscape professionals only, by appointment, Monday through Saturday. Landscapers may bring their clients. Availability list. Will drop-ship to nurseries and landscapers.

Redwood Valley Ground Cover Nursery

8060 Uva Drive, Redwood Valley 95470
(707) 485-5918
Harold Frisch
Wholesale

Plant specialties: Daphne—D. x burkwoodii 'Carol Mackie', D. odora (three varieties), D. caucasica, D. cneorum, D. collina, D. genkwa, D. giraldii, D. retusa, D. tangutica.

History/description: Harold Frisch never ever intended to be bored in retirement. He was fully prepared for life as a nurseryman after his career in teaching. He was raised on a farm, had taken courses in greenhouse methods, and knew lots about plant physiology having taught physical sciences for years. The small, backyard nursery did start out as an emporium for ground covers, hence its name, but Harold's interests have changed though the name has stuck.

How to get there: Call for directions.

General information: Open to wholesale customers only, by appointment. Plant list is available for SASE. Deliveries to nurseries only.

Regine's Fuchsia Gardens and The Orchid Bench

32531 Rhoda Lane, Fort Bragg 95437
(707) 964-0183
e-mail: paphlady@aol.com
Regine and Bruce Plows
Retail and Mail Order

Plant specialties: Fuchsias and orchids. Fuchsias include species, unusual cultivars and gall mite resistant varieties, e.g. F. excorticata and F. procumbens native to New Zealand, the new Dutch "Aubergine" hybrids, and 'Red Fanling', a smaller, mite-proof version of 'Fanfare'. The Orchid Bench offers seedlings, mericlones, and blooming orchids, with emphasis on species and primary hybrids of the genus Paphiopedilum.

History/description: These two orchid hobbyists left the Los Angeles area in 1980 for Fort Bragg. Well-known fuchsia hybridizer Annabelle Stubbs' nursery and home had just gone on the market. They fell in love with it and bought it, which explains this combination of plant specialties. This small nursery and display garden stresses quality over quantity. Plan also to visit the Ecological Staircase at the Pygmy Forest in Jug Handle State Reserve.

How to get there: From Highway 1 south of Fort Bragg, go east on Simpson Lane, south on George's Lane and west on Rhoda Lane.

General information: Open weekends from 10:00 am–5:00 pm. In winter and early spring it is best to call ahead. Weekday appointments are available. Their Paphiopedilum mail order listing is available by mail or e-mail.

Richards Landscaping and Gardening

32101 Highway 20, Fort Bragg 95437
(707) 964-0710 (office), (707) 964-2485 (nursery)
Charles Richards
Retail and Wholesale

Plant specialties: Rhododendrons, exclusively
Exbury seedlings, varieties, and some named
cultivars, plus R. occidentale in a wide variety of
forms, including some of the famous Mossman
azalea hybrids.

History/description: Bud Richards was a timber
faller for 36 years. He fell in love with the native
rhododendrons (R. occidentale and R. macrophyllum) he encountered in the forest. He began
hybridizing rhododendrons and azaleas as a hobby
in 1952 and is still at it, breeding for leaf and color
forms and fragrance. The family nursery, located at
Bud's house, has been run by son Charles since 1968
and will custom-grow for clients. The Richards
recommend you visit the Stagecoach Hill Azalea
Reserve near McKinleyville in Humboldt County to
get a good whiff of the powerful fragrance of R.
occidentale in bloom, March through May.

How to get there: The nursery is on Highway 20,
which connects Highway 1 with Highway 101
between Fort Bragg and Willits.

General information: Open April 1 through
June 1, every day, 8:00 am–5:00 pm.

Ros-Equus
40350 Wilderness Lodge Road, Branscomb 95417
(707) 984-6959
Virginia Hopper
Retail and Mail Order

Plant specialties: Antique and species roses—
gallicas, centifolias, damasks, bourbons, hybrid
perpetuals, teas, Chinas, and noisettes. All grown on
their own roots. Also deer-resistant perennials and
bulbs.

History/description: Virginia Hopper started
collecting roses from the many wonderful old
gardens in Mendocino and, with her sister, went into
a joint venture, selling old-fashioned roses (Heritage
Rose Gardens). Recently the sisters have separated
into individual ventures (see Heritage Roses of
Tanglewood Farms). The name Ros-Equus comes from
"rose horse", a four-legged frame used to support
climbing roses. It is also a tribute to the horses who
supply a great deal of primary soil amendment.
Ros-Equus has recently expanded its specialties and
now offers deer-resistant plants and bulbs.

How to get there: Directions given when appointment is made.

General information: Open by appointment only.
Call Tuesday or Thursday evenings to make arrangements for a free tour of the nursery and demonstration gardens. List of deer-resistant plants available for
large SASE. *Old Rose Catalogue* available for $1.

Sherwood Nursery
30480 Sherwood Road, Fort Bragg 95437
(707) 964-0800
Mike and Susan Peterson
Retail and Wholesale

Plant specialties: Rhododendrons—Ponticum
hybrids, Maddeniis, Yakushimanum crosses.

History/description: Trained as a forester, Mike
Peterson ran a Georgia Pacific tree nursery for 17
years. During this time he was a rhododendron
hobbyist and when the itch got to be "too much," he
opened this primarily wholesale business in 1984. He
is past-president of the local Rhododendron Society.

How to get there: Call for directions.

General information: Open by appointment only.
General public welcome by appointment only and
should not expect full retail services. Plant list
available.

Singing Tree Gardens
1975 Blake Road, McKinleyville 95519
(707) 839-8777
website: www.singtree.com
Ryan Scott, Don Wallace
Retail and Mail Order

Plant specialties: Rhododendrons—200 varieties
and many species, specializing in new hybrids and
fragrant varieties. Dwarf conifers.

History/description: Singing Tree Gardens was
launched in 1993, a direct result of the synergy
between Ryan's experience as a landscaper and Don's
rhododendron hobby. From the start their goal was
to educate clients about the galaxy of rhododendron
possibilities, as well as to make the best of these
available. They offer many of the newest hybrids,
including, R. 'Unique Marmalade' and 'Midnight
Mystique', and they introduced 'Patricia Marie" to
the trade. A display garden covers one fourth of the
nursery's 2 acres. They recommend you also visit
Prairie Creek Park, 30 miles north of Eureka.

How to get there: Fourteen miles north of Eureka
on Highway 101, take McKinleyville's Airport Road
exit. Stay to the right and take Airport Road to
Central Avenue. Take a right and then an immediate
left onto Norton Road. Norton bends to the left,
becoming Dow's Prairie Road. Blake Road is the
first road on the right. The Nursery is 1/4 mile on
the left.

General information: Open Wednesday through
Friday, 10:00 am–5:00 pm; Saturday, 9:00 am–5:00
pm. Open Sunday in April and May only, 11:00 am–
3:00 pm. Workshops and tours offered to plant
societies if booked well in advance. Local deliveries.

Specialty Oaks, Inc.
12552 Highway 29, Lower Lake 95457
(707) 995-2275, fax (707) 995-3566
John McCarthy
Wholesale

Plant specialties: California native oak trees—
Quercus agrifolia (coast live oak), Q. kelloggii
(black oak), Q. wislizenii (interior live oak),
Q. lobata (valley oak). Each year 2,500 choice
examples are selected from approximately 9,000
seedlings. Shaped and field grown for five years, the
result is a well-proportioned oak with a 1-1/2-inch
to 8-inch caliper.

History/description: Involved with a San Francisco
Peninsula tree-care service, John McCarthy noticed
the difficulty of replacing the many oaks falling
victim to age and suburban encroachment. Seizing
the opportunity, he switched to nursery production
in 1985. As an ISA Certified Arborist, he still gives
tree-care consultations.

How to get there: Call for directions.

General information: Open to wholesale customers, by appointment only. Plant list is available.
Deliveries to Northern California on orders of five
trees or more.

Summers Lane Nursery

20000 Summers Lane, Fort Bragg 95437
(707) 964-7526
James and Don Celeri
Retail and Wholesale

Plant specialties: Rhododendrons (100 varieties, species, hybrids), including R. macrophyllum and R. occidentale (California native rhododendrons) and R. 'Noyo Dream', their cross between R. yakushimanum and R. 'Mars'.

History/description: These brothers both worked in the lumber industry and realized there was need for a career change but did not want to forsake their relationship with plants. Local enthusiasm for rhododendrons and their suitability to the area convinced them to grow this plant. They have been in business since 1989 and recommend you schedule your visit to coincide with the rhododendron show held in the last week in April at the Dana Gray Elementary School in Fort Bragg. With 700 entries, it is the largest show on the West Coast.

How to get there: Call for directions.

General information: Open every day, by appointment only. Plant list available for SASE.

Tierra Madre

545 Shelter Cove Road, Whitethorn 95589
(707) 986-7215, fax (707) 986-7413
Greg Lattanza, Joe Whitney
Retail

Plant specialties: Perennials suited to Northern
California coastal areas and inland regions cold-
hardy to 15°, including Salvia (30 types) and
Penstemon (20), also deer- and drought-tolerant
plants. Organic vegetables. Over 30 types of medicinal herbs.

History/description: This pair of longtime organic
gardening enthusiasts moved to the Garberville area
in the early 1980s to work on a variety of landscape
projects. They linked up with Jayme Stark, previous
owner of this nursery, and helped her develop the
nursery's reputation as a purveyor of organically
grown goods. When the nursery came up for sale,
they were first in line to buy it.

How to get there: Take Highway 101 north past
Garberville to the Redway exit. Go left for 2 miles
to Redway. In Redway turn left onto Briceland-
Shelter Cove Road. Continue for 15 miles; nursery is
on Briceland-Shelter Cove Road, 1/2 mile past the
Whitethorn Rd. turnoff, in front of the lumberyard
at Whitethorn Construction Company. They recommend you also visit the BLM Visitor Center, 1/2 mile
further down the road, the King Range Conservation Area between Garberville and Shelter Cove and
Black Sands Beach.

General information: Open March through November, Tuesday through Saturday, 10:00 am–5:00 pm.

Ventrella Nursery/Gualala Nursery and Trading Co.

38870 South Highway One, Gualala 95445
P. O. Box 957, Gualala 95445 (mailing address)
(707) 884-4933, fax (707) 884-4023
Tony and Susan Ventrella
Retail and Wholesale

Plant specialties: California native plants suited to coastal mountain regions, and hardy perennials. Also, Australian and Mediterranean-climate plants.

History/description: Tony Ventrella's passion for plants was sparked by classes taken at Descanso Gardens when he was just a first grader. After college he worked in a nursery, then opened his own selling general landscape plants. He moved north in 1988, starting a larger nursery on 5 acres of raw land near Gualala. In full sight of the sea, the nursery gets its share of both 100° days and snow. Climate has definitely affected plant selection. The nursery now features California natives and hardy perennials and grows plants for several native plant nurseries in Southern California. Tony and Susan also have a new site on Highway 1 in Gualala. They offer the same plant selections and a gift shop.

How to get there: Directions will be given when appointment is made.

General information: Open Monday through Saturday, 10:00 am–5:00 pm, and Sunday, 9:30 am–4:00 pm. Plant list is available. Local deliveries possible; shipping can be arranged for large orders.

Watchwood Garden Design & Nursery

P. O. Box 21, Point Arena 95468
(707) 882-2415
Marilyn Bucher
Retail

Plant specialties: Orchids—Cattleyas (over 50 species and many hybrids), Oncidiums, Masdevallias, and many types of Pleurothallis. Rare plants. Bulbs.

History/description: Marilyn Bucher is a delightful, self-proclaimed plant addict who has been selling the labors of her love since 1982. She moved her huge collection of unusual plants to this coastal vacation property and opened for business, adding orchids to her collection in 1988. After the Big Freeze of 1990 destroyed her mother stock of subtropical landscape plants, she decided to devote her energies exclusively to orchids. Watchwood is located in the wild woods of the south Mendocino coast overlooking the sea.

How to get there: Call for directions.

General information: Open by appointment only, generally Wednesday and Saturday, 9:00 am–5:00 pm. Plants delivered from Point Arena to Bay Area. Orchid rentals. Future plans include a catalogue and mail orders.

Westgate Garden Nursery

751 Westgate Drive, Eureka 95503
(707) 442-1239
Catherine Weeks
Retail, Wholesale, and Mail Order

Plant specialties: Rhododendrons and azaleas
(species and hybrids), Chionanthus, Franklinia,
Halesia, Styrax, Stewartia, maples, Disanthus,
Drimys winteri, Desfontainea, Eucryphia,
Embothrium coccineum, Enkianthus 'Red Bells',
Exochorda, Fothergilla, Carpenteria californica
'Elizabeth', Cornus capitata, Michelia, Leucothoe,
Garrya, Kalmia, Viburnum. Introductions include
Rhododendron 'Teresa Elizabeth', R. 'Jeanette
Marie', and R. 'Catherine's Pride'.

History/description: Catherine Weeks continues
the business she started with her husband in 1963.
Their first home had a greenhouse and lath house
which encouraged their interest in plants. Intensely
curious and largely self-taught, they became successful propagators of rhododendron cuttings. This huge
collection of trees and shrubs fits on just a 2-1/2-acre
site. She continues to introduce new hybrids each year
(as she has done for the past 14 years) breeding
primarily for foliage and fragrance. She recommends
you visit the native azaleas in bloom in the Stagecoach Hill Azalea Preserve on Northridge Road.

How to get there: From Highway 101 south of
Eureka, take Elk River exit east. In 50 feet go right
on Elk River Road. After 1-1/2 miles, go left on
Westgate Drive.

General information: Open every day except
Wednesday, 8:30 am–6:00 pm. Catalogue available
for $4, refundable with purchase.

Nancy R. Wilson Species and Miniature Narcissus

6525 Briceland–Thorn Road, Garberville 95542
(707) 923-2407
Nancy R. Wilson
Retail and Mail Order

Plant specialties: Unusual species of narcissus
grown from seed or vegetative propagation; none
collected in the wild. Special attention to hybrids of
certain colors, smaller sizes, and rock garden-
compatible plants.

History/description: When you grow up with a
mother who has a well-developed bulb habit and the
first house you buy with your husband just happens
to have a rock garden packed with bulbs, you are
destined to be a bulb lover. This healthcare professional and her retired husband succumbed to their
destiny and started a nursery in 1990. Nancy Wilson
recommends you visit and support the embryonic
Humboldt Botanical Garden in Eureka.

How to get there: Call for directions.

General information: Open by appointment
anytime, although best bloom season is March and
April. Mail-order catalogue available for $1,
deductible from purchase. Site-specific consultation
by mail only.

HORTICULTURAL ATTRACTIONS

Mendocino Coast Botanical Gardens

18220 North Highway One, Fort Bragg 95437
(707) 964-4352

History/description: Originally the private garden
of Ernest and Betty Schoefer, these 47 landscaped
acres are now part of the Mendocino Coast Recreation and Park Department, but supported entirely
by memberships, entrance fees, retail sales, and
volunteer help. Located in the moist, coastal woodlands, their specialty is rhododendrons. Other
noteworthy plant collections include heaths and
heathers, roses, and perennials. The topography is
varied, ranging from breathtaking coastal bluffs to
fern-filled canyon trails. They offer garden walks,
lectures, workshops, docent tours for groups, and,
of course, the opportunity to volunteer.

Plant sales: Garden Store and Nursery is open all
year and sells unusual perennials and plants as seen in
the gardens. Biannual plant sales in October and
April, with monthly theme-sales throughout the
season.

General information: Open every day except
Thanksgiving, Christmas, and the Saturday after
Labor Day. November through February, 9:00 am–
4:00 pm; March through October, 9:00 am–5:00
pm. Well-behaved dogs allowed on leash and an
electric cart available for those with special needs.
Admission fee.

Azalea State Reserve
Highway 200, north of Eureka
(707) 488-2041

The home turf of Rhododendron occidentale. A 30-acre natural area of fragrant spring blossoms.

Fetzer Vineyards' Bonterra Garden
13601 Eastside Road, Hopland 95449
(707) 744-1250

Five acres of vegetable, flower, fruit, and herb gardens. A testimonial to organic farming.

Humboldt Botanical Garden
1626 E Street, Eureka 95502
P. O. Box 6181, Eureka 95502 (mailing address)
(707) 442-5139

Gardens recreating a variety of habitats from redwood forest to coastal dune will one day occupy this 44-acre disturbed site on a hillside next to College of the Redwoods. Though still in its planning stages, the project is already galvanizing the area's horticultural energy. Unusual plant sale in June and a garden tour in July.

Jug Handle State Reserve
Highway One, 3 miles north of Mendocino
(707) 937-5804

A 2-1/2-mile, self-guided nature trail—Ecological Staircase—travels over five uplifted terraces covering the evolution of California's ecology from beach to pygmy forest to developed coastal forest.

Kruse Rhododendron State Reserve

Near Fort Ross, 20 miles north of Jenner, 10 miles
south of Gualala
(707) 865-2391

Native rhododendrons colonizing second-growth
forest.

Montgomery Woods State Reserve

Comptche-Ukiah Road, 5 miles east of Comptche
(707) 937-5804

Huge old-growth coastal redwoods.

Richardson Grove State Park

Highway 101, 8 miles south of Garberville
(707) 247-3318

Old-growth redwood forest. Springtime wildflowers
include bleeding-heart and calypso lilies.

Stagecoach Hill Azalea Preserve

Humboldt Lagoon State Park, Kane Road between Big
and Dry Lagoons (off Highway 101 just north of Trinidad)
(707) 488-2041

Another effort to reintroduce the western azalea to its
native habitat, on a cleared slope in a spruce and
alder forest.

The Thompsons' Heather Garden

Manchester (about 30 miles south of Mendocino)
(707) 882-2345

California's signature heather garden is the master-
piece of Jim and Beverly Thompson. Best time to visit
is in August when the Callunas, Ericas, and
Daboecias bloom simultaneously, though heaths and
heathers offer year round interest. This is a private
garden. Visits by appointment only.

Trillium Lane

18855 Trillium Lane, Fort Bragg 95437
(707) 964-3282

This private garden of the doyenne of rhododendron
culture, Eleanor Philp, was formerly a nursery. Open
by appointment only, from April through June.

Sacramento Valley

Carmichael: 57
Chico: 43, 51, 57
Davis: 45, 56
Dixon: 55
Durham: 46
Elk Grove: 42
Folsom: 44
Galt: 54

North Highlands: 47
Oroville: 41
Paradise: 48
Pleasant Grove: 52
Redding: 58
Rumsey: 40
Sacramento: 49, 50, 53,
    56, 57, 58

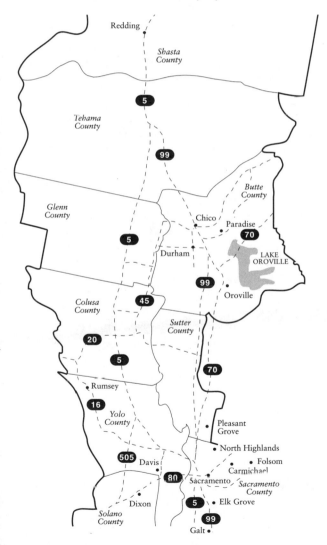

Cache Creek Nursery

2815 Rumsey Canyon Road, Rumsey 95679
P. O. Box 85, Rumsey 95679 (mailing address)
(530) 796-3521
Frances Burke
Retail and Wholesale

Plant specialties: Extremely hardy perennials, including herbs, Salvia, Lavandula, and Artemisia. Also, standard, heirloom, and traditional varieties of organic vegetable starts (in the spring).

History/description: Frances Burke and her husband moved to Rumsey from the Santa Cruz area in the early 1980s to farm oranges and nuts. They started a little sideline nursery business that prospered. A remarkable woman, she (and the 2-acre nursery) survived the freeze of 1990, floods, and the death of her husband. Frances now has 20 years experience cultivating long-blooming, heat-tolerant, and drought-resistant varieties. The emphasis here is on plants that flourish with little care, plants that are suitable to their garden environment. Cache Creek Nursery offers plants wholesale at the Marin and Davis Farmers Markets and at the California CNPS annual sale in Sacramento. Frances urges you not to miss the recreational pleasures of Cache Creek Regional Park, a wintering home for bald eagles, and the wildflower display in Bear Valley on Wilbur Hot Springs Road.

How to get there: From I-80, take I-505 north for 20 miles to the Madison/Esparto exit. Follow Highway 16 west for 25 miles to Rumsey. One mile past the town hall, turn right on Rumsey Canyon Road. The nursery is on your right in 1/4 mile.

General information: Open by appointment only. Plant lists available upon request.

Canyon Creek Nursery

3527 Dry Creek Road, Oroville 95965
(530) 533-2166, fax same
John and Susan Whittlesey
Retail and Mail Order

Plant specialties: Perennials—large selection of
Dianthus, Euphorbia, Aster, Campanula, Salvia, and
Geranium. Historical varieties of fragrant violets
and English violas.

History/description: In 1987 Susan and John
Whittlesey decided to start their own nursery and
growing grounds after having worked for a large
mail-order nursery in Washington state. Canyon
Creek has reintroduced many of the older, fragrant
cultivars of violas and violets, imported from
England. Most of their plants are field-grown and
hardy, sold in 3-1/2-inch to 5-inch pots. This acre
nursery is located at 800-foot elevation in an oak-
woodland canyon. Nearby Table Mountain is
known for one of the best displays of California
wildflowers, March through May.

How to get there: Call for directions or a map.

General information: Open by appointment only.
Catalogue available for $2. Mail orders shipped.

Cornflower Farms
P. O. Box 896, Elk Grove 95759
(916) 689-1015, fax (916) 689-1968
Ann and Jeff Chandler
Wholesale and Mail Order

Plant specialties: California native plants, ornamental grasses, perennials, drought-tolerant plants, California revegetation material and beneficial plants.

History/description: This business began in the early 1980s due to the demand for quality lining-out and container stock of California native and drought-tolerant plant material. A new container to encourage deeper rooting in plants (for greater drought tolerance) has been developed here. Today they sell only to landscapers and wholesale nurseries, and for site restoration projects. Cornflower's philosophy has always been to grow what everyone else will not or cannot grow. They also have been prime movers in the burgeoning beneficial plant movement, emphasizing plant selection which reduces pests and attracts beneficial insects. The nursery maintains a beneficial insect display border on their 5-acre site. They recommend you visit the rock garden at William Land Park and the UC Davis Arboretum.

How to get there: Call for directions.

General information: Open to the public once a year at their open house; call to get on mailing list. Open to wholesale trade by appointment only. Catalogue available for $3. Deliveries within California (call for minimum order requirements). The Chandlers do site-specific collection.

Covered Bridge Gardens

1821 Honey Run Road, Chico 95928-8850
(530) 342-6661
Betty and Harry Harwood
Retail and Mail Order

Plant specialties: Daylilies (1,000 registered cultivars).

History/description: Retired dentist Harry Harwood started collecting daylilies in 1981. Betty, the pragmatic partner, figured as long as they were working that hard on their collection, they might as well try to sell some, even if only to finance more plants. Their 2-acre garden has a 400-foot creek frontage and is a designated display garden of the American Hemerocallis Society. They introduce new cultivars each year, will contract grow and give slide talks. The nursery is named for a historical covered bridge 1/2 mile from their garden.

How to get there: From Highway 99 going north, take Paradise exit. Take Paradise Skyway for 1 mile. Left on Honey Run Road. After 5 miles the road forks at the covered bridge. Go right.

General information: Open June and July, every day, 9:00 am–4:00 pm. This business is predominately mail order; catalogue available for $1, refundable with purchase.

Digger Pine Nursery

7555 Baldwin Dam Road, Folsom 95630
(916) 988-6450
Bob and Beryl Adrian
Retail

Plant specialties: Camellia (japonica, sasanqua, and reticulata) and Azalea.

History/description: A lifelong camellia and azalea collector, Bob Adrian had no trouble deciding what to do in "retirement." With his knack for propagation and so many unusual goodies on-hand, a nursery business was born. The Adrians will be happy to share their enthusiasm and show you around their 1-acre garden nursery.

How to get there: From I-80, take the Greenback Lane exit. Go left on Folsom-Auburn Road. At the first stop sign, go left on Oak Avenue Parkway. Go right on Baldwin Dam Road. Go right on the dirt Digger Pine Road. The nursery is past the corral. Or from I-50, take the Folsom exit. Go left at the first stoplight. Continue to the first light after the Rainbow Bridge, which is Folsom-Auburn Road. Go right, then left on Oak Avenue Parkway and follow above directions.

General information: Open every day, 10:00 am until dark. Plant list available for SASE.

Flowers and Greens

P. O. Box 1802, Davis 95617
(530) 756-9238
e-mail: rmsachs@ucdavis.edu
website: www.members.tripod.com/~corbusoft/flowers/
Roy M. Sachs
Retail, Wholesale, and Mail Order

Plant specialties: Alstroemeria (Peruvian/Incan lily—rhizomes). Also some Acidanthera (aromatic gladiolus-corms), Watsonia, Calla, and Freesia alba, mostly grown at his weekend mini-nursery just west of Monte Rio on the Russian River—call ahead to visit on weekends, (707) 865-0433.

History/description: In 1988, four partners, all of whom were connected with the Department of Environmental Horticulture at UC Davis, started this nursery by selling salt- and freeze-tolerant eucalyptus. Roy, now the sole proprietor of the business, began to experiment with field production of alstroemeria rhizomes, which eventually became the main focus of the business. Having discovered that many of the older varieties developed for greenhouses were not suited to temperate-zone gardens, he continues to develop new colorful, vigorous hybrid varieties, that can be grown in various climates. Roy has two acres of cultivated alstroemeria fields on his 20-acre farm, well worth viewing in late spring.

How to get there: The nursery is located at 35717 Lasiandra Lane, off Road 96, 6 miles north and west of the UC Davis campus. From I-80, go north on Highway 113, west on Road 29, south on Road 96 and west on Lasiandra. Please call ahead.

General information: Open by appointment only. Mail-order catalogue available for SASE or for $2, credited to first order. Deliveries to nurseries within 40-mile radius of Davis. Nursery tours and demonstrations may be arranged.

Gold Run Iris Garden

P. O. Box 648, Durham 95938
(530) 894-6916
Kathy Hutchinson, Sara Skillin
Retail, Wholesale, and Mail Order

Plant specialties: Iris (1,000 varieties), primarily
tall bearded, standard dwarf bearded. Some aril-
bred, Louisiana, Spuria, Siberian, Dutch.

History/description: Kathy Hutchinson's iris
collection just outgrew her garden space. Requiring
more room and more money to finance her growing
collection, she went into business in 1989 with her
mother. The iris fields and display garden occupy 2
acres on a corner of the family's rice-growing ranch,
named "Gold Run" after an old canal on the property. Mother and daughter focus their hybridizing
efforts on increasing the color range of bearded iris.

How to get there: From Chico, go south on
Highway 99, past Highway 149 cutoff, past Nelson
Road. Watch for Skillin Lane on your right, marked
by "Gold Run" sign. Traveling north on Highway
99, Skillin Lane will be on your left past Gridley,
past Cottonwood Road.

General information: Open during bloom season,
late March through April, 10:00 am–5:00 pm, or by
appointment. Mail orders taken through July.
Catalogue available for $1, credited to purchase.
Nursery tours may be arranged.

M.A.D. Iris Garden

4828 Jela Way, North Highlands 95660
(916) 482-0562
Robert and Mary Dunn
Retail and Mail Order

Plant specialties: Iris—tall bearded and Louisiana hybrids.

History/description: Mary Dunn worked for a Sacramento nursery in the 1950s and developed an interest in irises. She joined the Iris Society, met hybridizers and began collecting. She and husband Robert have introduced 125 named bearded varieties and 75 Louisiana hybrids. They continue to register 8 to 10 new irises each year. Her efforts have won her the prestigious Mary Swords Debaillon award and the Hybridizer's Medal from the American Iris Society for introductions such as 'City Lights', 'Silhouette', and 'Vibrations'. He is noted for 'Crystalyn', 'Navy Blues', and 'Pagan'. Blossom time at this small rural nursery is quite a sight.

How to get there: Call for directions. The nursery is located 13 miles north of Sacramento, in a rural area near McLellan Airfield.

General information: Open late March to mid-May during bloom season (call for exact dates). Plant list available. Mail orders accepted.

Mendon's Nursery
5424 Foster Road, Paradise 95969
(530) 877-7341, fax (530) 877-3562
Jerry, Joanne, and John Mendon
Retail

Plant specialties: Trees and shrubs, including
unique collections of Japanese maples (more than 50
varieties), dwarf conifers, dogwood. Also ornamental grasses, perennials, roses, aquatic and bog plants.

History/description: After Cal Poly, the Mendons
started a small general nursery in San Gabriel. They
also had a professional tree-moving business (mostly
palms) creating many an instant oasis throughout
Los Angeles. Seeking a calmer, more rural environment, they found Paradise and vowed never to open
another nursery. They started selling fruits and nuts
harvested on their 8-acre property, got a few more
fruit trees, and sold a few to neighbors. Within four
years they were back in business. They alert you to
the Feather River Hospital Auxiliary and the Paradise
Garden Club's spring garden tour in Paradise and the
garden tour in Chico put on by St. John's Episcopal
Church. The seasons are not shy in Paradise, worth a
visit for the vibrant spring and fall displays.

How to get there: From Chico take Skyway to
Paradise. At traffic light go right for 1 block. Go
right on Foster for 1/2 mile.

General information: Open Monday through
Saturday, 8:00 am–5:00 pm, closed major holidays.
Pruning and drip-irrigation demonstrations may be
arranged. Rose catalogue available. Deliveries
within 25-mile radius. Some mail order.

Michael's Premier Roses

9759 Eldercreek Road, Sacramento 95829
(916) 369-7673 (ROSE)
website: www.michaelsrose.com
Michael and Darlene Fischer
Retail, Wholesale, and Mail Order

Plant specialties: Roses, including patented miniatures (300 varieties), old garden roses (200), species
hybrids, moss, gallicas, damasks, floribundas, hybrid
teas (200). Mostly ungrafted, grown on their own
rootstock.

History/description: A longtime rosarian, Michael
Fischer retired from commercial real estate to devote
himself full-time to his obsession with roses. He
opened a commercial nursery in 1993, in response
to the demand for interesting roses in the area.
Meanwhile, his wife has also parlayed her extracur-
ricular dreams into a business; she boards and trains
horses at an English equestrian center which shares
space with his roses on their 13-acre garden ranch.
The Fischers cross-pollinate and help out in each
other's businesses.

How to get there: From Highway 50, exit at
Bradshaw and travel 5 miles south. Go left on
Eldercreek.

General information: Open Friday through
Sunday, 10:00 am–5:00 pm. Free catalogue. Check
their website for articles about rose culture and on-
line catalogue. Pruning demonstrations offered every
Saturday in January. Nursery tours for interested
groups by arrangement.

Mighty Minis

7318 Sahara Court, Sacramento 95828
(916) 421-7284
Jeannie Stokes
Retail, Mail Order, and Wholesale (wholesale to violet clubs only)

Plant specialties: 800 varieties of miniature African violets (Saintpaulia) including 'Bustle Back', 'Wasps', trailers, variegated, and tiny, mostly registered forms. Also, other gesneriads, ferns, and begonias.

History/description: Jean Stokes has been growing African violets since 1970 when they were first hybridized. An avid collector, she started this business in 1985 and now with 8 to 12 greenhouses filled with multiplying miniatures, it is a full-time concern. She recommends you visit in January and February for best bloom.

How to get there: From I-80 in Sacramento, go east on Florin Road. Go right on Lindale. Sahara Court is off Lindale after the four-way stop.

General information: Open by appointment only. Yearly catalogue ready in January available for $2, credited to first order. Mail orders shipped on minimum order of 10 plants. Workshops, talks, and propagation clinics may be arranged for groups.

The Plant Barn
406 Entler Avenue, Chico 95928
(530) 345-3121, fax (530) 342-4558
Ilona and David Cronan
Retail and Wholesale (dba Chico Propagators)

Plant specialties: Unusual perennials, including
Lavandula, Artemisia, Aster, Thymus, Dianthus,
Verbena, Phlox. Large selection 6-inch-potted color.
Also, indoor tropicals.

History/description: Combine his degree in horticulture with her background in art accounts for this
profusion of growing color. Started in 1980, the
Plant Barn now covers 2 acres with poly Quonset
houses, a gift shop, and a brilliant display garden. In
December, 10,000 poinsettias make a grand holiday
statement. While you are in Chico, check out
Bidwell Park (east of Esplanade), Stansbury House
(west of Esplanade), and the Bidwell Mansion.

How to get there: From Highway 99 north, after a
golf course go left on Entler. Nursery is in 1 mile.

General information: Open Monday through
Saturday, 9:00 am–5:00 pm. Open Sunday, 1:00
pm–5:00 pm, in December and March through July.
They offer nursery tours, talks, and home landscape
consultations. Plant rentals available.

River Oaks Nursery
4827 Pacific Avenue, Pleasant Grove 95668 (mailing)
(916) 655-3591, fax (916) 655-3595
Bobbi Coggins
Wholesale

Plant specialties: California native plants, drought-tolerant plants, ornamental trees and shrubs.

History/description: Although River Oaks officially opened in 1990, Bobbi Coggins has been a plant broker since 1977. With a degree in horticulture from Sierra College and several years of experience at a local nursery, she decided to go into business for herself. She is also a revegetation specialist for Sacramento County, Cal Trans, and Nature Conservancy. Bobbi oversees 7 acres of production in the Valley flatlands. Much of her stock is custom-propagated for clients.

How to get there: Call for directions.

General information: Open to wholesale trade only by appointment, Monday through Friday, 8:00 am–5:00 pm. General public may visit with landscaper. Catalogue and availability list upon request.

Roris Gardens

8195 Bradshaw Road, Sacramento 95829
(916) 689-7460, fax (916) 689-5516
e-mail: roris@jps.net
website: www.jps.net/roris
Retail and Mail Order

Plant specialties: Tall bearded iris (more than 350 varieties).

History/description: Postcard perfect. Picture the old farmhouse next to a creek in the shade of mature hardwood trees, with wild peacocks, geese, ducks, and egrets feeding nearby. Then surround it all with 15 spectacular acres of irises in every color of the rainbow. All this just 14 miles from downtown Sacramento.

How to get there: From downtown Sacramento, take Highway 50 east. Take Bradshaw Road exit, go south on Bradshaw for 8 miles.

General information: Open during their Iris Festival from mid-April to mid-June, 8:00 am–5:00 pm. During the festival they also sell potted Japanese irises and daylilies. Color mail-order catalogue (72 pages) available for $5, refundable with first order.

Shepherd Geraniums

13470 Alabama Road, Galt 95632
(209) 748-2827
Doug and Terry Shepherd
Wholesale

Plant specialties: Pelargoniums, including scented, fancy-leaf, dwarf and miniature, stellar, and fancy-flowered (rosebud, cactus flowered, etc.). Some succulents.

History/description: After working for quite some time in retail and wholesale nurseries and with the children raised, the Shepherds decided to take a chance and start their own nursery in 1993. They began with bedding plants but soon got hooked on the versatility of pelargoniums. Now with 8,000 square feet under glass in the middle of gorgeous California ranchland, they and their business are going gangbusters.

How to get there: Call for directions.

General information: Open by appointment only to wholesale business. Nursery tours given.

Sunshine Nursery Growers
7820 Serpa Lane, Dixon 95620
(707) 678-4481, fax (707) 678-0825
Gary and Evelyn Bennett
Retail and Wholesale

Plant specialties: Perennials, ornamental grasses, shrubs, and trees. 1,250 species.

History/description: In the mid-1970s the Bennetts started a landscape contracting business. Evelyn had previously been a nursery manager in Davis, so she was quickly aware of the plants wanted but unavailable for their projects. They started growing and testing new perennials for California climates; the next step was a full-fledged nursery. A display garden surrounding their home is a primary attraction on their 10-acre site.

How to get there: From I-80 east, take the first Dixon exit. Bear left on West Dixon Avenue for 1-1/4 miles to Serpa Lane. From I-80 west, exit at West Dixon Avenue and bear right on West Dixon Avenue.

General information: Open Monday through Saturday, 8:00 am–4:30 pm; Sunday, 10:00–3:00 pm. Closed Sundays, November through March. Plant list is available for SASE. Nearby deliveries possible on wholesale orders of $500 or more. Nursery tours of new perennials gladly offered to interested groups.

HORTICULTURAL ATTRACTIONS

Capitol Park
1300 L Street, Sacramento
(916) 445-3658

History/description: These 40 acres which surround the capitol buildings, contain perhaps the largest and most extensive collection of mature trees in California. The historic insectary in the park's center provides visitors with self-guiding maps to 341 special trees; there are 200 more which do not even make the map. Planting began in 1870 and continues in a sporadic fashion. Their azalea collection in bloom has been described as "socko."

UC Davis Arboretum
TB-32, La Rue Road, University of California, Davis 95616
(530) 752-2498, fax (530) 752-5796
e-mail: arboretum@ucdavis.edu

History/description: Davis Arboretum has about 100 acres of themed gardens and special collections emphasizing drought-tolerant, low-maintenance plants. Gardens include the Native Plant Garden, the White Flower Garden, and a dry land demonstration garden. Special collections feature oaks, exotic conifers, Australian plants, and desert plants.

Plant sales: Big fall plant sale first Saturday in October, 8:00 am–2:00 pm. Monthly sales for Friends only, during academic year.

General information: Open every day. There is no admission charge, but there is a parking fee Monday through Friday. The Friends of the Davis Arboretum, a membership support group, organizes monthly lectures, Sunday tours, and workshops during the academic year.

Bidwell Park
Chico
(530) 895-4972

Ten-mile-long urban oasis with many old, stately trees. Picturesque canyon gorge alongside the Big Chico Creek.

Genetic Resource Center
US Forest Center, Chico
(530) 895-1176

Nature trail with many labeled examples of center's historic plant introductions.

C.M. Goethe Arboretum
California State University—Biology Department, Sacramento 95819-6077
(916) 278-6077

Six-acre collection of trees and shrubs.

Charles Jensen Botanic Garden
8520 Fair Oaks Boulevard, Carmichael
(916) 485-5322

Temperate, moist woodland plants along a creek.

William Land Park
Sutterville Road and Land Park Road, Sacramento
(916) 433-6305

Old rock garden and new color garden designed by
Daisy Mah in a municipal park with lofty trees in
midtown Sacramento.

McKinley Park Rose Garden
H and 33rd Streets, Sacramento 95816
(916) 277-6060

Modern roses and companion plants in park setting.

The Old City Cemetery Historic Rose Garden
Broadway and Riverside Boulevards, Sacramento
(916) 443-2146

A garden of old roses and found roses, organized by
famous rosarian Fred Boutin, now maintained by
Friends of the Old City Cemetery.

The Redding Arboretum
at the end of Travelled Way off North Market Street
P. O. Box 992360, Redding 96099-2360 (mailing
address)
(530) 2242-8850 ext. 2126   Rico Montenegro

A 210-acre open space on the Sacramento River.
Gardens are being developed to cover a third of this
area, the rest remaining as natural riparian and oak
savannah habitats with extensive trail system. Plant
sale at end of April.

Sacramento Garden and Art Center
3330 McKinley Boulevard, next to McKinley Park,
Sacramento 95816
(916) 443-9413

Site of about 50 garden and art groups' meetings,
shows, and sales. Big plant sale in March.

Mountain Region

Beckwourth: 63
Etna: 60, 62
Tahoe City: 64
Truckee: 65
Weed: 61

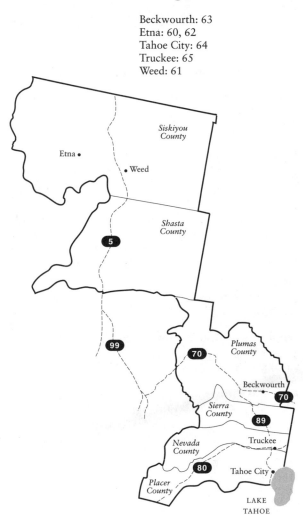

Cottage Gardens
520 Collier Way, Etna 96027
P. O. Box 160, Etna 96027 (mailing address)
(530) 467-3235
Barbara Coatney
Retail, Wholesale, and Mail Order

Plant specialties: Sempervivum, Sedum, alpines, and hardy plants; Dianthus, Geranium, Phlox, Campanula. Troughs and trough kits.

History/description: This nursery is the direct result of plant hobbyist Barbara Coatney's frustration with the lack of local supply of interesting plants. Her solution was to open a nursery herself in 1981. At this new location since 1996, she is still working on a display garden. She suggests a visit, while in Siskiyou County, to the garden of Jeanette Axton in Etna (open Sunday and Monday in summer) and to Mt. Etna summit, Scott Mountain, and Kangaroo Lake for best wildflower viewing in May and June.

How to get there: Take I-5 to Highway 3 to Etna, where Highway 3 becomes Collier Road. Nursery is on the right.

General information: Open April through June, every day, 9:00 am–5:00 pm. Rest of the year, open Tuesday through Saturday, 10:00 am–3:00 pm. Best to call first. Succulent and alpine lists for SASE (55¢). Trough-making clinics offered. Contract growing services.

Menzies Native Nursery

P. O. Box 9, Weed 96094
(530) 938-4858
Robert Menzies
Retail and Wholesale

Plant specialties: Riparian habitat plants, 208 species of montane California native plants.

History/description: An impeccably credentialed horticulturist, this Robert Menzies is grandson of Robert Menzies (founder of Save the Redwoods League), cousin of Arthur Menzies (of Strybing Arboretum fame), and distant relative of Archibald Menzies (pioneer plant explorer). With a background in viticulture at Davis, he started this nursery in Mill Valley in the 1970s and moved to Weed in 1980.

How to get there: Call for directions.

General information: Open Tuesday through Friday, 9:00 am–3:00 pm. They have a plant list and will ship your orders. Site-specific consultations and design assistance offered. Contract growing. Tours, lectures, and workshops also available.

Mountain Crest Gardens

1838 Eastside Road, Etna 96027
P. O. Box 724, Etna 96027 (mailing address)
(530) 467-3215, fax (530) 467-5733
Marsha Hayden
Retail, Wholesale, and Mail Order

Plant specialties: Succulents—Sempervivum (more than 400 varieties), Sedum (more than 100), Lewisia (4), Heuffeliis (25), Orostachys. Many hardy varieties.

History/description: This is a complicated business. It all started in Covelo as an enterprise called Cal-Forest raising pine trees for government reforestation projects. After the move to these 5 acres in Etna, a wholesale bedding plant and perennial business was added. In the mid-1990s Jim and Irene Russ's remarkable and extensive succulent collection went on the market and Cal-Forest snapped it up. The Sempervivum and Sedum section has continued to expand and is now a separate division called Mountain Crest Gardens. At present, the plants are available only through mail order, though nursery tours can be booked to see the plants in person and get residual views of the expanse of annual and perennial color.

How to get there: Located halfway between Medford, Oregon, and Redding, 30 miles southwest of the I-5 corridor in scenic Scott Valley. Call for directions.

General information: Not open to the public, though nursery tours may be arranged. Their bedding plants and tree operations are open to wholesale customers by appointment. Mail-order catalogue available for $2. Wholesale plant list.

Sierra Valley Farms

1329 County Road A23, Beckwourth 96129
P. O. Box 79, Beckwourth 96129 (mailing address)
(530) 832-0114, fax (530) 832-5114
e-mail: svfarms@psln.com
website: www.svfarms.com
Gary and Kim Romano
Retail and Wholesale

Plant specialties: Alpine plants. California native trees and shrubs suited to high elevations, especially Pinus, Cornus, Salix, and Ribes species. All Sierra conifers. Also Ceanothus cuneatus, C. velutinus, C. prostratus, Arctostaphylos patula, A. nevadensis, Prunus andersonii, Chrysothamnus, Purshia tridentata, Cercocarpus. Organic produce.

History/description: Sierra Valley Farms (formerly Sierra Valley Nursery) has added an organic produce farm to its extensive line of native plants. The 10-acre site includes both a wholesale/retail nursery and produce market. Gary Romano initially launched a landscape business specializing in revegetation projects. The nursery was started in 1990 to supply plants for his landscape work and has grown to contain a significant collection of high-elevation natives. Sierra Valley Farms will also contract grow.

How to get there: Beckwourth is on Feather River Highway 70 (35 miles from Quincy and 45 miles before Reno). From Highway 70, take the Calpine turn-off and travel one mile south on Country Road A23 to the nursery.

General information: Open May through September, Thursday through Saturday, 10:00 am–6:00 pm. From October through April, open by appointment only. Please call ahead. Catalogue and plant list available. Plants delivered within 100 miles on minimum orders of $500. Plants shipped COD-FOB Beckwourth.

Tahoe Tree Company

401 West Lake Boulevard, Tahoe City 96145
P. O. Box 5325, Tahoe City 96145 (mailing address)
(530) 583-3911, fax (530) 583-0557
Leslie and John Hyche
Retail and Wholesale

Plant specialties: California native plants, ornamental trees and shrubs, cold-hardy perennials.

History/description: David and Katherine McBride started this nursery in 1954 as an offshoot of his tree service business, her interest in perennials and California native plants, and their combined desire to supply local gardens with healthy plants suited to the area. The second generation now directs the operation. Daughter Leslie manages the retail nursery and gift shop. Leslie's husband, John, supervises the wholesale backyard and specializes in the propagation of native plants. The 12-acre property includes a variety of garden displays, a native plant propagation area, growing area, and retail shop with restaurant. They recommend Julie Carville's *Lingering in Tahoe's Wild Gardens* as a guide to nearby wildflower walks.

How to get there: Located 1/4 mile south of Tahoe City on corner of Highway 89 and Granlibakken Road.

General information: Open year-round. The nursery is closed in winter, but the retail store and gift shop with restaurant are open daily. Catalogue available for wholesale trade. Gardening talks offered in summer. Group nursery tours by arrangement. Newsletter available.

The Villager Nursery
10994 Donner Pass Road, Truckee 96161
(530) 587-0771, fax (530) 587-7439
Sarah Trebilcock, Eric Larusson, Rob Van Dyke
Retail and Wholesale

Plant specialties: California native plants suited to
the montane region, Sierra alpines, perennials, cold-
hardy plants.

History/description: Sarah Trebilcock, a UC-
Davis-educated botanist and ecologist, bought a
florist shop in 1975 and started converting a good
piece of property in back of the shop into a nursery.
In 1980 she obtained her contractor's license and
opened a landscape business. At the start, the
landscape business drove the demand for plants but
in the past five years, local gardening interest has
surged. Now the nursery is concentrating on its
retail business, searching the Sierra for seeds and
cuttings of hard-to-find native plants to propagate
for customers. The flower business sold in 1991.
The nursery has a display garden and produces an
informative newsletter about High Sierra gardening.
Sarah suggests you explore the local native ecosystems of alpine, high desert, wildflower, and riparian
areas to get a better sense of the microclimate
around your home.

How to get there: From the train depot in downtown Truckee, go west under freeway on Donner
Pass Road (Main Street). Nursery is on top of hill
behind Old Gateway Center on the right.

General information: Open in summer, 9:00 am–
6:00 pm. Fall and spring, open according to the
weather (call first). Plant lists available. Free classes
offered in June and July on topics such as vegetable
gardening, perennials, fruits, and berries. Big sales in
the spring and fall. Consulting services for revegetation with native plants.

Foothills

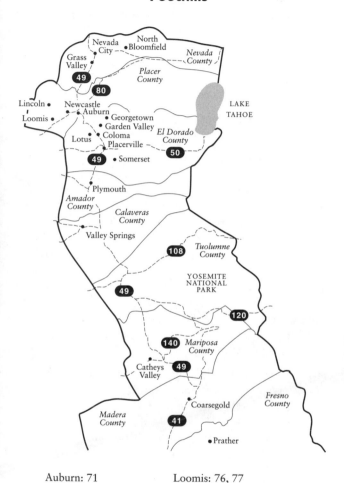

Auburn: 71	Loomis: 76, 77
Catheys Valley: 87	Lotus: 80
Coarsegold: 83	Nevada City: 88, 90
Coloma: 89	Newcastle: 79, 82
El Dorado: 85	North Bloomfield: 89
Garden Valley: 86	Placerville: 75, 81
Georgetown: 84	Plymouth: 68
Grass Valley: 72, 73, 89, 90	Prather: 78
	Somerset: 69
Lincoln: 74	Valley Springs: 70

Amador Flower Farm

22001 Shenandoah School Road, Plymouth 95669
(209) 245-6660, fax (209) 245-6661
e-mail: deaver@daylilyfarm.com
website: www.daylilyfarm.com
Jeanne and Ken Deaver
Retail and Mail Order

Plant specialties: Daylilies (650 varieties) and
perennials (300+ varieties).

History/description: Longtime gardener Jeanne
Deaver got into the daylily business quite by happenstance. While buying plants at Alpine Gardens in
Santa Rosa, she discovered this business was for sale
and bought it. Amador opened in 1994 as a mail-
order-only business. Since 1996 the nursery, located
at the edge of the foothills surrounded by vineyards
(Ken is a grape grower), has been open for retail
business in a big way. Four acres of theme gardens
(fragrant, white, cut-flower, wine-colored, and a
huge lawn with perennial beds) have already been
developed, as well as a gift store, pumpkin patch,
pond, and picnic tables.

How to get there: Take Highway 16 into Ply-
mouth. Go right on Shenandoah Road (main
intersection) and continue for 6 miles out of town.
Shenandoah School Road is U-shaped and crosses
Shenandoah Road twice, take the *second*
Shenandoah School Road right.

General information: Open every day, 9:00 am–
4:00 pm. Mail-order catalogue available, call or write.

Bluebird Haven Iris Garden
6940 Fairplay Road, Somerset 95684
(530) 620-5017
Mary and John Hess
Retail and Mail Order

Plant specialties: Bearded iris—tall, border, dwarf varieties. Specializing in historic and antique varieties (600).

History/description: This garden nursery has been in its present location since 1988, although it previously existed, primarily as a bird sanctuary, for nine years elsewhere. The display garden has 2,300 varieties of irises planted midst Victorian gazebos, benches, archways, and costumed employees reflecting a turn-of-the-century civility. Three miles of landscaped walkways provide a pleasant stroll and can help you walk off whatever damage was done in the surrounding wine country.

How to get there: From Highway 50 just west of Placerville, take the Missouri Flat exit. Turn south on Missouri Flat Road to Pleasant Valley Road. Turn left on Pleasant Valley Road. In about 12 miles, turn right on E16 (also known as Mt. Aukum Road). Turn left on Fairplay Road; continue for 1/4 mile.

General information: Open during bloom season (usually second weekend in April to fourth weekend in May), daily, 10:00 am–5:00 pm. Rest of year by appointment. Will ship anywhere in USA (minimum order $10). General catalogue available for $1. Informational flyer with map free upon request. Iris Seminar held, usually in July. Will grow your iris sample for identification.

Calaveras Nursery
1622 Highway 12, Valley Springs 95252
(209) 772-1823
Mick and Pat Stoppard
Wholesale and Retail

Plant specialties: Specialty oaks (27 varieties) from all over the world, redbud, toyon.

History/description: Mick Stoppard helped finance his way through college by working at Boething Treeland. Armed with degrees in zoology and plant science, he launched Calaveras Nursery in 1977. Worth a visit for its gardenlike setting in the foothills (700-foot elevation), this 10-acre nursery is nestled in a wooded area with a fine creek. Worth a visit as well is Indian Grinding Rock State Historical Park, just north of Jackson off Highway 88 and Micke Grove Park in Stockton.

How to get there: From Highway 99, go east on Highway 12. Nursery is 2 miles past the town of Valley Springs, approximately 35 miles south of Sacramento and 11 miles north of Stockton.

General information: Open by appointment only. Wholesale hours: 8:00 am–5:00 pm, Monday through Friday. A plant list is available.

Dry Creek Herb Farm
13935 Dry Creek Road, Auburn 95602
(530) 878-2441, fax (530) 878-6772
Rick and Shatoiya de la Tour
Retail and Mail Order

Plant specialties: Herbs—mostly medicinal, some culinary.

History/description: Shatoiya's interest in herbalism started when she took over her grandfather's farm in Poway in what was then rural San Diego County. Her friends and neighbors there, mostly women of Eastern European descent, were well steeped in folk-healing and herbal traditions. She learned from them and also studied under Rosemary Gladstar and the California School of Herbal Studies. Having moved to Auburn, she and her husband grow and sell herbs from their 2-1/2-acre garden and offer a nine-month apprenticeship in herbalism, several other classes, and craft workshops. A gift shop sells their dried herbs and teas.

How to get there: From I-80, go north on Highway 49 towards Grass Valley. Go east on Dry Creek Road. Or you can take the Dry Creek Road exit from I-80, east of Auburn.

General information: Open Saturday and Sunday, 9:00 am–5:00 pm. Catalogue and plant list are available. Mail orders accepted.

Emerald Hill Gardens

12890 Greenhorn Road, Grass Valley 95945
(530) 272-4326, fax (530) 272-4326
Catherine Knight
Retail, Wholesale, and Mail Order

Plant specialties: Perennials (90 genera), including Penstemon (10 varieties), Phlox, Hemerocallis. Perennials for cut flowers.

History/description: Catherine Knight thinks she's taking it easy. She and her husband retired from their retail nursery business in Willows and moved to Grass Valley. She wanted to be more selective about what she grew and about her use of time. So she opened this small perennial nursery and cut-flower business, only open by appointment.

How to get there: Directions given when appointment is made.

General information: Open by appointment only. Plant catalogue is available. Mail orders (bare root only) accepted November to April. Local deliveries on orders of $150 or more. The nursery can offer design support and will give garden talks. Twice a year, it holds big plant sales—during the first week in October and over Memorial Day weekend.

Foothill Cottage Gardens
13925 Sonntag Road, Grass Valley 95945
(530) 272-4362
e-mail: csinger@jps.net
website: www.fcgardens.com
Carolyn Singer
Retail and Mail Order

Plant specialties: Wide variety of perennials resistant to deer, drought, and cold (to 10°), including Penstemon, Artemisia, Achillea, Santolina, Lavandula, and Thymus. Mediterranean plants, rock garden plants, and alpines.

History/description: This longtime gardener who had worked the soil in Sebastopol, Colorado, and Montana, moved to Grass Valley for the solitude and for horticultural therapy. One thing led to another. She taught gardening classes; students wanted her plants. And so this garden nursery started in 1977 on the site of the old Sonntag homestead. Country borders frame the house, while the front yard plays host to a variety of gardens demonstrating Mediterranean, very drought-tolerant, rock garden, and alpine plants. Carolyn Singer continues to design gardens and teach at the nursery offering classes on a whole range of gardening subjects. Somewhere she finds the time to write for *Fine Gardening* and *Garden Gate* magazines. She recommends you visit the many gardens in Empire Mine State Park and the old rose gardens on the east side of St. Joseph's Cultural Center in Grass Valley.

How to get there: Call for directions.

General information: Open year-round by appointment only. Very detailed plant lists are available for $3 which includes exposure and irrigation requirements. The mail-order list specializes in deer-resistant plants. Plants shipped March to May and September to November.

Gold Country Orchids

390 Big Ben Road, Lincoln 95648
(530) 645-8600, fax (530) 645-7076
Alan Koch
Retail and Wholesale

Plant specialties: Orchids—miniature Cattleyas,
Phalaenopsis, Oncidium intergenerics. Brand-new is
their Hawkinsara 'Keepsake'.

History/description: In 1970, Alan Koch was
introduced to orchids by his Sacramento State
botany professor. He went on to get degrees in
public administration and law, meanwhile starting a
sideline orchid business in 1978 in Southern California. He moved back north in 1988, spending ever
increasing amounts of time on his nursery endeavor
until it warranted his full-time attention. His
introductions include—Sophrolaelia 'El Dorado
Sunrise' and Sophrolaeliocattleya 'Pink Doll'. He is
now studying oenology and viticulture at UC Davis,
so who knows what is next. Alan recommends you
visit the Gladding-McBean clayworks nearby,
purveyors of terra-cotta architectural detail to many
historic buildings in California.

How to get there: From I-80 take Highway 65
north to Lincoln. Go right on Gladding Road. At first
stop sign go right on Wise Road. At next stop sign
go left on McCourtney. Go right on Big Ben Road.

General information: Open Tuesday through
Saturday, 9:00 am–4:30 pm. Wholesale by appointment only. Catalogue available for $2, credited to
your purchase. Wholesale orders shipped (minimum
$250). Write for information about their nursery
tours and workshops.

Gold Hill Nursery
6000 Gold Hill Road, Placerville 95667
(530) 622-2190
Al Veerkamp
Retail and Wholesale

Plant specialties: Japanese maples, dogwoods, unusual trees and shrubs, including Chinese magnolias, weeping forms of beech, ginkgo—"oddball stuff for hot summers and cold winters."

History/description: Born and raised in Placerville, Al Veerkamp worked for the Department of Agriculture following his graduation from UC Davis. In 1957 there was no nursery in El Dorado County so he started growing general nursery stock. Over a period of time, he started to specialize in unusual grafted conifers and deciduous trees. His display garden, a miniature arboretum, offers a feast for the connoisseur. The nursery is just 2 miles from the town of Coloma, where gold was first discovered.

How to get there: West of Placerville on Highway 50, take the Placerville Drive exit. Go north on Placerville Drive 1/2 mile past Raley's grocery store. Left on Pieroz Road. Left at stop sign on Cold Springs Road. Continue 7 miles to Gold Hill Road.

General information: Open Friday through Sunday, 9:00 am–5:00 pm, or by special appointment.

Golden Pond Water Plants
3275 Sierra College Boulevard, Loomis 95650
(916) 652-5459
Sue Golden
Retail

Plant specialties: Aquatic plants (more than 250
varieties). Bog plants (including the elusive
Lysimachia ciliata, Potentilla egedii, and Carex
nudata), hardy and tropical water lilies (over 50
varieties), ornamental grasses (including evergreen,
Miscanthus, and Bouteloua).

History/description: Yet another well-trained Cal
Poly graduate in landscape design, Sue Golden
enjoyed detailing water features and started growing
aquatic plants to supply her projects. Proving
successful at dividing her own stock, she started the
nursery and its display ponds in 1990. She also
creates miniature gardens for indoor use.

How to get there: From I-80, take the Sierra
College Boulevard exit and go north for 2-1/2 miles.

General information: Open April through October,
Friday through Sunday, 10:00 am–4:00 pm, or by
appointment. Nursery tours are welcomed and can
be arranged during the summer months.

High Ranch Nursery, Inc.
3778 Delmar Avenue, Loomis 95650
(916) 652-9261, fax (916) 652-6771
e-mail: sales@highranchnursery.com
John C. Nitta
Wholesale

Plant specialties: General woody ornamentals.
California natives suited to the foothills and High
Sierra. Oaks (12 varieties), hardy and drought-
tolerant perennials (Coreopsis—4 varieties),
Buddleia (6 cultivars), asters, penstemons, lavenders,
daylilies (20 varieties). Mediterranean plants,
shrubs, trees, including Lagerstroemia 'Seminole',
L. 'Cherokee', and the mildew-resistant form of
crepe myrtle, L. indica 'Muskogee', 'Tuscarora',
'Natchez'. Alpine and rock garden plants.

History/description: Educated at UC Davis, John
Nitta started High Ranch Nursery in 1976 as a
shade-tree nursery. Increased public interest and
general unavailability of choice plants shifted his
focus to feature California natives. He is now
working to develop an extensive selection of hardy
perennials. The 30-acre nursery includes display
plantings and container displays.

How to get there: Call for directions.

General information: Open to wholesale trade
only, Monday through Friday, 7:00 am–5:00 pm,
and March through November, Saturday, 8:00 am –
noon. Retail customers welcome only with a landscape professional. Nursery tours may be arranged.
Catalogue available. Deliveries within 100 miles on
minimum order of $500. Contract growing.

Intermountain Nursery
30443 Auberry Road, Prather 93651
(559) 855-3113, fax (559) 855-8809
Raymond G. Laclergue, Bonnie L. Bladen
Retail and Wholesale

Plant specialties: California native plants suited to
the foothill, alpine, and Central Sierra regions. Bog,
riparian, drought-tolerant, and Mediterranean plants.
Carpenteria californica, native perennial bunch
grasses, and hard-to-find annuals and perennials.
Erosion control and revegetation plants available.

History/description: Ray started the nursery in
1979, joined 10 years later by Bonnie. Both have a
strong commitment to native habitat preservation
and restoration. This 5-acre site includes several
display gardens and a garden supply and gift shop
selling organic products and soil ammendments,
Korean hand plows, and books on growing native
plants. The Flower Shop florist, a new addition,
offers fresh arrangements using native plants and
grasses. Visitors can picnic down by the creek or just
rest by the fish pond. They recommend you visit the
McKenzie Table Top Preserve and Black Mountain
Carpenteria Preserve, both managed by the Sierra
Foothills Conservancy, and the nearby Native Plant
Demonstration Garden in Auberry.

How to get there: Prather is located on Highway
168 between Clovis and Shaver Lake, about 27 miles
east of Clovis. Auberry Road is a mile past Prather on
the left.

General information: Open Monday through
Saturday, 8:00 am–5:00 pm; Sunday, 10:00 am–4:00
pm. Plant list available for SASE. Plants delivered
within a 100-mile radius on minimum orders of
$500. Consultations given on site-restoration
projects. Brochure describes the many classes offered,
from propagation of native plants to bat ecology.

Lake's Nursery

8435 Crater Hill Road, Newcastle 95658
(530) 885-1027, fax (530) 887-1511
e-mail: david@lakesnursery.com
David and Tsutako Judy Lake
Retail

Plant specialties: Japanese maples (Acer palmatum—100+ varieties, 4- to 24-inch boxes). Bamboo, other shrubs and trees.

History/description: In 1975, Judy Lake got tired of Dave's vegetable seedlings growing in the bathroom. So he got a greenhouse and moved his propagation efforts outside. Soon he was growing more vegetables than the family could eat. The Lakes began selling them. When customers noticed their landscape plants, they started to propagate and sell these, too. Hence, the vegetable stand became a nursery—a full-time venture since 1983. Today visitors will delight in the parklike grounds, Japanese garden, waterfall, and major koi pond. Too busy to propagate anymore, the Lakes can help you plan a Japanese garden of your own.

How to get there: The nursery is in Ophir. Call for directions, if needed.

General information: Open every day except Christmas and New Year's, 8:00 am–5:00 pm.

Lotus Valley Nursery & Gardens

5606 Peterson Lane, Lotus 95651
P. O. Box 859, Lotus 95651 (mailing address)
(530) 626-7021
Bob Davenport, Joe House
Retail

Plant specialties: Ornamental grasses, drought-tolerant plants, perennials, shrubs, and trees, featuring many California native plants.

History/description: These two delightfully compulsive gardeners started selling just a few plants from their own rich and varied garden. Word obviously got out. Now they are full-time plant producers, operating in a 4-acre valley near the south fork of the American River with a beautiful view of the mountains. Their rock garden was created from granite blasted to prepare a building site for the original Victorian ranch house (since burned). Their garden grows like topsy, using Mediterranean plants in all sorts of unusual combinations, in the ground and in a variety of unique pots. The stone sculptures throughout the garden are hand-cast at the nursery. They suggest you combine your visit with a trip to the nearby Marshall Gold Discovery State Park.

How to get there: Highway 50 east to Shingle Springs. Follow signs to Lotus. Turn left on Bassi Road. Right on Peterson Lane. From Auburn: Take Highway 49 to Lotus. Right on Lotus Road. Right on Bassi Road. Right on Peterson Lane.

General information: Open Wednesday through Sunday, 9:00 am–5:00 pm. Nursery tours may be arranged.

Maple Leaf Nursery

4236 Greenstone Road, Placerville 95667
(530) 626-8371, fax same
e-mail: maple_lf@inforum.net
Robert Barnard, Susan Iversen
Retail

Plant specialties: Salvias (40 varieties), unusual and hard-to-find perennials, Japanese maples (100 varieties), medicinal and ornamental herbs, Cornus (20 varieties), English roses, West Coast native lilies.

History/description: Well-seasoned in the nursery business for 20 years, Bob Barnard, started Maple Leaf in 1987 for the sole purpose of introducing new and different plants to the public. He and Susan now run the nursery which consists of a small sales area and an acre of growing grounds surrounded by oak-studded woodlands.

How to get there: Nursery is located 1/2 mile south of Highway 50 on the west side of Greenstone Road, between the towns of Shingle Springs and Placerville.

General information: Open by appointment only. Plants available also at area farmer's markets (call or write for information). Groups are welcomed.

Matsuda Landscape and Nursery
4888 Virginiatown Road, Newcastle 95658
(916) 645-1820
Hiroshi Matsuda
Retail

Plant specialties: Bonsai stock and mature specimens of Japanese maples, elms, and Pinus thunbergii. More than 300 finished bonsai and miniature landscapes. Bonsai accessories also available.

History/description: Hiro Matsuda has been a bonsai pottery importer, landscape designer/installer, bonsai nurseryman, potter, artist, and instructor. He has introduced two new bonsai art forms: bonarte and bonniwa. Bonarte, bonsai in a container, removes the artistic restrictions of traditional bonsai. Bonniwa, a miniature landscape in a tray, differs from other such landscapes (Saikei) in that it is a complete Japanese garden, including traditional rocks, mounds, and plants, as well as a ceramic bridge, lantern, tsukabai, waterfall, and stream. Opened since 1991, the nursery sells traditional bonsai, Chinese penjing, bonarte, bonniwa, Zen gardens, and Japanese painting—all the work of one remarkable man. Given the title, "Bonsai Guru" by the Sacramento Bee, Hiro Matsuda teaches classes in bonsai and Japanese gardening. Here you can find Eastern artistic tradition in harmonious blend with the ruggedly western, rolling hills of Placer County.

How to get there: Take I-80 to Sierra College Boulevard. Left on Sierra College Boulevard. Right on Highway 193. Left on Fowler Road. In .5 mile go right on Virginiatown Road. Nursery in .2 mile.

General information: Open Thursday through Saturday, 9:30 am–5:00 pm, or by appointment. Hiroshi Matsuda gives bonsai classes at the nursery. Free group tours may be arranged.

Orchid Species Specialties
42314 Road 415, Coarsegold 93614
(559) 683-3239
Walter Rybaczyk
Retail, Wholesale, and Mail Order

Plant specialties: Species orchids of many genera. His collection is collected in the wild (with permits from many foreign governments) and purchased from grower friends in South American countries.

History/description: Though Walter Rybaczyk was always interested in gardening and a self-described "frustrated botanist," his preoccupation with orchids began after his wife came home with two little plants bought at Sears & Roebuck in 1947. While he was an electrical power consultant for the city of Los Angeles, he took courses at the Arboretum, joined orchid societies, and began to travel and collect. His first fully-permitted plant expedition was to Belize in 1952. He has since been to 15 countries with botanists from the Los Angeles County Arboretum and other orchid specialists. The nursery was started in 1962 in Arcadia and moved to Coarsegold upon his retirement in 1976.

How to get there: Call for directions.

General information: Open every day, 8:00 am–5:00 pm, but it's wise to call ahead. General nursery list available for $1. Specific mail-order lists for different genera (e.g., Laelia, Paphiopedilum, Phragmipedium, Cattleya) available for $1 each. Minimum mail order is $50. Workshops offered.

Redbud Farms

1100 Four Wheel Drive, Georgetown 95634
(530) 622-3470
Martha and David Cox
Retail and Wholesale

Plant specialties: Cut flowers, fresh and dried roses. Also, organically-grown culinary and medicinal herbs, including seedling Ginko biloba (so they can remember what they are doing). Fruit available in the early fall.

History/description: Now settled into their new home on a 20-acre farm, the Coxes are back in the business of fruitful living. Located at 3,000-foot elevation in the Sierra Nevada foothills, beyond the PG&E grid plat, they operate their business and live completely on alternate energy systems. Worth a visit to observe this serenity. No traffic jams. Abundant wildflower walks. And the fishing is great. They will tell you where.

How to get there: The nursery is located 6 miles northeast of Georgetown (near Placerville). Call for directions.

General information: Open May through October, by appointment only.

Rose Acres
6641 Crystal Boulevard, El Dorado 95623
(530) 626-1722
Muriel and Bill Humenick
Retail and Mail Order

Plant specialties: Roses, especially the single (five-petaled) varieties and the hybrid musks.

History/description: The Humenicks have been busy judging and lecturing on the subject of roses since 1957. In 1980 they started this nursery to supply customers with unique and unusual cultivars. They now have 5,000 roses, including many species and old-fashioned types, on their 4-acre site. They still host their annual Rose and Wine tour on the Saturday before Mother's Day and suggest you check out the several interesting cemeteries with unusual, old plantings nearby. In recent years, Father's Day has become an additional Open Garden Day.

How to get there: Take Highway 50 east from Sacramento for about 30 miles to El Dorado Road exit. Right on El Dorado Road for 2 miles until it dead-ends. Left onto Pleasant Valley Road. Right at stop sign onto Highway 49. Continue south on Highway 49 for 5 miles. Right onto Crystal Boulevard; continue for 1 mile.

General information: Open by appointment only. Best viewing time is mid-April through June. Plant list available in October for SASE. Mail orders shipped December through February. Plants available for pick-up on site all year long. Pruning lectures and consultations. Slide talks available for interested groups.

Roses and Wine
8070 Fair Pines Lane, Garden Valley 95633
(530) 677-9722, fax (530) 676-0608
Barbara and Wayne Procissi
Retail and Mail Order

Plant specialties: Old garden roses, especially rebloomers, trailing and semi-procumbent ground cover roses.

History/description: Landscape architect and contractor Barbara Procissi and husband recently moved to their dream location, a 12-acre former Christmas tree farm, perched in the conifer forest at 2,000-foot elevation. In spite of personally moving 1,600 roses, she has not lost her enthusiasm for this beautiful piece of property. In addition to the rose gardens, a 2-acre vineyard and pond (with complimentary canoe) are in the works.

How to get there: The nursery is located 4 miles east of Georgetown, off Highway 193.

General information: Open by appointment only. Bare-root plants shipped January and February. They also ship plants for Rose Acres. Mail-order catalogue available for SASE. The 1-1/2-acre rose garden is available for rental for special occasions.

Superstition Iris Gardens

2536 Old Highway, Dept. WOE, Catheys Valley 95306-9738
(209) 966-6277
e-mail: randrcv@sierratel.com
Rick Tasco
Retail, Wholesale, and Mail Order

Plant specialties: Iris—bearded (1,300 varieties), rebloomers, historic iris, Louisianas, Siberians, Spurias.

History/description: Rick Tasco lived at the base of the Superstition Mountains, east of Phoenix, Arizona, and was a weekday computer programmer analyst and a weekend iris breeder. He moved to this 1-acre garden site in Catheys Valley for better growing conditions in 1990, bringing his iris business with him. He introduces new varieties each year. Some of his biggest winners are I. 'Mariposa Skies' and I. 'Ruffled Goddess'. The most recent are I. 'Mariposa Autumn' and I. 'Dream Express'.

How to get there: From the Bay Area, take the following routes: 101 to 152 to 59 to 99 to 140 to Old Highway, or 580 to 132 to 99 to 140 to Old Highway.

General information: Open April 1 to May 16, Thursday through Sunday, 10:00 am–5:00 pm. A catalogue is available February through August for $1.50. Mail-order plants shipped July and August.

You Bet Farms
14340 Boquest Drive, Nevada City 95959
(530) 292-9450
Rodger L. Rollings
Retail

Plant specialties: Hardy perennials (over 500 species) and California native plants. Also, alpines and drought-, deer-, heat-, and fire-resistant plants. Ornamental grasses, bog plants, succulents, ferns, and shade plants. Of special interest are the Penstemon, hardy Geranium, Achillea, Artemisia, and Campanula collections.

History/description: Coming from a family of gardeners and florists, Rodger Rollings has had a lifelong familiarity with plants. His English-style display garden is brimming with 4,000 plants which cater to the climate of the Sierra Foothills. Everything here is organically grown and he will gladly show you how to prepare soil with composted material. Nearby points of interest include Empire Mine State Park, Malakoff Diggins State Park, and Independence Trail.

How to get there: Go through Grass Valley and Nevada City on Highway 49. As you go through Nevada City, turn left at Downieville sign. Go approximately 13 country miles and turn right on Tyler Foote Road. After 3 miles, go right on Purdon Road. Go 1 mile to Boquest Drive and turn left. The nursery is the second driveway on the left.

General information: Open April through October, Wednesday through Sunday, 9:00 am–4:00 pm. Please call ahead. Rodger will give tours at the garden, explain soil preparation, and offer specific plant selection advice.

HORTICULTURAL ATTRACTIONS

Bourn Mansion
Empire Mine State Park
Empire exit off Highway 49, Grass Valley
(530) 273-8522

Another Willis Polk-designed home for mining magnate William Bourn (see Filoli, San Francisco, Peninsula & South Bay region). Thirteen acres of European-style parkland in the ponderosa forest, including several noteworthy gardens of roses and perennials.

Malakoff Diggins State Historical Park
Derbec Road, North Bloomfield
(530) 265-2740

Three thousand acres of foothill forest with incense cedars, ponderosa pines, and oaks, including old mining site and old apple orchards.

Marshall Gold Discovery State Historical Park
Highway 49, Coloma
(530) 622-3470

Wildflower displays on the canyon slopes of the American River, where gold was first discovered, in a countryside of oak and chaparral.

Rose Gardens at St. Joseph's Cultural Center

410 South Church Street, Grass Valley 95945
(530) 272-4725

Large Victorian-style garden, divided into four parts
by boxwood hedgerows in the form of the Celtic
harp, with many old, well-tended roses, other
flowering plants, and large trees.

South Yuba River Independence Trail

Eight miles north of Nevada City on Highway 49
P. O. Box 1026, Nevada City 95959 (mailing address)
(530) 265-9398

Once a canal and series of flumes to carry water
from the Yuba River to a mining site downstream,
this is now a 4-1/2-mile, wheelchair-accessible
wilderness trail through rolling, forested hills from
Nevada City area to North San Juan. Call for map.

San Joaquin Valley

Clements: 95
Fresno: 93, 100
Kerman: 96
La Grange: 97
Lodi: 92, 98
Micke Grove Reg. Park (Stockton): 100
Sanger: 94
Visalia: 99

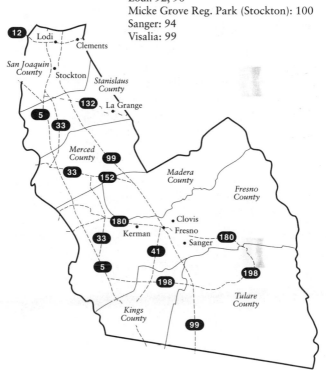

Cactus by Dodie
934 East Mettler Road, Lodi 95242
(209) 368-3692
Dodie and Dick Suess
Retail and Mail Order

Plant specialties: Cacti and succulents, rare stock from seed including Haworthia, Crassula, Conophytum, Euphorbia. Large cactus collection.

History/description: Dodie Suess was a cacti and succulent hobbyist, as were her parents. She and her husband started a retail nursery by buying the stock and mail-order list of a going-out-of-business nursery in 1981. They have a small display garden, though most plants are in greenhouses.

How to get there: Call for directions.

General information: Open Thursday through Saturday, 9:00 am–5:00 pm. Mail-order catalogue available for $2.

Hill 'n Dale

6427 North Fruit Avenue, Fresno 93711
(559) 439-8249, fax same
e-mail: cembra@ix.netcom.com
Dale Kloppenburg
Retail, Wholesale, and Mail Order

Plant specialties: Primarily Hoyas (Asclepiadaceae), about 300 varieties. Also, Dischidia, Aeschynanthus (lipstick plant).

History/description: Dale Kloppenburg has done more than most. With a degree in genetics from UC Berkeley, he started his career as a rose and fruit-tree breeder. In 1957 he opened an arts and crafts store, which he ran until 1968. Then came a stint as research agronomist for Northup King Seeds. In 1979, he followed the lure of his new hobby, Hoyas, traveling to Australia, Singapore, Malaysia, and elsewhere in search of all varieties of this genus. He has written *Hoyas of the Philippines* and *Hoya Handbook,* the final word on this versatile plant which can be succulent, thin-leafed, vining, or even epiphytic.

How to get there: Call for directions.

General information: Open by appointment only. Mail-order catalogue available for $1.

Kelly's Plant World
10266 East Princeton Avenue, Sanger 93657
(559) 292-3505
Herbert Kelly, Jr.
Retail and Wholesale

Plant specialties: Perennials. Eclectic and unusual collection of plants and bulbs from around the globe. Canna (125 varieties), Crinum, Gardenia (more than 25), Hymenocallis, Hedychium (gingers), Siberian iris, Lycoris (more than 150), Amaryllis belladonna (150 clones), cold-hardy palms. The country's largest collection of Aspidistra (15 varieties). Many variegated and unusual foliage types.

History/description: A collector since childhood, hybridizer Herb Kelley grew up gardening in his grandmother's garden in Fresno. Largely self-taught and very influenced by the writings of Luther Burbank and the tutelage of Mr. Henderson of Henderson's Experimental Gardens, Herb Kelly opened his nursery in the early 1970s. He has created the first yellow hybrid Crinum (Crinum 'Yellow Triumph'). All plants are field grown on 16 acres of land. In addition to the 1,000 varieties of unusual nursery plants, Herb Kelly is creating a botanical garden with 60-year-old crepe myrtles among the hundreds of rare and old trees. Well worth a visit.

How to get there: Highway 99 south to Herndon exit. Go left over railroad tracks to Herndon Avenue. Continue east for 13 miles through Fresno and Clovis to McCall Avenue. Right on McCall. After the Ashland stop sign, go about a mile and turn left on Princeton.

General information: Open every day, 8:00 am–5:00 pm. Catalogue available for $1, refundable on first order. Plants shipped. Slide talks for groups.

King's Mums

20303 East Liberty Road, Clements 95227
P. O. Box 368, Clements 95227 (mailing address)
(209) 759-3571
Ted King
Retail and Mail Order

Plant specialties: Chrysanthemum morifolium (mums)—250 different cultivars. Sold in 6-1/2-inch pots or as rooted cuttings in spring. Football types, spiders, cascades, bonsai types, and cushions. Bonsai.

History/description: King's was started in 1964 in Castro Valley as a sideline to Ted King's pest control business, for the purpose of locating fellow chrysanthemum hobbyists. King's has become the largest producer of chrysanthemum cultivars. Their annual fall King's Mums Show (October 1 to November 24) is well worth a visit to see the fields of flowers growing on California's rolling Sierra foothills in this land of wine and gold. A display garden illustrates the many styles of chrysanthemum culture—cascade, tree, bonsai, hanging basket, and espalier. All is not lost if you pass by there in the spring; he suggests you visit Daffodil Hill near Volcano further east on Route 88.

How to get there: One mile west of intersection of Highway 88 and Liberty Road. Eleven miles east of intersection of Highway 99 and Liberty Road.

General information: Open October 1 through November, every day, 9:00 am–5:00 pm. Catalogue available for $2, refundable with purchase. Mail orders shipped in spring. Deliveries throughout continental US on minimum order of $10. Large bus tours may be scheduled.

Planet Earth Growers Nursery
14178 West Kearney Boulevard, Kerman 93630
(559) 846-7881, fax (559) 846-9567
Cathy and John Etheridge
Retail and Wholesale

Plant specialties: Australian plants, California
native plants for foothills and desert areas, South
African plants, perennials, ornamental grasses,
drought-tolerant plants. Large collections of Acacia
(15 species), Ceanothus (10), Eucalyptus (15),
Grevillea (10), Hakea (6), and Eremophila (8).

History/description: The Etheridges began experimenting with Xeriscape plants when they opened
their nursery in Arizona in the 1970s. Moving to
California, they founded Planet Earth in 1987. The
nursery sits on 5 acres of growing fields, 3 of which
contain a demonstration garden testing plants for
their temperature tolerance (17° to 104°). All plants
are labeled and a network of paths provides easy
access. They suggest you visit Kearney Park, just 8
miles east on the same road.

How to get there: From Fresno take Highway 99
south to Shaw exit. Go west approximately 10
miles. Left on Dickenson Road. Right on Kearney
Boulevard. Nursery is in 4 miles.

General information: Open Tuesday through
Sunday, 9:00 am–5:00 pm. Tours for groups may be
arranged. Call about occasional demonstrations in
the garden.

The Rose Ranch
P. O. Box 326, La Grange 95329
(209) 852-9220
Alice Hinton, Anthony Hinton
Retail and Mail Order

Plant specialties: Over 800 varieties of old garden roses, especially centifolia, English, damask, bourbon roses. Some hybrid tea and floribunda roses.

History/description: Alice Hinton's father grew old roses for 65 years and she shares the family passion. When he became ill, she took over. Joined by her son, she opened for business in 1992, on their old family place in Salinas. In 1998, the Hinton's moved their entire rose collection to this dream location, on 20 acres of rolling foothills, below the snow and above the fog. They hope eventually to have the whole property under cultivation, but are now madly at work cultivating 5 acres, planting 1,000 roses with perennials and iris and shade trees for protection from the very hot summers. They will re-open to the public in the fall of 1999, maybe even sooner. The Tuolumne River is nearby for fishing and the old gold-mining town of La Grange is an historical landmark.

How to get there: Call for directions.

General information: Open by appointment only. Catalogue available for $3. Plant list available for SASE. Plants shipped year-round.

Seiju-en Bonsai Nursery
23181 North Davis Road, Lodi 95242
(209) 369-4168
Kevin and Angela Stroh
Retail, Wholesale, and Mail Order

Plant specialties: Bonsai plants grown from seeds, cuttings, grafting, division, layering, or from collected specimens (Ulmus, Azalea, Acer, Diospyros particularly). Field and container grown to develop caliper, the stock includes primarily pre-bonsai, partially trained and limited finished bonsai. Seedlings to 17-gallon trained specimens.

History/description: Carl Young, the previous owner, spent 20 years in Japan where he studied with the world's foremost bonsai masters. He was a registered teacher of bonkei (tray landscapes) and co-authored a book on chrysanthemum bonsai. He started the nursery in 1969 and introduced Ulmus parvifolia 'Seiju', propagated from a sport. Kevin and Angela Stroh purchased the nursery in January 1996 and are continuing under Carl's direction.

How to get there: Call for directions

General information: Open by appointment. Plants shipped on minimum order of $25.

Sequoia Nursery—Moore Miniature Roses

2519 East Noble Avenue, Visalia 93292
(559) 732-0309, fax (559) 732-0192
Ralph S. Moore
Retail, Wholesale, and Mail Order

Plant specialties: Miniature roses (over 300 varieties), specializing in those hybridized by owner, as well as a line of old or unusual roses.

History/description: For as long as he can remember, Ralph Moore has always been interested in roses. Son of a farmer, he established a general nursery of landscape plants in 1937 and planted the trees for which the nursery is named. By the 1950s, the allure of roses prevailed and the nursery was devoted entirely to them. Over the past 60 years, he has developed over 400 varieties of roses, mostly miniatures, registered by the American Rose Society, many named for the good folk in and around Visalia. Most are very unusual, very floriferous, and often everblooming. Featured as an American original in Charles Hillinger's book *America,* Mr. Moore will be 92 in 1999 and is still going strong. He also breeds lilacs, crepe myrtles, and amaryllis, though none of these plants are for sale.

How to get there: From Highway 99, take Highway 198 east for about 8 miles. Take Ben Maddox exit to Noble Avenue. Go left on Noble for 1/2 mile. You will see the sequoias.

General information: Open Monday through Friday, 8:30 am–4:30 pm; Saturday and Sunday, 10:00 am–4:00 pm, except for major holidays. Mail-order catalogue and supplemental plant lists available for SASE.

HORTICULTURAL ATTRACTIONS

Forestiere Underground Garden
5021 West Shaw, Fresno 93727
(559) 271-0734

This old garden planted in the 1920s next to an underground house includes a variety of plants and trees grown well below grade with their canopies above ground for various experimental reasons. Open weekend afternoons. Tours. Admission fee.

Micke Grove Regional Park
11793 Micke Grove Road (between I-5 and Highway 99)
North of Stockton
(209) 331-7400, (209) 953-8800

Large oak grove, 3-acre Japanese garden containing a distinctive collection of camellias, and small rose garden—all in a 259-acre park with zoo and museum.

Roeding Park
890 West Belmont, Fresno
(209) 498-1551

Impressive, old, labeled trees.

Shin Zen Japanese Friendship Garden
Woodward Park, Fresno
(209) 498-1551

Four garden sections, combining plants from the East and West, highlight the separate seasons with a serenely Japanese touch. Admission $1. Call for seasonal hours.

East Bay

Berkeley: 102, 106, 114, 117, 129, 130, 131
Concord: 110, 122, 131
Danville: 118, 123
El Sobrante: 124
Fremont: 111, 126
Hayward: 112
Kensington: 105, 129
Livermore: 103, 120, 125
Martinez: 108
Moraga: 107, 116
Oakland: 109, 115, 121, 130, 131
Richmond: 104
Tilden Park (Berkeley): 128
Walnut Creek: 113, 119, 127, 128

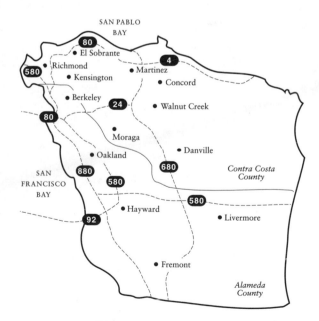

Alpines
1646 10th Street, Berkeley 94710
(510) 524-1969
John Andrews
Retail

Plant specialties: Bulbs and alpine plants from around the world, including Campanula, Penstemon, Eriogonum, Primula.

History/description: An entomologist at UC Berkeley, John Andrews became interested in alpines while backpacking in the high country. He started gathering seed, joined the American Rock Garden Society, and was suddenly in the nursery business. All of his plants are propagated from seed, still collected by himself or trusted experts in the field, and grown in a special soil and gravel mix.

How to get there: From Highway 80, take University Avenue exit. Go east on University, then north (left) on 10th Street.

General information: Open by appointment only. Plant list is available for SASE.

Jeff Anhorn Nursery
P. O. Box 2061, Livermore 94551
(925) 447-0858, fax (925) 447-1854
Jeff and Renee Anhorn
Wholesale

Plant specialties: California native plants, perennials, woody ornamentals. 400–500 types of plants, from 4-inch through 15-gallon sizes.

History/description: A graduate of the Landscape Architecture Department of UC Berkeley, Jeff Anhorn comes from prime horticultural stock. His uncle, Louis Gravello, owned many plant patents. The nursery markets plants through local brokers and directly to landscape contractors.

How to get there: Call for directions to their growing grounds in Sunol.

General information: Open to wholesale trade only, by appointment. Retail customers may visit with a landscape professional. Plant list available for SASE.

Annie's Annuals
P. O. Box 5053, Richmond 94805
(510) 215-1326
Annie and Alejandro Hayes
Wholesale

Plant specialties: Annuals (unusual and obscure) and some perennials.

History/description: Annie was lured west during the good times of the folk/rock music era and led a predictably interesting life. She settled in the Bay Area with her husband and worked at Berkeley Horticultural Nursery for a number of years. "Endlessly fascinated by seed," they started propagating and pretty soon had flats all over their front and back yards. The nursery was inevitable and opened in 1990. They continue to relish the challenge of propagating unusual plants from seed; 99% of their business is seed-propagated.

How to get there: Directions given when appointment is made.

General information: Open by appointment only. Deliveries on minimum order of eight flats.

Michael Barclay & Associates
400 Yale Avenue, Kensington 94708
(510) 524-0888, fax (510) 524-5999
Michael D. Barclay
Retail

Plant specialties: Rhododendrons—Maddenii and Vireya species and hybrids. Alpines and ground covers, especially those used as lawn substitutes, including Rubus tricolor, R. nepalensis, Acorus species. Perennials and drought-tolerant plants.

History/description: Opera scholar and aficionado Michael Barclay has transferred his robust sense of histrionics into the garden. Intentionally overgrown, his garden is a collector's paradise of more than 2,000 species and varieties of plants. An exotic woodland, a dry slope of perennials and other plants (watered only three times a year), rule-breaking planting strips, a mixed border containing the artwork of regional luminaries, a variegated rock garden, and a patio ground-cover demonstration garden are packed into his Eden. Still evading maturity, Michael has been the subject of many articles and is an encyclopedic plantsman. His designs for plant-prolific gardens have won many awards; his generosity of spirit has won many friends.

How to get there: Call for directions.

General information: Open by appointment only. Garden talks and tours are a specialty. Design services offered.

Berkeley Horticultural Nursery

1310 McGee Avenue, Berkeley 94703
(510) 526-4704
e-mail: berkhort@sirius.com
website: www.berkeleyhort.com
Doty family
Retail

Plant specialties: Large and varied plant selection, including annuals, perennials, vines, shrubs, bulbs, ground covers, rock garden plants, cacti and succulents, aquatic, carnivorous, and shade plants. California natives, Mediterranean and other drought-tolerant plants. Large collection of rhododendrons, (especially Vireya, Maddenii), roses (300 varieties including old roses), camellias, and vegetables.

History/description: This business was started in 1922 and is now in its fourth generation of family ownership. The Dotys are responsible for the palm plantings at Hearst Castle in San Simeon and have introduced hundreds of fuchsia varieties to the Bay Area, as well as the Vireya rhododendron 'George Budgen'. The nursery, almost 2 acres in size, has a "tropical" courtyard and rockery display. Although few plants are grown on-site, Berkeley Hort has a cadre of growers who contract-grow specially for them. Their emphasis has always been on unusual and appropriate plants.

How to get there: From I-80, take the Gilman Street exit (northernmost of the Berkeley exits). Go left on Hopkins when Gilman ends. After 3 blocks, go right on McGee and look for street parking.

General information: Open March through September, every day, 9:00 am–5:30 pm. Winter hours, every day but Thursday, 8:30 am–5:00 pm. Local deliveries may be arranged. Workshops and classes announced in bimonthly newsletter.

Copacabana Gardens

P. O. Box 323, Moraga 94556
(925) 254-2302
Lee Anderson, James Larsen
Retail and Wholesale

Plant specialties: Unusual subtropical and drought-tolerant plants from the Southern Hemisphere, (South Africa, South America, Australasia, and the Philippines). Seedlings to 24-inch boxes.

History/description: Like many specialty growers, Copacabana Gardens started because there was a need for more interesting plant material suited to the many Bay Area microclimates. Open since 1987, their concentration on Southern Hemisphere flora has already yielded new plant possibilities for California gardens. This partnership also offers site consultations, design, and landscape construction. They recommend you also visit Hacienda de las Flores in Moraga.

How to get there: Call for directions.

General information: Open by appointment only. Closed December and January. Deliveries on orders over $200 throughout the Bay Area.

Cottage Garden Plants

2680 Franklin Canyon Road, Martinez 94563
212 Ludell Drive, Walnut Creek 94596 (mailing address)
(925) 946-9136
Tim Torres
Retail and Wholesale

Plant specialties: Perennials, native grasses, shrubs, and trees.

History/description: Landscape contractor Tim Torres could not find acceptable numbers of well-grown plants for his projects and so started propagating in his backyard. He discovered he was a whiz at grafting and propagation, a desirable trait inherited from his farmer grandfather. Now with a 3-acre location of its own, the nursery occupies an increasingly large share of his time and interest. His greenhouses are enhanced by vacuum hoses sucking in carbon dioxide from compost piles outside. Trained at Cal Poly Pomona in hotel and restaurant management, Tim has recently started to propagate culinary herbs.

How to get there: Take Highway 680 to Highway 4 to Martinez. Take the Alhambra Avenue exit south. Go right (west) onto Franklin Canyon Road for 1.7 miles. Go right on Wolcott Lane. Follow the signs.

General information: Open Friday and Saturday, 9:00 am–4:00 pm. Wholesale availability list. Retail catalogue.

The Dry Garden
6556 Shattuck Avenue, Oakland 94609
(510) 547-3564
Richard Ward
Retail

Plant specialties: Unusual, rare, hard-to-find, and "queer" plants. Cacti and succulents for seasonally dry climate, Mediterranean plants, ornamental grasses.

History/description: This self-confessed plant and garden maniac is having a lot of fun growing and searching for weird and interesting plants. His garden nursery has enlivened almost an entire acre on a previously dead corner of North Oakland. Richard opened the nursery with his late partner, Keith Cahoon, in 1987. Both were Chattanoogans who knew each other from their student and early working days there. Both became obsessed with collecting cacti and succulents. When they reconnected in California many years later, they combined their collections and the nursery was born.

How to get there: From I-80 east, exit on Ashby. Follow Ashby. Turn right on Shattuck. Nursery is 3 blocks on left. From Highway 580 west, take Highway 24 east off-ramp. Exit at Martin Luther King/51st Street. Turn right onto 51st, then left onto Shattuck. Nursery is 2 blocks after third light on right. Only 10 minutes more to the UC Botanical Garden and the Regional Parks Botanic Garden.

General information: Open Tuesday through Sunday, 10:00 am–5:00 pm. Deliveries to the Bay Area arranged for fee.

Exotic Flora Landscape and Nursery, Inc.

4081 Golden Avenue, Concord 94521 (mailing address)
(925) 299-9433
Gary Gragg
Retail and Wholesale

Plant specialties: Subtropical plants, including palms
(50 varieties), bananas, bromeliads, cycads, cannas,
flowering trees, and vines. The only Bay Area source
for cold-hardy Heliconia and Archontophoenix,
Phoenix rupicola (cliff date palm), Ficus macrophylla,
Cinnamomum glanduliferum.

History/description: As a little kid, Gary Gragg was
fascinated by tropical plants, especially palms, and
started collecting. His interest grew at San Diego
State where he took some horticulture courses and
did landscaping on the side. After college he started
work as a landscaper, then as a landscape contractor.
He started to sell the overflow plants propagated for
his projects; in 1993 he opened the nursery. This
energetic young man has done installations at the
Oakland Zoo and many other places. His well-tended,
well-organized nursery includes a demonstration
garden filled with examples of the plants he grows.

How to get there: Call for directions.

General information: Open by appointment. Plant
list available for SASE. Deliveries on minimum order
of $150 to $250. Design and installation services.

Four Winds Growers

P. O. Box 3538, Fremont 94539
(510) 656-2591, fax (510) 656-1360
website: www.fourwindsgrowers.com
Don Dillon, Sr. and Jr.
Wholesale and Mail Order

Plant specialties: Citrus—dwarf and standard, avocado, Daphne.

History/description: This major citrus growing business started in a Carmel backyard as a retirement hobby of Don Dillon's father. By 1949 he had contracted with a Ventura grower to produce plants for retail nurseries. The nursery was moved to Fremont in 1954 and now specializes in dwarf citrus, grown in the ground on cultivar specific dwarfing rootstocks. Four generations have worked here. Don Dillon's activities have not been restricted just to plants; he is a past mayor of Fremont and past president of the Association of Bay Area Governments. Don Dillon, Jr. is currently president of the California Citrus Nurserymen's Society.

How to get there: Your landscaper must call for directions.

General information: Open to wholesale trade only. Visit with your landscaper. Catalogue and booklet on growing citrus available for SASE. Group tours, garden talks, and slide shows may be arranged.

Grove Way Bonsai Nursery

1239 Grove Way, Hayward 94541
(510) 537-1157
John Uchida
Retail

Plant specialties: Bonsai, specializing in Pinus thunbergii and Juniperus species.

History/description: John Uchida has been collecting and sculpting bonsai since 1959, having studied the art under the bonsai master, Toichi Domoto. Primarily occupied for a good part of this time as a landscape contractor, he opened the nursery in the early 1970s. This small nursery includes a display garden.

General information: Open Thursday through Saturday, 9:00 am–5:00 pm. Pruning demonstrations offered. House calls may be arranged, Monday through Wednesday.

How to get there: Take the Hayward exit (Highway 238) off of Highway 580. After two lights, go right on Grove Way for 1-1/2 blocks.

Harlequin Gardens
P. O. Box 2155, Walnut Creek 94595
(925) 947-2958, (925) 932-7673 (office)
fax (925) 932-2863
Donald Rose
Wholesale

Plant specialties: Perennials, with particular emphasis on variegated plants and plants with unusual foliage.

History/description: Donald Rose knows his way around gardens, having worked in some of the best. Always fascinated by plants with striking foliage, he had amassed a robust collection of hard-to-get and unusual plants. In 1991, with the help of his wife Kristina as well as horticulturalist Janet Edwards, he began propagating the collection. In 1993 this 1-acre commercial site became available and his long-time dream of starting a nursery became reality. The nursery has introduced Verbascum 'Harlequin Hybrids' and Aurinia saxatilis (Alyssum saxatile) 'Harlequin'. Stay tuned to this guy's plans—he's already talking about a larger space.

How to get there: Call for directions.

General information: Open to wholesale customers only, by appointment. An availability list will be sent upon request. Local deliveries may be arranged.

Magic Gardens
729 Heinz Avenue, Berkeley 94710
(510) 644-1992, fax (510) 644-1568
Aerin Moore; Don Sayer, nursery manager
Retail

Plant specialties: Perennials (750 varieties, including 21+ varieties of Salvia). Camellias, ferns, and other shade plants. Also aquatic plants, rock garden plants, ornamental grasses, annuals, succulents, shrubs, trees, and houseplants. Always a good sale selection.

History/description: Aerin Moore was taught good gardening practices by his grandfather and has been a gardener ever since. Impressed by what he could not find for his landscape clients, he started the nursery in 1982. Since the early 1990s with the acquisition of a test garden in the Oakland Hills, Magic Gardens has been propagating in earnest. Recently acquired growing grounds have resulted in an expanded inventory. The beautifully landscaped rockery surrounding the nursery gives visitors the chance to see potential purchases in a garden setting.

How to get there: From Interstate 80, take Ashby exit to first stoplight. Go left on on 7th Street for 3 blocks. Go left on Heinz. Off-street parking.

General information: Open Monday through Saturday, 9:00 am–5:30 pm. Sunday, 10:00 am–5:00 pm. Winter hours: Monday through Saturday, 9:00 am–5:00 pm, Sunday 10:00 am–5:00 pm. Informative newsletter available. Full schedule of classes and talks offered at the nursery.

Merritt College Landscape Horticulture Department

12500 Campus Drive, Oakland 94619
(510) 436-2418, fax (510) 436-2631
Retail and Wholesale

Plant specialties: Perennials, focusing on rare finds, grafted magnolias, roses (old and new), bulbs, orchids, houseplants, and vegetables.

History/description: Merritt College's Landscape Horticulture Department continues to grow in stature, adding courses to keep up with California's fast-changing horticultural landscape. In addition to design and plant identification, courses here cover the practicalities of landscaping, from the aesthetics of pruning to nursery management. There are many short-term, one-day courses offered for professionals and homeowners. For 30 years, Merritt College has trained generations of talented landscapers who have made their craft an art. There are 7-1/2 acres of gardens for viewing full-size specimens and completely renovated, state-of-the-art greenhouses and a weather station.

How to get there: Take Highway 580 east to 35th Avenue exit (which becomes Redwood Road). Go left over freeway up Redwood Road. Right on Campus Drive. Take first available left, go left again past Child Care Center. Go left at the T. Parking costs 50¢.

General information: Open Monday through Friday, 8:00 am–10:00 pm, and on Saturday if a class is taught that day. Call first. Big sales in early May and October. Exact dates and class schedules listed on their website. Wholesale contact: Susan Ashley, (510) 524-3627. Docent tours available upon request.

Moraga Garden Center
1400 Moraga Road, Moraga 94556
(925) 376-1810
Ken Murakami
Retail (courtesy discounts to landscapers)

Plant specialties: Unusual conifers and dwarf conifers, including Pinus strobus 'Blue Shag'. Trees, especially Japanese maples. Perennials (500+ varieties), Hosta, Camellia, bamboo, roses on their own rootstock, daylilies (100+ varieties), irises, Epimedium, and oddball things such as Carpinus koreana.

History/description: Ken Murakami's father started the nursery in 1972 as a sideline to his career as a landscape architect. This made Ken's career choice delightfully simple. He had always enjoyed working with plants, studied biological sciences in college, and was well trained by past work at the nursery. He has been working here full-time since 1986 and has extended the nursery's selection, collecting plants hard to find at the wholesale level. Sharing his finds with other growers, he has helped get many interesting plants into the trade.

How to get there: From Highway 24 eastbound, take the Orinda/Moraga exit. Turn right on Camino Pablo. Continue on Camino Pablo past McDonald's Nursery into the Moraga Shopping Center. Nursery is on the far left side.

General information: Open every day except Tuesday, 9:00 am–5:00 pm. Shorter hours in winter. Plants delivered locally on minimum orders of $250.

Native Here Nursery
101 Golf Course Drive, Berkeley 94708
(510) 549-0211
California Native Plant Society, Charli Danielsen
Retail and Wholesale

Plant specialties: Locally collected and grown native species from Alameda and Contra Costa counties.

History/description: Native Here Nursery was started in 1993, an outgrowth of an older nursery called D.A.W.N. (Design Associates Working with Nature). Its purpose is to propagate plants from locally collected seed and cuttings for revegetation projects in Alameda and Contra Costa counties. Owned by the California Native Plant Society, the nursery is administered by Charli Danielsen, a former state chairman of CNPS, and operated with the assistance of many volunteers. Their success at propagation has resulted in many excess plants, which are for sale here. The plant inventory changes according to which revegetation project is currently underway.

How to get there: Located opposite the golf course in Tilden Park, southeast of Shasta Road.

General information: Open Friday, 9:00 am–noon, and second Saturdays.

No Nonsense Nursery

1779 St. Helena Drive, Danville 94526 (mailing address)
(925) 838-8873, fax (925) 820-1843
Pat Thompson
Retail

Plant specialties: Ornamental grasses—150 species
and varieties. Perennials—500 types, including
Salvia (30 varieties), Rudbeckia, heat-tolerant
Helichrysum and types well suited to woodland
gardens. Also Buddleia, shrub roses on their own
rootstock.

History/description: Some career changes seem
made in heaven. A junior-college horticultural
program convinced Pat Thompson to shift gears.
She gave up teaching to start a landscape maintenance business. At the same time a young air-traffic
controller opted for a less stressful career in the
great outdoors and began to work in tree care. They
met on a job, got married, and launched No Non-
sense Horticultural Services, offering garden design,
installation, maintenance, and arborist services.
(They are both certified arborists.) The nursery is an
outgrowth of their propagation efforts to supply
plants for their projects. The naturalistic garden
surrounding their home uses low-maintenance
plants to provide habitat for birds.

How to get there: Call for directions.

General information: Open by appointment and
on the first Thursday of each month. Local deliveries
on minimum orders of $100. Nursery tours offered.

Noodle Dog Gardens

1451 Springbrook Road, Walnut Creek 94596 (mailing)
(925) 930-6022
Johnny Marchant
Retail and Wholesale (depending on how much of
his time you take)

Plant specialties: Alpine plants, rock garden plants,
unusual perennials (small amounts).

History/description: Johnny Marchant just could
not stifle a long-simmering delight in plants. This
self-taught horticulturist, artist, and garden designer
has amassed a very eclectic collection of rare and
unusual plants which he will sometimes part with if
you are a discerning plant nut. The nursery opened
in 1994 after he purchased his home and garden. He
has now taken over the neighbor's yard for growing
and keeps his own for display purposes. Currently,
he is testing new plants for their suitability to East
Bay conditions. Some grow, some go. He has also
hybridized and introduced several Pacific Coast iris
hybrids.

How to get there: Call for directions.

General information: Call for an appointment as
John is usually out, somewhere or another, gardening and mumbling his mantra: If you know it, we
don't grow it. Loves to talk plants.

The Orchid Ranch: Orchids Orinda, Fordyce Orchids, Tonkin's Orchids, Inc.

1330 Isabel Avenue, Livermore 94550
(925) 447-7171
Helen and Maynard Michel, the Fordyce family, and
Mrs. W. J. Tonkin
Retail, Wholesale, and Mail Order

Plant specialties: Orchids, primarily those useful as
houseplants. Specifically Phalaenopsis (butterfly or
moth orchid), Cattleya and its intergeneric hybrids,
Paphiopedilum (lady slipper), Dendrobium, Oncidium.

History/description: This collaborative venture
started with the founding of Orchids Orinda in the
1970s as a retirement caper for the Michels. They
were quickly joined by the Fordyce family upon Mr.
Fordyce's decision to re-establish his own business
after many years working for a major orchid grower.
The Tonkins joined in 1985. Sounds like more fun
than Rossmoor. All three families do their own
hybridizing and have produced many well-known
orchid hybrids and awarded clones. Their 31,500
square feet of greenhouses are located in the
Livermore Valley.

How to get there: From Highway 580 east, take
Portola Avenue exit. At stoplight, turn right at North
Murrieta Boulevard. After a mile, turn right at East
Stanley Boulevard. After another mile, turn left at
Isabel Avenue. Proceed 9 miles to nursery on the left.

General information: Open Tuesday through
Sunday, 10:00 am–5:00 pm. (Tonkin's open Friday,
Saturday, and Sunday only.) Plant list occasionally
available for SASE. From time to time seminars and
culture sessions offered at Orchids Orinda and
Fordyce Orchids. Group tours and presentations may
be arranged.

Orchidanica

P. O. Box 13151, Oakland 94661 (subject to change, check website)
(510) 482-0408, fax (510) 482-5233
e-mail: orchid3@uclink4.berkeley.edu
website: www.orchidmall.com/orchidanica
Larry Moskovitz
Retail, Wholesale, and Mail Order

Plant specialties: Orchids—miniature, Cattleya, Masdevallia, Oncidium. Unusual genera include Zygopetalum, Laelia. Rare species.

History/description: Larry Moskovitz' studies in photography, botany, and ornamental horticulture combined with a lifelong fascination with orchids eventually led him into the nursery business. Opened in 1985, the nursery will make house calls throughout the Bay Area to repot your orchid. Past president of the San Francisco Orchid Society, Larry gladly shares his knowledge with visitors.

How to get there: Mail order and shows only.

General information: Free plant list available. Mail-order catalogue is on-line and is the same as paper catalogue but has color photos and links to orchid growing sites, plus other information.

San Miguel Greenhouses
936 San Miguel Road, Concord 94520
(925) 798-0476
Pamela and James Leaver
Retail, Wholesale, and Mail Order

Plant specialties: Rare, epiphytic bromeliads
(Tillandsia, Aechmea, Vriesea), some hybrid
Neoregelia.

History/description: This family business is an
extension of Pamela Leaver's bromeliad hobby
which first outgrew her home, then outgrew her
rented greenhouse, and now happily lodges in a
9,000-square-foot greenhouse in Concord. Of
course, her growing space is much greater than that,
since epiphytic bromeliads can grow almost anywhere. Visitors will enjoy the riotous color inside.

How to get there: Take Highway 24 to Highway
680 north. Take Treat Avenue exit. After 12 traffic
lights, go left on San Miguel until number 934. Go
right over canal behind gate to number 936.

General information: Open every day, 1:00 pm
until dark, but call first to make sure they are there.
Plants shipped by mail. Mrs. Leaver loves to give
talks about bromeliads.

Sunset Color
1435 San Ramon Valley Boulevard, Danville 94526
(925) 831-3574, fax (925) 831-8616
Judy Sandkuhle
Retail and Wholesale

Plant specialties: Pelargoniums (fancy-leaf, dwarf, and scented varieties), Hosta, and Alstroemeria "butterfly" hybrids.

History/description: The daughter of nurseryman Herman Sandkuhle (proprietor of Sunset Nursery in Oakland), Judy got a genetic head start in the business. After studying ornamental horticulture at Cal Poly San Luis Obispo, she worked for 10 years as a grower for her dad. She opened her own nursery in 1995 on the last remaining bit of country-side between Danville and San Ramon. She has developed her own soil mix which she sells, along with individual plants and "color bowls."

How to get there: From Highway 680, take the San Ramon Valley Road exit. The nursery is located on the west side of the freeway between Crow Canyon and Sycamore Valley Roads.

General information: Open Tuesday through Saturday, 8:30 am–5:00 pm. Plant list available for SASE. Deliveries on wholesale orders.

Terra Viridis
4726 Hilltop Road, El Sobrante 94803
(510) 222-9438
Bob Johannessen, Carol Morse
Retail and Wholesale

Plant specialties: Bamboo (140+ species in the collection, including the genera Bambusa, Phyllostachys, Fargesia, Sasa, and Pleioblastus). Herbs, California natives, vegetables, ornamentals, and ferns, including Pyrrosia and Adiantum.

History/description: Yet again, passionate plant hobbyists discover they can profit from their pleasures. In 1981 Bob Johannessen, influenced in his youth by the fern collecting of his mother, got hooked on bamboo thanks to a sale by the Northern California chapter of the American Bamboo Society at Strybing Arboretum. But he also never lost his interest in ferns, having served as a past president of the now defunct San Francisco Fern Society. Carol Morse, a botanist by training, has been propagating plants for most of her life. Their plants are sold also at the Sunday farmer's market in Oakland's Jack London Square, and at the Tuesday farmer's market in Concord. This crowded, 1/4-acre backyard nursery reflects their combined interests and their contributions towards improving Terra Viridis, Latin for green earth.

How to get there: Directions given when appointments are made.

General information: Open on weekends, by appointment only.

Up Sprout Geraniums

1378 South Livermore Avenue, Livermore 94550
(925) 447-3575
Sylvia Musso
Retail and Wholesale

Plant specialties: Pelargoniums (800 varieties), including mini, dwarf, ivy, fancy-leaf, and scented, as well as other members of Geraniaceae family. Also, reblooming, tall bearded iris (165 varieties).

History/description: In 1978, while recovering from a bad accident sustained while training her Tennessee walking horse, Sylvia Musso saw an ad for a 4-by-7-foot greenhouse kit. To fill the greenhouse, she decided to grow something which was not easily available, something which would require her expected year of recuperation to mature and something which would use little heat. Hence pelargoniums. A full-time business since 1981, she now has 20,000 plants under polyethylene, on her 3-acre site. While you are in the area, plan to visit the well-landscaped Concannon and Wente Wineries.

How to get there: Highway 580 to North Livermore Avenue. Go south to 1378 South Livermore Avenue. Turn left; follow dirt road 1/2 mile to end.

General information: Open by appointment only. Nursery tours, propagation, and on-site workshops offered. Bus tours welcome.

Valencia Ranch Nursery
P. O. Box 3442, Fremont 94539
(925) 656-7703
James and Susan Gearhart
Wholesale

Plant specialties: Ornamental grasses (80 species), including Festuca, Carex, Stipa, Elymus.

History/description: The Gearharts got John Greenlee to design a garden around their home to feature their collection of grasses. The 2-1/2-acre result shows both the beauty and practicality (grasses are a good firebreak) of using ornamental grasses as landscape plants. The nursery was an outgrowth of the garden and the enthusiastic response of its visitors. A Master Gardener, James Gearhart lectures and offers on-site plant consultations.

How to get there: Call for directions.

General information: Open to wholesale trade only. Other customers may visit with a landscape professional, by appointment. Plant list and contract growing services available. Deliveries within 100 miles on minimum orders of $100. Will ship plants beyond 100 miles for a fee.

HORTICULTURAL ATTRACTIONS

The Ruth Bancroft Garden
P. O. Box 30845, Walnut Creek 94598
(925) 210-9663

History/description: In 1972, with his walnut orchard in decline and her 1,000 plants in pots proving too time-consuming to care for, the Bancrofts began this exquisite 3-acre garden of cacti, succulents, and companion plants. Preeminent plantsmith Lester Hawkins laid out the mounded beds for Ruth Bancroft to place her collection of plants. Now in her nineties, she still works in the garden every day, tending her 2,000 plants, undaunted by the setbacks of frost and floods. The garden was the inspiration for the founding of the Garden Conservancy, a national organization dedicated to the preservation of significant private gardens. In 1993, a nonprofit group, The Ruth Bancroft Garden Inc., was formed to manage and maintain the garden; Mrs. Bancroft has deeded this part of her historic ranch property to them.

General information: Garden is open from mid-April to mid-October. Reservations required for all tours and events. Docent tours available on Fridays and Saturdays. Plant sales at 11:00 am on tour days.

The Gardens at Heather Farm

1540 Marchbanks Drive, Walnut Creek 94598
(925) 947-1678

History/description: Heather was a horse and this was her farm, owned by Mr. Marchbanks, a famous breeder of thoroughbreds. Since 1970 it has been a public-education garden. Twenty demonstration gardens, located throughout the 5.4-acre hillside site, include California Natives, Water-Conserving, Butterfly, Sensory, and Children's Multicultural Gardens. A nonprofit volunteer organization, the Gardens also provides outreach programs in horticulture, conservation, and ecology.

Plant sales: Plant sales are held in the spring and fall.

General information: Gardens are open daily from sunrise to sunset. Self-guided tour brochure or guided group tours available by calling (925) 947-6712. Office and horticultural reference library open weekdays from 9:00 am-1:00 pm.

Regional Parks Botanic Garden

Wildcat Canyon Road at foot of South Park Drive, Tilden Park, Berkeley 94708
(510) 841-8732

History/description: Part of the East Bay Regional Park District, the Botanic Garden is devoted exclusively to California native flora. Not surprisingly, it has been zealously supported by the California Native Plant Society. Tours of the 10-acre garden can be arranged for groups of 10 or more. They have a winter lecture series from November to February. 1990 marked the garden's 50th anniversary.

Plant Sales: Plant sale held at the Botanic Garden on the third Saturday of April.

General information: Garden is open daily, 8:30 am–5:00 pm. Their annual journal, *The Four*

Seasons, devoted to the botany, ecology, and culture of California native plants, is available for purchase.

UC Blake Garden
70 Rincon Road, off Arlington, Kensington 94707
(510) 524-2449

History/description: Formerly the home of Mr. and Mrs. Anson Blake, this 11-acre garden and house is the official residence of the president of the University of California system and used as a teaching lab for the UC Berkeley Department of Landscape Architecture. The garden was designed in the mid-1920s by Mrs. Blake's sister, one of the first UC Berkeley landscape architecture students. The house was situated to take advantage of the spectacular views and to serve as a windbreak for the garden. A great variety of microclimates makes possible a variety of garden rooms, including a redwood canyon, dry Mediterranean garden, Italianate formal garden, and Australian hollow. Groups can arrange tours.

General information: Open Monday through Friday, 8:00 am–4:30 pm, closed university holidays.

UC Botanical Garden
University of California
Centennial Drive, Berkeley 94720
(510) 642-3343

History/description: A venerable century old, this 34-acre garden has special collections of California native, New World desert, Meso-American, and Asian plants. Also, a South African hillside, an old growth redwood forest, native and alpine rock gardens, and greenhouses devoted to orchids, ferns, tropical, and carnivorous plants. Free docent tours, 1:30 pm, Saturday and Sunday. Their active membership support group arranges a wide variety of lectures and workshops.

Plant sales: Big plant sales in the fall and on
Mother's Day weekend; smaller sales are held
throughout the year. The visitor center has a garden
shop selling plants, books, and other garden items.

General information: Garden is open every day
except Christmas. Visitor center is open from 10:00
am–4:00 pm every day except Monday.

Berkeley Municipal Rose Garden
Euclid Avenue at Bay View Place, Berkeley 94708
(510) 644-6530

Three thousand roses on terraced amphitheater.

Dunsmuir House and Gardens Historic Estate
2960 Peralta Oaks Court, Oakland 94605
(510) 615-5555

Fifty-acre historic landscape designed by John
McLaren for the I. W. Hellman, Jr. family, owners
of the property from 1906 until the late 1950s.
Call for hours.

Firestorm Memorial Garden
Intersection of Hiller Drive and Tunnel Road, Oakland
(510) 843-3828

Garden of California natives and Mediterranean-
climate plants designed by Ron Lutsko, with
memorial sculptures commemorating the devastat-
ing 1991 Oakland/Berkeley Hills fire. Several other
firescape gardens are in the works, including the
succulent garden by David Schwartz at the entry to
Kaiser school. The energetic nonprofit North Hills
Landscape Committee one day hopes to have a fire-
resistant greenway bordering both sides of Highway 24.

Lakeside Park Garden Center
666 Bellevue Avenue, Oakland 94610
(510) 238-3187

Five-acre ornamental demonstration garden including a fruit and vegetable education garden; venue for meetings, shows, composting and gardening workshops; sales by bonsai, cacti, dahlia, orchid, rose, iris, lily, and African violet societies. Garden hours—winter: Monday through Friday, 10:00 am–5:00 pm, Saturday and Sunday, 10:00 am–4:00 pm. Summer: Monday through Friday, 10:00 am–6:00 pm, Saturday and Sunday, 10:00 am–5:00 pm.

Markham Regional Arboretum
1202 La Vista (off Clayton Road), Concord
3503 Half Moon Lane, Concord 94518 (mailing address)
(925) 681-1551

Both an arboretum and creekside nature park on 16 acres, including displays of roses, herbs and an international garden.

Morcom Amphitheatre of Roses
700 Jean Street, Oakland

Five hundred varieties of roses on 7 acres.

Our Own Stuff Gallery and Garden
3017 Wheeler Street, Berkeley 94705
(510) 540-8544

A collector's garden, packed with unusual plants and the sculptured art of Marcia Donahue and Mark Bulwinkle. Open Sunday afternoon, noon–5:00 pm.

North Bay

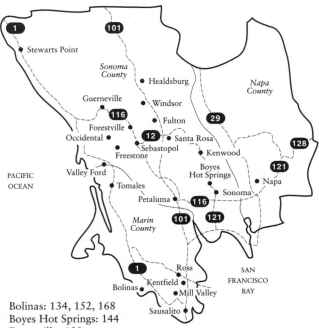

African Plants, Ltd.
Bolinas
(415) 332-4515, fax (415) 331-3163
Dr. Herman Schwartz; David Schwartz, director
Retail

Plant specialties: Succulents—hardy to the Bay
Area (more than 60 varieties); collector's specimens
(more than 1,000 varieties). Large collection of
Aloe, Euphorbia, and Stapelia, as well as good
collections of Agave, Bulbine, Cotyledon, Dudleya,
and Echeveria.

History/description: Given 10 succulent plants by a
grateful oncology patient in 1972, this former fern
hobbyist switched suits. Within 10 years he had
more than 200,000 plants in three greenhouses on
13 acres in Bolinas. As he admits, "finding plants in
habitat is intoxicating to a botanist" and so he
traveled to exotic parts of the world to collect
specimens. While still practicing medicine, he
published a book about Euphorbia and since
retirement has authored 11 additional books about
succulents; he has plans for 10 more. The exceptional location and individual provide another great
reason to visit Bolinas, if you can find it. Son David
Schwartz and his wife Isis are landscape designers
based in Sausalito and have recently opened the Mill
Valley Sculpture Gardens where these plants are also
available.

How to get there: Call for directions.

General information: Open by appointment only.
Plant list available. Design and installation services.

Appleton Forestry
1369 Tilton Road, Sebastopol 95472
(707) 823-3776
Harold and Patricia Appleton
Retail and Wholesale

Plant specialties: California native plants, mostly trees, some shrubs for shade. Large collections of Quercus (oaks), Fraxinus (ash), Sambucus (elderberry), Acer (maple), and redwood seedlings.

History/description: As a registered state forester and erosion-control expert, Harold Appleton discovered the need for well-grown native trees. He still produces revegetation and mitigation plans, while Patricia manages the nursery. Together they propagate all their plants in super-cels, dee-pots, and tree-pots and are available for site-specific consultations. This small nursery located in the hilly area west of Sebastopol has some display plants set against the natural background of oak woodland.

How to get there: Call for directions.

General information: Open by appointment only. Plant list available upon request. Deliveries can be arranged.

Bamboo Ridge Nursery
P. O. Box 832, Occidental 95465
(707) 874-1045, fax (707) 874-1533
Hastings Schmidt
Wholesale and limited Retail

Plant specialties: Bamboo (280 varieties), including
Phyllostachys, Bambusa, Thamnocalamus, Otatea,
and Arundinaria alpina. Also Phormium, Canna.

History/description: Hastings Schmidt inherited his
father's bamboo-collecting habit. A licensed landscape contractor since 1975, he opened the nursery
in 1990. Though still a sideline to his landscape
business, the nursery, just over an acre, includes a
display garden and reflects two lifetimes of collecting. Hastings Schmidt does root-barrier and propagation demonstrations for the American Bamboo
Society.

How to get there: Call for directions.

General information: Open for retail customers on
Saturday, by appointment only. The nursery has a
plant list available for SASE. Large wholesale orders
shipped.

Bamboo Sourcery

666 Wagnon Road, Sebastopol 95472
(707) 823-5866, fax (707) 829-8106
website: www.bamboo.nu
Jennifer and Chris York, Joshua Bol, Jesus Mora
Retail and Mail Order

Plant specialties: Bamboo—both running and clumping types from all over the world. Bamboos range from dwarf ground covers to giant timber varieties, 50+ feet tall. They come in shades of green, yellow, red, blue, and black with variegations on the culm (stem) as well as the leaf.

History/description: The origins of Bamboo Sourcery lie in the plant collecting passion of one exceptional individual, Gerald Bol, whose untimely death in 1996 was a tragic loss to horticulturists worldwide. He made myriad trips to South and Central America and the Far East with other bamboo experts, making important contributions to the understanding and classification of bamboo, while amassing this amazing collection. The nursery opened in 1984 on five sloping and terraced acres in the coastal forest and now holds more than 300 mature species of bamboo. Jesus Mora, Gerald's right-hand man and bamboo expert in his own right, and Jennifer York, Gerald's daughter, are now in charge.

How to get there: Please call first. Heading north on Highway 101, take the Highway 116 West/Rohnert Park/Sebastopol exit. Turn left, travel west for 8-1/2 miles to first traffic light in downtown Sebastopol. Turn left onto Sebastopol Road which becomes Bodega Avenue/Highway for 4 miles and turn left onto Wagnon Road (easy to miss) for 1/2 mile. The Bamboo Sourcery is on the left.

General information: Open by appointment only. Will ship within the USA and Canada. Price list and 20-page descriptive catalogue available free from website or send $2. Deliveries within Bay Area.

Burgandy Hill Nursery
4577 Hall Road, Santa Rosa 95401
(707) 579-3790, fax (707) 579-3792
Kim and Becky Hill
Wholesale

Plant specialties: Dwarf conifers, ornamental grasses, California native plants, daylilies, shrubs, perennials, and aquatic plants.

History/description: About 1986, speech therapist Kim Hill decided he would rather talk to plants than to people and started growing choice specimens at home in Sebastopol. Burgandy Hill Nursery now occupies 10 acres west of Santa Rosa.

How to get there: Take Highway 101 to Highway 12 west toward Sebastopol. Turn right onto Fulton Road and go to second signal. Turn left onto Hall Road. The nursery is 3/4 mile on the right.

General information: Wholesale customers only, but general public may visit with landscaper. Monday through Friday, 8:00 am–5:00 pm and Saturday by appointment. Current plant availability list sent upon request. They deliver throughout Sonoma, Napa, and Marin Counties; San Francisco; the Peninsula; and to Vallejo, Berkeley, and Walnut Creek.

California Carnivores
7020 Trenton-Healdsburg Road, Forestville 95436
(707) 838-1630
website: www.californiacarnivores.com
Peter D'Amato, Marilee Maertz
Retail and Mail Order

Plant specialties: Over 400 varieties of carnivorous and bog plants, specializing in Sarracenia (American pitcher plants), Drosera (sundews), Dionaea (Venus-flytraps), Pinguicula (butterworts), Utricularia (bladderworts), and Nepenthes (tropical pitcher plants).

History/description: Grower Peter D'Amato began his interest in insect-eating plants at the age of 12, growing up near the New Jersey Pine Barrens. The nursery was opened after his successful display at the 1989 San Francisco Landscape Garden Show. California Carnivores is the only nursery of its type open to the public and houses one of the world's large collections. There are picnic grounds in the beautiful setting of the surrounding Mark West vineyard. Books, T-shirts, and supplies are also for sale, as is Peter's book, *The Savage Garden: Cultivating Carnivorous Plants* (Ten Speed Press, 1998).

How to get there: Highway 101 north past Santa Rosa to River Road exit. Turn left on River Road for 5-1/2 miles and take a right onto Trenton/ Healdsburg Road at the Mark West Winery sign. Nursery located at Mark West Winery.

General information: Open every day, 10:00 am–4:00 pm. Call ahead in winter.

California Flora Nursery
2990 Somers Street, Fulton 95439
P. O. Box 3, Fulton 95439 (mailing address)
(707) 528-8813, fax (707) 528-1836
Philip Van Soelen, Sherrie Althouse
Retail and Wholesale

Plant specialties: California native plants mostly
from the coastal ranges, unusual perennials, shade
plants, ornamental grasses, Mediterranean-climate,
drought-tolerant, and deer-resistant plants. Large
collections of Ceanothus, Arctostaphylos, Ribes,
Cistus, Lavandula, Heuchera, Salvia, Zauschneria,
Tiarella, and more.

History/description: Sherrie Althouse and Philip Van
Soelen started California Flora in 1981, to produce
California native plants, though now their horticultural interests and offerings have greatly expanded.
Both have been past presidents of the local chapter of
the California Native Plant Society. Phil's background
in environmental studies combined with his engaging
artistry produced a children's ecology book, *Cricket
in the Grass*, now regrettably out of print. Sherrie
and Phil have discovered and introduced Achillea
millefolium 'Calistoga', Ceanothus 'Hearts Desire'
and C. 'Coronado', Monardella villosa 'Russian
River', Oxalis oregana 'Smith River White', and Vitis
californica 'Russian River'.

How to get there: Highway 101 north to River
Road exit (first exit north of Santa Rosa). Go west on
River Road for a mile. Go left on Somers Street just
before the traffic light. Nursery at corner of Somers
and D Streets.

General information: Open weekdays, 9:00 am–
5:00 pm; weekends, 10:00 am–4:00 pm. Winter
hours: Monday through Friday, 10:00 am–4:00 pm.
Free plant list available. Wholesale deliveries in Bay
Area. Tours may be arranged.

Circuit Rider Productions, Inc.

9619 Old Redwood Highway, Windsor 95492
(707) 838-6641, fax (707) 838-4503
Betty Young, manager
Retail and Wholesale

Plant specialties: Oaks and other California native woody plants. Site-specific collections for restoration of disturbed or developed areas. Most sold in super-cel tubes to encourage proper root development.

History/description: This nonprofit organization has a win-win prospectus. They are revegetation specialists who for 15 years have propagated and sold plants to restore disturbed areas. Profits from this enterprise go to address human resource needs, such as job training, employment counseling, drug prevention, and summer youth employment. Not many enterprises set out to solve both the problems of the earth and its inhabitants. We laud their efforts and success.

How to get there: Take Highway 101 north past Santa Rosa to Windsor exit. Continue west on Old Redwood Highway for 1/2 mile.

General information: Open by appointment only.

Cottage Garden Growers
4049 Petaluma Boulevard North, Petaluma 94952
(707) 778-8025, fax (707) 778-1826
Bruce Shanks and Daria Morrill
Retail and Wholesale

Plant specialties: More than 300 varieties of perennials, clematis vines (45 types), old and new roses, hydrangeas (15 varieties). Drought-tolerant, Mediterranean-climate plants; herbs and grasses, rock garden, shade, and deer-resistant plants.

History/description: This family business opened in 1990 on an enchanting hillside setting overlooking the Petaluma Valley. A cascade of fieldstone terraces covers the 1-acre site where perennials mingle with staked clematis vines. Informative signage takes the guesswork out of creating a perennial border. In the year 2000, the nursery will move to a new 4-acre site directly behind the existing location, in order to accommodate increased inventory and demonstration gardens.

How to get there: Heading north on Highway 101, take Penngrove exit. Go left over freeway onto Petaluma Boulevard North. Continue for 1/2 mile and go right on Pine Tree Lane. Nursery is up the hill on the left.

General information: Open every day, 9:00 am–5:00 pm. Winter hours, 10:00 am–4:00 pm. Plant list available. Deliveries to Bay Area available upon request.

Cray Croft Gardens

P. O. Box 82, Stewarts Point 95480 (mailing address)
Greenhouses in Gualala and Richmond
(707) 884-1127, fax (707) 884-9167
Jerry and Barbara Gonce, Neal Tadlock
Retail and Mail Order

Plant specialties: Orchids, especially Cymbidium and Masdevallia, and other cool-growing genera.

History/description: Cray Croft Gardens has been in business since 1989, but reflects a 15-year personal passion for orchid collecting. Among their many accomplishments, the Gonces have successfully hybridized orchid cultivars in wondrous sunset colors. Cray Croft has two permanent locations, with greenhouses both in Gualala and Richmond and, during the winter, at farmer's markets in Oakland, San Francisco, and Marin.

How to get there: Directions given when appointment is made.

General information: Open by appointment only. Please call 24 hours in advance. For the Gualala greenhouses, call the number listed above. For the Richmond greenhouses, call Neal Tadlock (510) 215-9260.

Marca Dickie Nursery

P. O. Box 1270, Boyes Hot Springs 95416
(707) 996-0364
Marca and Mike Dickie
Retail, Wholesale, and Mail Order

Plant specialties: 190 cultivars of grafted Acer palmatum (Japanese maple), dwarf, shrub, mounding, and tree forms. One-gallon to 36-inch boxes. Also, cultivars of Acer japonicum (fullmoon maple), A. circinatum (vine maple), A. buergeranum (trident maple), A. mono (painted maple) and several trifoliate species.

History/description: During her ornamental horticultural studies, Marca Dickie discovered that she had a knack for propagation and grafting. In 1979 she decided to go into the nursery business for herself, choosing to specialize in maples because their graceful forms appealed to her art-trained eye. Both Marca and Mike use their design backgrounds in the siting of maples throughout their property, a 10-acre canyon nestled above Sonoma Valley. Their nursery is one of the few in California that allows you to view large specimen-size cultivars. The Dickies suggest you visit the native plants in the garden of the Sonoma Mission and the Sonoma town square to see its interesting and labeled trees.

How to get there: Call for directions.

General information: Open by appointment only. Nursery tours may be arranged. Occasionally workshops offered. Catalogue and plant list available. One-gallon plants shipped for mail orders only in midwinter. Design services and site-specific consultations also available.

emerisa gardens

555 Irwin Lane, Santa Rosa 95401
retail (707) 525-9644, wholesale (707) 525-9600
fax (707) 525-0300
Muchtar and Rohana Salzmann
Retail and Wholesale

Plant specialties: 1,000 varieties of herbs, ornamental grasses, heaths and heathers, and perennials, featuring Penstemon, hardy Geranium, Cistus, Campanula, Lavandula, Salvia, and a wide variety of drought-tolerant and cold-hardy plants.

History/description: After raising eight children, working as a flagman, pizza maker, and teacher, Muchtar Salzmann could still muster the energy to return to school (Cal Poly) and earn a degree in crop science. After working as a field assistant for agricultural extension programs, he bought a small nursery in Sebastopol in 1990. In 1996 he moved his largely wholesale nursery to this 20-acre site in Santa Rosa. In 1997 he added a seasonal, retail nursery on the same property to keep up with the growing demand for emerisa's plant material. Named after Muchtar's parents, Emerson and Marisa, the nursery is truly a family affair with Muchtar, his nephew, and three of his brood all working there.

How to get there: From Highway 101 in Santa Rosa, take the Highway 12 exit (Sebastopol/Sonoma) toward Sebastopol. Follow Highway 12 for about 3 miles. At stoplight, turn right onto Fulton Road, then left onto Occidental Road. In about a mile, turn right onto Irwin Lane.

General information: Call for retail hours and information, (707) 525 9644. Wholesale summer hours: weekdays, 8:00 am–5:00 pm; Saturday, 10:00 am–4:00 pm. Wholesale winter hours: weekdays, 8:00 am–4:00 pm; Saturday 10:00 am–2:00 pm. Inquire about plant list, catalogue, and deliveries.

Enjoy Rhododendrons
890 Joy Ridge Road, Occidental 95465
(707) 874-3055, fax (707) 874-1575
e-mail: joyridge@monitor.net
website: www.monitor.net/~joyridge/
Paul Molinari
Wholesale

Plant specialties: Rhododendrons—exceptional collection of Maddeniis, "big leafs" (R. falconeri, R. grande), and the early-blooming R. arboreum series.

History/description: Located on a coastal woodland ridge, this well-tended nursery offers visitors the chance to see over 45,000 rhododendrons in perfect growing conditions. The 8-1/2-acre site slopes down a canyon; cascading R. maddenii and garden drifts planted with almost all the sections of the genus Rhododendron contrast with the native redwood forest. Paul Molinari continues to select and evaluate his extensive collection, looking for good habit, good flower, and dependability. He planted his first garden of vegetables with his Italian grandfather and has been in love with plants ever since. He chucked an early career as a university psychologist for a chance to start this nursery in 1975.

How to get there: Call for directions.

General information: Open to wholesale customers, by appointment only. General public may visit with landscape professional. Availability lists and descriptions sent to wholesale customers. Tours of the garden and nursery may be arranged in advance.

Farwell and Sons Nursery

12983 Bodega Avenue, Freestone 95472
(707) 823-8415
website: www.rhododendron.com
Gary Farwell
Retail

Plant specialties: Rhododendron—hybrids selected
for general West Coast landscape use. R. 'Inherit-
ance' hybridized by owner. 2- and 5- gallon sizes.

History/description: Conscripted for nursery
chores by his father, Everett Farwell, the well-known
rhododendron grower in Woodside, Gary Farwell
obviously thrived under forced labor. He has been in
business on his own since 1977 and has several
hybrids to his credit. The nursery occupies about 3
of his property's 10 acres in the rolling, wooded hills
of the Freestone Valley. All plants are container-
grown, in 5- and 7-gallon sizes. He recommends you
visit the Kruse Rhododendron State Preserve near
Fort Ross.

How to get there: From Highway 101, go west on
Highway 12, which becomes Bodega Avenue.
Continue through Sebastopol. Nursery is 6 miles
west of Sebastopol on the left side.

General information: Open daily in April, May
and June, 10:00 am–6:00 pm. Open Friday through
Monday, July through March, 10:00 am–5:00 pm.

Fiori Lane Farm
12450 Fiori Lane, Sebastopol 95472
(707) 874-2010, fax (707) 874-2075
e-mail: fiori_lane@aol.com
Nancy Hill, Steve Isaacson
Retail and Wholesale

Plant specialties: Rhododendron (250 cultivars, some species), especially varieties with interesting leaves and good plant shape.

History/description: These landscapers and rhododendron hobbyists bought Manning's Heather Farm in 1992. By that time the old venerable nursery was nothing more than a sloping site on the edge of redwoods—perfect for rhododendron cultivation. Of their 11 acres, 4 are covered with nursery stock, with cuttings grown in raised beds and larger plants sold in containers. They continue to seek specimens for foliage and shape, avoiding undue emphasis on the plant's transitory flower.

How to get there: Directions given when appointment is made.

General information: Open by appointment only, 9:00 am–5:00 pm. Plant list is available. Deliveries throughout the Bay Area for a minimum order.

Garden Valley Ranch Nursery

498 Pepper Road, Petaluma 94952
(707) 795-0919, fax (707) 792-0349
e-mail: gvr@ap.net
website: www.gardenvalley.com
Rayford Reddell
Retail, Wholesale, and Mail Order

Plant specialties: Roses—hybrid tea, floribunda,
English, heirloom, climbers, miniatures.

History/description: Roses were just a hobby of
Ray Reddell's until 1981 when he planted fields of
roses for the cut-flower market; better colors and a
longer-lived flower result when roses are not hot-
house-grown. The nursery is a later addition. The
ranch, originally an old dairy ranch owned by one
of General Vallejo's lieutenants, is a genuine destination location. 8-1/2 acres of roses are organized into
various sections and gardens, including pergolas,
fountains, a pond, fragrance garden, and the only
official All American Rose Selection test garden
(AARS) in Northern California. On weekends the
nursery is often rented out for weddings and other
special events. Ray Reddell is also a noted lecturer,
columnist, tour leader, and author *(The Rose Bible,
Full Bloom, A Year in the Life of a Rose)*.

How to get there: Highway 101 north to Old
Redwood Highway/Penngrove exit. Go left back
over freeway to second stoplight. Go right on Stoney
Point Road for 1-1/4 miles. Go left on Pepper Road.
Ranch on right, 1/4 mile ahead.

General information: Open Wednesday through
Sunday, 10:00 am–4:00 pm. Free catalogue is
available in September. Mail orders accepted for
bare-root roses, shipped January through February.
Self-guided and group tours offered for $4. Gift
shop with rose-related items.

Geraniaceae

122 Hillcrest Avenue, Kentfield 94904
(415) 461-4168, fax (415) 461-7209
e-mail: geraniac@pacbell.net
website: www.freeyellow.com/members/geraniaceae
Robin Parer
Retail

Plant specialties: Geraniums, erodiums, pelargoniums (scented-leaf, angel, pansy, and night-scented). Over 300 selected forms of hardy geraniums.

History/description: Robin Parer is a delight and unquestionably the number-one fan of the hardy geranium. Her indefatigable efforts as lecturer, collector, propagator, and exhibitor have made the once-lowly geranium a garden favorite. She has been on plant-collecting trips to remote areas of Australia, Europe, and the Andes and continues to track down new resources in the UK, Europe, and Australia. With 300 species and selected forms of hardy geraniums, her 1-acre garden/nursery contains the largest collection of geraniums and erodiums in the country. The garden has mixed perennial and shrub borders and a woodland section, illustrative of the versatility and landscape use of the family Geraniaceae.

How to get there: Call for directions.

General information: Open by appointment only, from early spring to late fall any day of the week. Catalogue available for $3. Nursery tours and workshops offered. Lectures and demonstrations arranged for groups.

The Great Petaluma Desert

5010 Bodega Avenue, Petaluma 94952
(707) 778-8278, fax (707) 778-0931
e-mail: jerry@gpdesert.com
website: www.gpdesert.com
Jerry and Eiko Wright
Retail and Mail Order

Plant specialties: Cacti and succulents. Specializing in plants from Africa and Madagascar, such as aloes, Euphorbia, pachypodiums, and other rarities.

History/description: Courtesy of the US Army, Jerry moved to California in 1974 and renewed his interest in cacti. As his personal collection and his contacts with fellow hobbyists grew, he started to help out at a local succulent nursery. He got a business license and tested the waters with a few plant orders. Response was so great that five years later he retired and entered the nursery business full-time. In 1994, he started mail-order sales of his plants, and in 1996, went on-line with his own mail-order internet site. The nursery has a small display garden and can help you plan yours.

How to get there: From Highway 101, take the East Washington exit and head west towards Bodega Bay. East Washington Street becomes Bodega Avenue as you leave Petaluma. The nursery is approximately 5-1/2 miles from Highway 101.

General information: Open Friday, Saturday, and Sunday, 10:00 am–5:00 pm. Winter hours: 10:00 am–4:00 pm. Plant list available for $1 (no cacti). Mail orders shipped within the country ($35 minimum order).

Larner Seeds
P. O. Box 407, Bolinas 94924
(415) 868-9407
Judith Lowry
Retail and Wholesale

Plant specialties: California native plants, especially suited to the coast, including wildflowers, grasses, trees, and shrubs. Limnanthes douglasii var. sulphurea (Point Reyes meadowfoam), Calandrinia ciliata (red maids), and Eschscholzia californica var. maritima (coastal California poppy) uniquely offered here.

History/description: Judith Lowry went into the seed business in 1977 to perpetuate the horticultural gene pool for the revegetation of West Marin and the North Coast. She opened the nursery in 1986 in response to requests by landscapers for actual plants grown from her wide variety of native seeds. In addition to seeds, plants, and books, the nursery sells a point of view—that gardening and restoration ecology can find a meeting place in California's backyards. They have a constantly changing, 1-acre demonstration garden of California native plants and will custom-grow plants from seed collected by landowners for site-specific restoration. Judith's book, *Gardening with a Wild Heart: Restoring California's Landscapes at Home,* just might make you rethink the subject of gardening.

How to get there: Call for directions. They are included in the catalogue.

General information: Open Tuesday and Thursday, 10:00 am–2:00 pm; Saturday, noon–4:00 pm; or by appointment. Catalogue available for $2. Workshops offered. Spring open house in May. Consultations, design, and installation services offered to homeowners wishing to restore their native landscape.

Lone Pine Gardens

6450 Lone Pine Road, Sebastopol 95472
(707) 823-5024, fax (707) 824-1677
Ian C. Price, Janet M. Price
Retail and Wholesale

Plant specialties: Cacti, succulents, and bonsai (seedlings and cuttings for bonsai starters and field-grown, larger pre-bonsai stock).

History/description: The British background of this family mandated its gardening interest. Educated in botany and horticulture in the UK and US (specializing in desert plants), the Prices returned to England to operate a nursery there. A nostalgia for the opportunity to grow desert plants out-of-doors brought them back to the West. Their 4-acre nursery opened in 1975 and affords visitors a spectacular panoramic view of the coastal mountains.

How to get there: Highway 101 north to Highway 116 west (Rohnert Park/Sebastopol exit). Go 4-1/2 miles. Left on Lone Pine Road. Nursery is in 1-1/2 miles at the top of the hill.

General information: Open Thursday, Friday, and Saturday, 10:00 am–5:00 pm. Price list available for wholesale customers. Wholesale orders delivered to Bay Area, Sacramento Valley, Foothills, and Monterey area.

McAllister Water Gardens
7420 St. Helena Highway (Highway 29), Napa 94558
(707) 944-0921, fax (707) 944-1850
Vicky and Walt McAllister
Retail and Wholesale

Plant specialties: Aquatic plants—including
containerized water lilies (hardy Nymphaea—50
varieties), water iris (20 varieties—I. ensata, I.
virginica, I. pseudacorus, and Louisiana hybrids),
bog plants (100 varieties). Plus an assortment of
dwarf conifers, bamboo, and Japanese maples. Pond
goldfish, too.

History/description: The McAllisters started this
business to provide a local, wholesale source for
container-grown aquatic plants. Out-of-area cata-
logue-sales companies ship their plants bare-root
which diminishes their survival rate. Now the largest
seller of aquatic plants in Northern California,
McAllister supplies 75 to 80 nurseries. The success
of the wholesale business spawned a need for a retail
enterprise dedicated to water gardening. Display
ponds, waterfalls, and bog gardens on-site illustrate
the many landscape uses of water plants. Recently,
dwarf conifers, bamboo varieties, and Japanese
maples have been added as complimentary plants
for a pond environs. In the middle of the Napa Valley,
the McAllister's water gardens offer a welcome and
water-conserving relief for hot, dry areas.

How to get there: The nursery is located on
Highway 29, 2 miles north of Yountville, across
from Mustards Grill and Cosentino Winery.

General information: Open March through September, Thursday through Sunday, 9:00 am–4:00 pm.

Miniature Plant Kingdom
4125 Harrison Grade Road, Sebastopol 95472
(707) 874-2233, fax (707) 874-3242
e-mail: mpk@neteze.com
Becky and Don Herzog
Retail, Wholesale, and Mail Order

Plant specialties: Miniature roses, bonsai starters, dwarf conifers, alpines, dwarf perennials, and rock garden plants.

History/description: The Herzog's decision to start a nursery of miniature plants was based, in part, on the successful results of a college project to create a miniature rose greenhouse. In 1986, they expanded their sphere of interest and started to grow plants other than roses. At the present, they usually have over 1,000 varieties in stock. Their 2-1/2-acre nursery, perched on a mountaintop and surrounded by apple orchards, is the result of more than a quarter century of hard work. They are well connected with Sonoma County growers and generous with their knowledge.

How to get there: Take Highway 101 north to Highway 116 (about 5 miles north of Petaluma). Go left (west) on Highway 116 through Sebastopol. Left on Graton Road for 5-1/2 miles. Right on Tanuda Road at crest of mountain. At end of block go right for one block, then left. Their driveway is on the right in 1/2 mile. Sign at driveway says Occidental Nursery. At end of driveway, they are on the left.

General information: Open Monday, Tuesday, Thursday, and Friday, 9:00 am–4:00 pm; Saturday and Sunday, noon–4:00 pm. Not open for wholesale on Saturday or Sunday. Catalogue available for $2.50.

Misty Hill Farms—Moonshine Gardens
5080 West Soda Rock Lane, Healdsburg 95448
(707) 433-8408
Jack and Phyllis Dickey
Retail, Wholesale, and Mail Order

Plant specialties: Bearded irises, Iris x germanica.
Introductions include I. 'Miss Lemon'.

History/description: Master Gardener Jack Dickey
grew up growing things in Healdsburg. In the early
1980s, he and his wife started a vineyard ("Misty
Hill") on their 4-acre farm. Iris lovers, they decided
the iris would be a perfect companion plant for their
grapes. Their iris collection was enriched by the
purchase of longtime iris grower Monty Byers'
Moonshine Gardens. The Dickeys opened the
nursery in 1991 and now work with their two
children to develop Mr. Byers' seedlings of
rebloomers and space-agers.

How to get there: Call for directions.

General information: Open mid-April through
mid-May, every day except Wednesday. A catalogue
is available for $2, credited to your purchase. Mail
orders shipped during the dormant season, July
through October.

Momiji—Japanese Maples
2765 Stony Point Road, Santa Rosa 95407
(707) 528-2917, fax (707) 527-8968
Sachi and Mike Umehara
Retail and Mail Order

Plant specialties: Grafted varieties of Japanese maples (over 200+ cultivars of Acer palmatum) in a complete range of sizes (dwarf, semi-dwarf, and standard) and colors (bright red, burgundy, variegated, green). Good selection of A. palmatum dissectum (cascading form). In 1-, 2-, 5-, 15-, 20- and 24-gallon containers.

History/description: Although only open to the public since 1986, Momiji Nursery represents the Umeharas' lifelong interest in Japanese maples. They grow their own understock seedling for grafting and graft all their own maples, thereby producing many maple selections not generally available. The large specimen plants on their 3-acre property are exquisite.

How to get there: From the Bay Area: take Highway 101 north to Sonoma County. Take the Yolanda Hearn exit and turn left onto Santa Rosa Avenue. At the first light, turn left onto Hearn Avenue for 1-1/2 miles to Stony Point Road. Go left on Stony Point Road for 1/4 mile and the nursery is on the right. From the north: take Highway 101 south, to Highway 12/ Sebastopol exit. Continue west towards Sebastopol for 1 mile. Go left (heading south) on Stony Point Road. Nursery is on your right in 1-1/2 miles.

General information: Open by appointment only. Plant list available for SASE. Minimum mail orders, $25. Site-specific consultations offered. Bus tours welcomed. Custom grafting by arrangement.

Mostly Natives Nursery

27235 Highway One, Tomales 94971
P. O. Box 258, Tomales 94971 (mailing address)
(707) 878-2009, fax (707) 878-2079
Walter Earle, Margaret Graham
Retail and Wholesale

Plant specialties: Drought-tolerant plants, especially coastal California native plants. Native shrubs and trees (1- and 5-gallon), perennials (1-gallon and 4-inch pots), native bunch grasses (1-gallon and 4-inch pots). California annuals in spring (4-inch pots). Organic vegetables in spring and fall.

History/description: This partnership has been operating on a 1/2-acre site in the heart of downtown Tomales since 1984. With horticulturally minded owners and a location near the sea, Mostly Natives is in a good position to supply coastal gardens in western Marin and Sonoma Counties with plants that will really grow. They even know which deer will eat what.

How to get there: Highway 101 north to Petaluma/Washington Street exit. Continue west to Two Rock. Follow signs to Tomales.

General information: Open every day but Tuesday, 9:00 am–5:00 pm; Sunday, 10:00 am–4:00 pm. In the winter, shorter hours (10:00 am–4:00pm) and closed Tuesday and Wednesday. Plant list available. Deliveries to the North Bay. Talks may be arranged for interested groups.

Muchas Grasses

P. O. Box 683, Occidental 95465 (mailing address)
(707) 874-1871, (415) 383-4777, fax (415) 388-5283
Retail outlets:
Mill Valley Sculpture Garden (415) 381-9922
Roseland Garden Center in Santa Rosa (707) 527-5866
Bob Hornback
Retail and Wholesale

Plant specialties: Ornamental grasses of all kinds, including native species. Phormiums (New Zealand flaxes—41 varieties). Bob has introduced several new grasses, including the miniature Cortaderia selloana 'Evita' and Miscanthus sinensis 'Cat's Pajamas', as well as the dwarf Phormium tenax 'Toney Tiger' and the very dark P. t. 'Morticia'.

History/description: Bob Hornback, a true horticultural pioneer, lectures at Merritt College and has a wholesale plant brokerage, design, and consultation business. His respected Muchas Grasses nursery is now associated with friend David Schwartz's Mill Valley Sculpture Gardens (see Horticultural Attractions). He sells his plants there and at the Roseland Garden Center. He also stores his creations at the MVSG nursery yard on Rosemont Avenue in Mill Valley and, annually, opens it to the public for a plant sale. Bob Hornback is admittedly nuts about variegated foliage so you will find plenty of this.

How to get there: To get to the Mill Valley Sculpture Garden, take the Mill Valley/Stinson Beach/Highway 1 exit from Highway 101. Follow Shoreline Highway west for 1/2 mile and turn left at Video Droid.

General information: Mill Valley Sculpture Garden is open Wednesday through Sunday, 10:00 am–6:00 pm, and is available for special events. Tour groups hosted by appointment.

Neon Palm Nursery

3525 Stony Point Road, Santa Rosa 95407
(707) 585-8100
Dale Motiska
Retail, Wholesale, and Mail Order

Plant specialties: Palms, cycads, conifers, cacti, and succulents. Subtropical plants.

History/description: Dale Motiska grows rare and unusual plants in all sizes—from seedlings to mature specimens over 40 feet tall. He can transplant large specimens by crane and will transplant mature palm trees of any age. In business since 1984, Dale continues to make important contributions to the diversification of palm species. Allow time to visit Neon Palm's 2-acre botanical garden; guided tours are on Sundays.

How to get there: Highway 101 to Santa Rosa. Take Todd Road exit. Go west 1 mile to stoplight and turn right on Stony Point Road. Nursery is on the left in a block.

General information: Open Tuesday through Saturday, 10:00 am–5:00 pm; Sunday noon–5:00 pm. Nursery tours may be arranged. Catalogue available for $2. Mail orders shipped anywhere in the continental United States (minimum order, $50). Site-specific consultations offered for fee.

North Coast Native Nursery
2710 Chileno Valley Road, Petaluma 94952
(707) 769-1213, fax (707) 769-1230
David Kaplow
Retail and Wholesale

Plant specialties: California native trees, shrubs, grasses, and flowering perennials for landscaping and revegetation of prairie, wetland, forest, and chaparral habitats.

History/description: The North Coast Native Nursery was established in 1989 as the plant propagation facility for Pacific Open-Space, Inc., an environmental planning and habitat restoration firm. Dave Kaplow founded Pacific Open-Space, Inc., in 1987 and now designs and implements restoration of plant and wildlife habitats for public agencies and private landholders throughout California. Dave is also a part-time college instructor of restoration design and technology, and offers workshops for Master Gardener classes. Located in the Chileno Valley of West Marin, the 2-acre nursery stocks a wide variety of California native plants.

How to get there: Call for directions.

General information: Open to restoration and landscape professionals primarily. Open for retail sales by appointment only. Wholesale and retail plant availability lists are available. Interested groups may schedule nursery tours.

Oasis

84 London Way, Sonoma 95476
(707) 996-8732
Shirley and Kermit Puls
Retail and Wholesale

Plant specialties: Cacti and succulents, all genera
represented. Trichocereus shaferi fa. monstrosus is
uniquely offered here. A hardy, robust grower, it
arose in a batch of T. shaferi seed sown in 1977—a
unique must for all monster lovers.

History/description: A full-time nursery since
1983, the breadth of selection at Oasis reflects the
Puls' 25-year collecting hobby that admittedly "got
out of hand." They started propagating from seed
when so many plants desired for their collection
proved to be unavailable. When they realized their
success with seeds had spawned 600 different
varieties, they began to think sales. All plants are
propagated on the premises and grown locally under
polyethylene or shade cloth, producing a full winter
dormancy; this, we are told, produces a hardier
plant with better color and spination.

How to get there: Call for directions.

General information: Mostly wholesale. Retail
business limited to the serious collector, by appointment only, March through October. Local deliveries.

O'Brien Iris Garden
3223 Canfield Road, Sebastopol 95472
(707) 824-9223, fax (707) 824-9035
Retail and Mail Order

Plant specialties: Bearded iris (over 700 varieties, including 21 introductions).

History/description: With little time to devote to her painting when the children were small, Lois O'Brien turned to the garden to ease her artistic frustrations. Learning to hybridize from an article in *Sunset* magazine, she discovered that by extending the color range of available irises, she could "paint" with flowers in the garden. That was 30 years ago. Her passion for iris landed her leadership roles in local iris societies and required ever more space for her expanding collection. Now located on 8 acres in the rolling coastal hills, Lois and retired engineer husband Dan have three demonstration terraces planted with iris and large growing fields beyond. Realizing that she had many old-fashioned varieties unavailable elsewhere, she opened for business in 1993.

How to get there: From Highway 101 north, take Cotati/Sebastopol exit. Take Highway 116 left toward Sebastopol. Continue to intersection of Hessel and Blank Roads. Take a hard left onto Blank Road; continue for 2.8 miles. Go right onto Canfield Road, up the hill to the nursery. From Highway 101 south, take the Highway 12 exit to Sebastopol. Turn left onto Highway 116. In 1.7 miles, turn right onto Bloomfield Road. After 1.4 miles, turn left onto Canfield Road.

General information: Open during bloom season only, usually from the first week in April through the first week in June, Wednesday through Saturday, 10:00 am–5:00 pm, and Sunday, 11:00 am–5:00 pm. Catalogue $1 by mail or free at garden. Special tours and lectures for groups on Mondays and Tuesdays by arrangement. Bus space.

Petaluma Rose Company

581 Gossage Avenue, Petaluma 94975
(707) 769-8862, fax (707) 769-0394
e-mail: PRoseCo@aol.com
website: www.sonic.net/~petrose
Rick Weeks
Retail, Wholesale, and Mail Order

Plant specialties: Roses (300 varieties), including
hybrid teas, floribundas, David Austins, climbers,
and old roses. Rosa 'Petaluma' is his hybrid.

History/description: Rick Weeks was well prepared
to start his own rose business in 1993. His family
grew roses in Southern California; he studied
horticulture and plant genetics at Cal Poly before
working for rose growers in Northern California.
The 2-acre site is exceedingly picturesque, with
rustic wooden cottages rising above and among a
sea of roses. Rick can help you plant and maintain
your purchases.

How to get there: Take the Penngrove exit off of
Highway 101. Go left on Petaluma Boulevard North
for about 1-1/2 miles. Go right on Gossage, going
up and down a hill. Number 581 will be on your
left. If you drive fast, you'll miss it.

General information: Open Monday, Wednesday
through Saturday, 9:00 am–4:00 pm (closed Sunday
and Tuesday). A catalogue and schedule of pruning
and rose-care classes are available. Mail orders
accepted year-round.

Petite Plaisance—Orchids

P. O. Box 386, Valley Ford 94972
(707) 876-3496, fax (707) 876-3496
e-mail: orchids@sonic.net
website: www.sonic.net/orchids/
Jim Hamilton, Ron Ehlers
Retail, Wholesale, and Mail Order

Plant specialties: Species orchids—rare and un-usual. Orchid supplies.

History/description: In 1981 these orchid hobby-ists became partners in a nursery nestled in the rolling hills of Sonoma County, 2 miles from Bodega. They tramp the globe to collect and propa-gate orchids in order to preserve endangered species. Travels have taken them to Peru, Ecuador, Mexico, and Southeast Asia. Orchids comprise the largest number of flora on the planet—some 35,000 species have been identified—and these guys want them all! They also have some pretty interesting tales to tell about orchid pollination.

How to get there: Call for directions.

General information: Open by appointment only. Mail orders shipped worldwide. Plant list available. Talks and demonstrations offered to groups.

Petite Vines
766 Westside Road, Healdsburg 95448
(707) 433-6255, fax (707) 433-1618
Steve Mandy; Keith Pratt, manager
Retail, Wholesale, and Mail Order

Plant specialties: Bonsai grapevines and grafted vines for fruit production. Bonsai vines range from young 12-inch plants to 40-year-old specimens up to 26 inches.

History/description: When Colorado dermatologist Steve Mandy saw his first bonsai grapevine at Vin Expo in France in the early 1990s, he sensed it was an idea that would catch on in California. He called an old friend in Healdsburg (who used to give his daughter dressage lessons—but we digress), and asked if he knew of any property for sale. The friend did and, thus, the enterprise was launched on this 10-acre parcel in the middle of the Russian River valley surrounded by chardonnay vineyards. Keith Pratt, who has been in the nursery business all his life, is the resident horticulturist and has this venture off and running.

How to get there: From Highway 101 south, take the Westside Road exit and go west on Westside for 1 mile. From Highway 101 north, take Central Healdsburg exit. Go left (west) on Westside Road for 1-1/2 miles.

General information: Open weekdays, 9:00 am–5:00 pm; weekends, 10:00 am–4:00 pm. Best to call ahead. Price list available. Custom grafting on selected rootstock and budwood.

Pic-A-Lily Gardens

2401 Schaeffer Road, Sebastopol 95472
(707) 823-3799, fax (707) 823-4350
e-mail: picalily@sonic.net
Jan Nahmens
Retail, Wholesale, and Mail Order

Plant specialties: Over 500 varieties of Hemerocallis (daylilies).

History/description: Bud and Jan Nahmens changed their careers as a dairyman and travel agent respectively, as a result of a Sunday drive in 1993. Seeing an advertisement for a daylily sale, the just-retired Nahmens decided to check it out. Their purchase blossomed into a hobby that has since rebloomed into a business. They think the daylily just might be the perfect plant, since it is hardy and drought-tolerant, has few pests or diseases, requires minimum care, adds color to the garden, and has edible flowers. Located on beautiful oak-studded property with scenic views to the surrounding hills, the gardens here are ablaze with color during peak bloom season (June through July).

How to get there: From Highway 101, take Highway 116 West/Rohnert Park/Sebastopol exit. Turn left at stoplight. Continue on Highway 116 to Hessel/Blank Roads. Turn left, and make an immediate left onto Blank Road. Continue 2.8 miles to Canfield Road. Turn Right on Canfield and travel one mile to Schaeffer Road. Turn right on Schaeffer. Just before Schaeffer curves sharply to the left, take the gravel driveway on the right and continue .3 miles to the nursery.

General information: Open May through August, Thursday through Sunday, 10:00 am–4:00 pm. Call for appointment at other times of the year. Daylilies can be purchased March through October. Free catalogue available. Shipping throughout the US.

Plants from the Past

195 Aspen Road, Bolinas 94924
P. O. Box 372, Bolinas 94924 (mailing address)
(415) 868-1885, fax (415) 868-1951
Sarah Hammond
Retail

Plant specialties: Perennials, Mediterranean plants, shade plants, vines, and select roses.

History/description: Impeccably credentialed in the world of horticulture, Sarah Hammond apprenticed at several well-known English gardens. She worked for three years with Marshall Olbrich at Western Hills Nursery and was the founding director of the nursery at Smith & Hawken, managing it for seven years. British born, she shares her country's passion for new plant discovery. Each year she returns home to search for plants which combine the "English" look with a tolerance for our dry climate. Lavatera 'Barnsley' was one of her good finds. Her 1/2-acre display garden will inspire your purchase.

How to get there: Call for directions.

General information: Open by appointment only. Call for details about workshops, demonstrations, and nursery tours. Hourly design consultations may be arranged.

Sonoma Antique Apple Nursery

4395 Westside Road, Healdsburg 95448
(707) 433-6420, fax (707) 433-6479
e-mail: tuyt20b@prodigy.com
Carolyn and Terry Harrison
Wholesale and Mail Order

Plant specialties: Antique apples, pears, peaches, plums, and other fruits and nuts.

History/description: Located in the hills west of Healdsburg, this nursery is certified organic. Starting with just a couple of trees 20 years ago, the Harrisons now grow 100 varieties of antique apples, pears, peaches, and plums on their 25-acre farm. You'll never have to settle for golden delicious again. They hold apple tastings in the fall at various Bay Area locations. Consult their catalogue for details.

How to get there: Directions given when appointment is made.

General information: Open to wholesale trade by appointment only. General public may visit with landscaper. Plants shipped bare-root. Catalogue available. Talks about antique fruits offered to groups.

Sonoma Horticultural Nursery

3970 Azalea Avenue, Sebastopol 95472
(707) 823-6832, fax (707) 823-4865
Polo de Lorenzo, Warren Smith
Retail and Wholesale

Plant specialties: Rhododendrons (1,200 kinds), azaleas (600), unusual trees, shrubs, and companion plants.

History/description: Anyone looking for a real springtime show should plan a visit to Sonoma Hort's 7 acres of gardens and shade houses. In addition to the fields of rhododendrons, azaleas, and other ericaceous blossoms, there is an impressive laburnum walk, maple allee, and birch woodland. Visitors will also enjoy the owners' 20-plus years of accumulated knowledge.

How to get there: Take Highway 101 north to Highway 116 west. Go 4 miles west on Highway 116. Left on second Hessel Road. After a block, right on McFarlane. After 6 blocks, right on Azalea Avenue.

General information: Open year-round; during March, April, and May, every day, 9:00 am–5:00 pm; from June through February, open Thursday through Monday. Catalogue available for $2.

Urban Tree Farm Nursery

3010 Fulton Road, Fulton 95439
(707) 544-4446
Stanley Bradbury, Ruthie Martin
Travis Woodard, manager
Retail

Plant specialties: Specialists in big trees, broad-leaved evergreens, flowering trees, fruit trees, palms, conifers, shrubs. 5-gallons up to 48-inch boxes. Height up to 15 feet.

History/description: Former farmer Stanley Bradbury worked for years for the Sonoma County Agricultural Department while growing Christmas trees at home for sale. Originally more of a hobby than enterprise, the growing of conifers expanded to broad-leaved trees. After his retirement from the Ag Department, he opened a retail nursery. By 1990 he was ready to either grow the business or retire. Enter Ruthie, an old friend who owned a solar company in Florida. She became an equal partner in the business, making the decision to grow. In 1991, Urban Tree Farm expanded to this new location and now grows 30,000 trees on 17 acres with a featured display garden. The partnership seems to be working. They are now husband and wife.

How to get there: From Highway 101, go west on River Road, then south on Fulton Road for 1/4 mile.

General information: Open Monday through Friday, 8:00 am–5:00 pm; Saturday and Sunday, 10:00 am–5:00 pm. Closed Tuesdays.

Vintage Gardens

2833 Old Gravenstein Highway South, Sebastopol 95472
(707) 829-2035, fax (707) 829-9516
website: www. vintagegardens.com
Gregg Lowery, Louise Eisen, Gita Bradford Phy
Retail, Wholesale, and Mail Order

Plant specialties: 3,000 varieties of roses, specializing in the old, unusual, and hard to find. Also annuals, antique fruit trees and espaliers (especially Malus), perennials (especially Dianthus), vines, Mediterranean plants, and flowering shrubs.

History/description: Always interested in horticulture, Gregg Lowery took a while to get there. This former high school teacher, social worker, and offset printer started in the nursery and landscape design business in 1982. He had a cut-flower farm in San Francisco, moved to Sebastopol, and founded Vintage Gardens as a small backyard operation in 1984. In 1991 they started mail orders and in 1994 opened a retail site. His display garden is located elsewhere and only open in the spring (call nursery for exact dates), but the nursery itself is beautifully laid out and well worth seeing.

How to get there: Take Highway 101 north to Highway 116 West/Sebastopol exit. Go left at light on Gravenstein Highway (Highway 116) and take a right in a couple of miles on Old Gravenstein Highway. Nursery is on a little road on the right, about one hour north of San Francisco.

General information: Open Tuesday through Sunday, 9:00 am–5:00 pm. Fall and spring newsletters announcing workshops, pruning demos, slide shows, and sales. Free spring and fall availability lists. Catalogue $5. Mail orders shipped within the US. Custom rooting services offered.

Western Hills Nursery
16250 Coleman Valley Road, Occidental 95465
(707) 874-3731
Maggie Wych
Retail

Plant specialties: Wide selection of unusual perennials, shrubs, vines, and trees.

History/description: Back in 1960 Marshall Olbrich and Lester Hawkins started to propagate plants for their own extensive garden, being among the first to introduce Mediterranean and Australian plants. Western Hills has been on the cutting edge of plant introductions ever since. The knowledge shared by these beloved horticulturists spawned a whole generation of specialty growers and plant hobbyists. Upon the death of surviving partner Marshall Olbrich, the nursery was willed to Maggie Wych who had worked with him for 11 years. Western Hill's 3-acre strolling garden is a virtual botanical garden, chock-full of mature specimens of rare and unusual plants. They are located in the coastal redwood country, 60 miles north of San Francisco.

How to get there: Highway 101 north to Rohnert Park/Highway 116 West exit. Follow Highway 116 through Sebastopol to Occidental Road. Left on Occidental for 5 to 6 miles to village of Occidental. Turn right on Coleman Valley Road; continue for about a mile.

General information: Open Thursday through Sunday, 10:00 am–4:00 pm. Call for winter hours.

Wildwood Farm

10300 Sonoma Highway, Kenwood 95452
(707) 833-1161
website: www.wildwoodmaples.com
Ricardo and Sara Monte
Retail, Wholesale, and Mail Order

Plant specialties: Trees—Japanese maples (more than 180 cultivars, and species), Abies, Picea, Cryptomeria, Fagus (many unusual, pendulous, contorted forms), Cornus kousa, and natives (including madrone, Cornus nuttallii). Cold-hardy perennials and specialty shrubs.

History/description: The evolution of a plantsman as lived by Ricardo Monte: start with a degree in history from UC Berkeley, become a fledgling dress designer, shift to garden design, start growing rare and unusual specimens for use in your landscape projects, sell some, collect even more, then open a nursery on 15 rural acres. Now a family-run affair with wife Sara working full-time assisted by their wonder son Joseph, the 3-1/2-acre nursery includes growing grounds and display gardens surrounded by vineyards and grazing land. The garden and terrace may be rented for special occasions. The nursery now offers a variety of stone art, including imported lanterns and water basins.

How to get there: Take Highway 101 north to Highway 12 east (Sonoma Highway). Nursery is on the Glen Ellen side of Kenwood.

General information: Open March through October, Tuesday and Wednesday, 9:00 am–2:00 pm; Thursday through Saturday, 9:00 am–5:00 pm; Sunday, 10:00 am–4:00 pm. Winter hours seasonal, call ahead. Catalogue available on the website or for $2 credited to purchases of $20 or more. Deliveries made. Nursery tours may be arranged.

HORTICULTURAL ATTRACTIONS

Luther Burbank Home and Gardens

Corner of Santa Rosa & Sonoma Avenues, Santa Rosa
P. O. Box 1678, Santa Rosa 95402 (mailing address)
(707) 524-5445

History/description: Hybridizing wizard Luther
Burbank slept here. This pioneer of plant introduction put Mother Nature into fast-forward. His home
and garden were given by his family to the city of
Santa Rosa and are now a registered landmark. The
1-1/2-acre gardens were revitalized in 1991 to
include signage and demonstration beds, worth a
visit even when the home is closed. This guide to
plant specialties would be incomplete without a
mention of California's greatest plant specialist. The
Luther Burbank Home and Garden Volunteer
Association runs the Carriage House and museum.

Plant sales: Plants are occasionally sold on site.

General information: Garden is open Tuesday
through Sunday from April 1 to October 31 during
daylight hours. Home, Carriage House gift shop,
and museum are open 10:00 am–3:30 pm. Tours,
required for entry to the house, are given Wednesday through Sunday, from the first Wednesday in
April to mid-October. Visits to the garden are free;
there is an admission charge for house tours.

Green Gulch Farm

Off Highway One, between Mill Valley and Muir Beach,
1601 Shoreline Highway, Sausalito 94965
(415) 383-3134 (office)

History/description: Green Gulch is a Zen Bud-
dhist center and organic farming community.
Produce from their 8-acre farm appears in the best
restaurants and health-food stores. The smaller
garden, separating the living quarters from the farm
and sea beyond, includes rose arbors, a formal
herbal circle, espaliered fruit trees, and masses of
flowers. Saturday classes are offered on such subjects as composting and wreath making. A robust
garden volunteer program gives everyone a chance
to be part of this serene and successful tending of
the earth.

Plant sales: Their big plant sale is in April and
occasionally there is a sale in the fall, although some
plants are always available for self-service sales.

General information: Open every day.

Ferrari-Carano Winery

8761 Dry Creek Road, Healdsburg 95448
(707) 433-6700

Five acres of gardens including annual beds for
seasonal show (6,000 tulips and 12,000 daffodils,
for instance), a series of mixed California borders,
rose garden, formal courtyard, and meandering
stream with ponds and waterfall.

Goldridge Farm

7781 Bodega Avenue, Sebastopol
(707) 829-6711

Operated by the Western Sonoma County Historical

Society, this is Luther Burbank's experimental farm which produced the plumcot, the fast-growing Paradox walnut, the spineless cactus and, of course, the Shasta daisy. Open all year for self-guided tours. Group tours available by appointment.

Korbel Champagne Cellars Garden

13250 River Road, Guerneville 95446
(707) 824-7000

A century-old garden beautifully restored in 1979 by Korbel Horticulturist, Phillip Robinson, under the guidance of Valerie Heck. Situated on a hillside surrounding the historic home of the original Korbel family, the garden overlooks majestic redwood forests and the Korbel vineyards in the Russian River Valley, featuring antique roses and cottage-style perennial beds. Garden tours Tuesday through Sunday, at 11:00 am, 1:00 pm, and 3:00 pm, April through October (weather permitting).

Marin Art and Garden Center

30 Sir Francis Drake Boulevard, Ross 94957
(415) 454-5597

Ten acres of old trees and memorial gardens; venue for shows and plant sales put on by different garden groups.

Matanzas Creek Winery

6097 Bennett Valley Road, Santa Rosa 95404
(800) 590-6464

Acre and a half of terraced lavender fields. Large strolling garden through naturalized landscape of perennials, ornamental grasses, herbs, and natives. Self-guided tours. Open during daylight hours.

Mill Valley Sculpture Gardens

219 Shoreline Highway, Mill Valley 94941
(415) 381-9922, fax (415) 381-2821

Bay Area landscape designers David and Isis Schwartz
have created a garden that delights in the interplay of
art and nature. Full of sculpture, fountains, exotic
succulents grown by David's father, Dr. Herman
Schwartz, and New Zealand flax and ornamental
grasses developed by Bob Hornback. Plants from
several small growers are for sale here. Open Wednesday through Monday, 10:00 am–6:00pm.

Mom's Head Garden

4153 Langner Avenue, Santa Rosa 95407
(707) 585-8575, fax (707) 585-1264
e-mail: momshead@ap.net

Vivien Hillgrove has created a healing herb walk,
using medicinal and culinary herbs, based on the
folk traditions of Europe, China, East India, South
and North America. The county has temporarily
shut down her sales, but her wild and amusing
garden (named after a cat named Mom and in a
parody of the word 'Brideshead' and the proper
English approach to gardening) remains open
Sundays, 11:00 am–5:00 pm, May through October.
She offers classes on herbal medicine and has co-
founded the Sonoma County Herb Association and
a fall event, the Sonoma County Herb Festival. Take
the Todd Road exit from Highway 101. Follow the
overpass to the west side of the freeway, staying left.
Go left onto Moorland, which turns into Scenic. Go
right on Langner.

San Francisco, Peninsula & South Bay

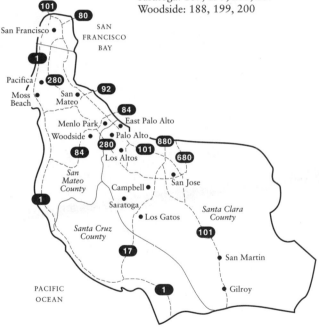

Acer Acres
Los Altos
(650) 941-4221
Robert Iacopi
Retail

Plant specialties: Acer palmatum (50 unusual varieties), specializing in 2-year grafts.

History/description: Bob Iacopi has been a maple hobbyist since the 1970s when his fascination and success with grafting resulted in quite a collection of Acer species. No one else was grafting at that time and the challenge was too great for this avid gardener to ignore. As often happens when a collection grows too large, sales happen, and they did in the mid-1980s. This backyard operation has captured more of his attention since retiring from a long career at Chevron where he was publisher of Ortho Books. Few are so happy both in the halls of corporate America and in the stalls of local farmer's markets.

How to get there: Call for directions.

General information: Open by appointment only. A perk to purchasing here is that you may bring back your plants for pruning and re-potting.

C. H. Baccus
900 Boynton Avenue, San Jose 95117
(408) 244-2923
Charles Baccus
Retail, Wholesale, and Mail Order

Plant specialties: Bulbs—Calochortus (50 species) and other California natives.

History/description: Charles Baccus, fresh out of horticulture studies at Foothill College in 1977, started a part-time business in native orchids while doing landscaping full-time. This eventually became a native bulb business. Now retired from his regular job, he hopes to establish growing grounds in other states. His display garden is best to see during bulb blooming season.

How to get there: Call for directions.

General information: Open by appointment only. Business is primarily mail order. Plant list available for SASE.

Baylands Nursery

1165 Weeks Street, East Palo Alto 94303 (nursery)
P. O. Box 50155, Palo Alto 94303 (mailing address)
(650) 323-1645
Day Boddorff
Retail and Wholesale

Plant specialties: California native plants, including
Ceanothus, Arctostaphylos, Cercis. Ornamental
grasses (over 50 varieties). perennials, daylilies,
trees, and shrubs, including Leucadendron and
Protea.

History/description: Baylands is an outgrowth of
Day Boddorff's desire to have more interesting
plants available for his landscaping business. His
knowledge of plants has been enriched by his far-
flung past. Five years of living in South Africa
studying botany and soils gave him more than a
passing familiarity with proteas. A master's degree
from the University of Florida in agronomy, studying soils and pastures, explains his fascination with
grasses. His move to California explains the rest.
Baylands will special order plants at no extra charge.

How to get there: Baylands Nursery is located a
block west of the Bay Road/Pulgas Avenue intersection in East Palo Alto. Call for directions.

General information: Open Monday through
Saturday, 8:00 am–4:30 pm. Delivery to most of San
Mateo and Santa Clara counties with minimum
order (please inquire).

Briarwood Nursery

1910 San Martin Avenue, San Martin 95046
(408) 683-2632, fax (408) 683-9326
Craig and Lolita Pierce
Wholesale and Mail Order

Plant specialties: Culinary herbs (more than 100 kinds) and scented geraniums.

History/description: Craig Pierce decided growing plants was much more interesting than working in a retail nursery. His training as a botanist has found successful application. This 3-acre nursery currently supplies the herbs for Williams-Sonoma, the Herb Farm, and other catalogue sales. Soon they will be on-line with a farmer's market group known as Farmacopia. Hecker Pass Family Specimen Tree Park is nearby off Hecker Pass Road (Highway 152).

How to get there: From Highway 101 take San Martin exit and go east for 1-1/3 miles.

General information: Open to wholesale customers only, by appointment. Local deliveries.

Brookside Orchids
2720 Alpine Road, Menlo Park 94026
(650) 854-3711
Jim Heierle
Retail, Wholesale, and Mail Order

Plant specialties: Orchids (25 genera).

History/description: Jim Heierle followed both his
father and grandfather into the orchid business,
working as they did at Niven's Nursery in Marin
County. He opened his own business in 1981 after
studying ornamental horticulture here and in Europe
and working for the Orchid House in Los Osos. He
has introduced Miltonia 'Jim Heierle' and several
heat-tolerant Odontoglossom hybrids. Occasionally
you might catch his newest introductions at a local
farmer's market.

How to get there: Take the Alpine Road exit off of
Highway 280. Continue east on Alpine Road. The
nursery is next-door to Heritage Garden Growers.

General information: Open Monday through
Friday, 8:00 am–4:30 pm. A plant price list is avail-
able for SASE. Mail orders filled for retail customers.
Wholesale orders over $400 will be delivered.

Carman's Nursery

16201 East Mozart Avenue, Los Gatos 95032
(408) 356-0119
Ed Carman
Retail and Wholesale

Plant specialties: Perennials, rock garden plants, bonsai starters, dwarf conifers, herbs. Hostas, Wisteria (7 named cultivars), kiwi vines. Fruit trees including figs (14 varieties), olives, pomegranates, and pawpaw. Large collection of Rhodohypoxis cultivars from New Zealand and England. Hypertufa troughs for alpine plants.

History/description: The history of Carman's reflects the evolution of the nursery trade in Northern California, albeit Carman's has always been a bit ahead of the times. The business, started by Ed's father in 1937, began with bedding plants, then shifted to selling herbs in pots to retailers. In the 1960s they began to focus on perennials. In 1970 the nursery moved to this 3/4-acre intensely stocked site. Now it grows the old standby perennials along with many unusual vines and fruit trees. Nearby horticultural attractions include Hakone Gardens in Saratoga, Japanese Tea Garden in San Jose, Vasona Park in Los Gatos, and Villa Montalvo in Saratoga.

How to get there: Take Highway 85 to Bascom Avenue exit. Left on Bascom Avenue. Continue to White Oaks Road and make a U-turn, reversing your direction on Bascom. Go right on Mozart.

General information: Open Tuesday through Saturday, 10:00 am–5:00 pm.

Checkerspot Nursery
725 Oddstad Boulevard, Pacifica 94044
(650) 738-1191, fax (650) 747-9718
Delmar and Elizabeth McComb
Retail and Wholesale

Plant specialties: Unusual shrubs and perennials, especially Salvia, Heuchera, Abutilon.

History/description: A class in nursery management at Cal Poly and a stint with the Sherman Library and Gardens, whetted Delmar McComb's appetite to someday have a nursery of unconventional plants. Never losing his dream and always on the prowl for new plants, he worked for almost a decade for a private estate in the South Bay, until he could open his 2-acre nursery in 1996. In his other life, Delmar sings opera for a variety of local companies, his talent having been discovered and encouraged by his mother-in-law, a composer of classical music.

How to get there: From Highway 1 heading south, go left onto Linda Mar Boulevard and continue to its end. Go left onto Oddstad. The nursery is 1-1/2 blocks on the left.

General information: Open Tuesday through Saturday, 9:30 am–5:00 pm; Sunday, 10:00 am–5:00 pm. Tours of the nursery can be arranged. Wholesale plant list available. Wholesale deliveries throughout the Bay Area on orders over $250. Landscape design services offered.

Christensen Nursery Company

16000 Sanborn Road, Saratoga 95070
(408) 867-4181
Jack Christensen; Albert Sotelo, manager
Retail and Wholesale

Plant specialties: California native plants, including Ceanothus, toyon, Myrica, Fremontodendron, Carpenteria, madrone, Arbutus 'Marina', manzanita, oaks, maples, dogwoods. Camellia specialties, including japonica, sasanqua. General line of ornamental trees and shrubs.

History/description: This venerable family operation was founded by Jack Christensen's father in 1938, moving to Belmont in 1947 and to Saratoga in 1960. Though the business is almost entirely wholesale, they welcome knowledgeable plant enthusiasts.

How to get there: From Saratoga, go west on Route 9 for 2 miles. Opposite Saratoga Springs picnic area, go left on Sanborn Road.

General information: Open Monday through Saturday, 8:00 am–4:30 pm.

Farwell's Rhododendron Nursery
13040 Skyline Boulevard, Woodside 94062
(650) 851-8812
Mrs. Everett E. Farwell, Jr.
Retail

Plant specialties: Rhododendrons and azaleas, mostly ungrafted hybrids, some species and unusual varieties, three year plants to very large specimen sizes, all field-grown. Pieris (5 forms).

History/description: In 1946 the Farwells decided to go into business for themselves, choosing to pursue Everett Farwell's avocation of rhododendron hybridizing. At that time, the only rhododendrons available in California were large-sized plants from Oregon. The Farwells were the first in California to sell two-year-old, field-grown specimens. Farwell's has a well-established display garden on this 1-acre site containing several large, 65-year-old rhododendrons. The nursery's location at a 2,000-foot elevation encourages the culture of cold-hardy plants. Mrs. Farwell reminds visitors to visit Filoli, just below them.

How to get there: From Highway 101, go west on Highway 92. Go south on Skyline Boulevard for 4-1/2 miles.

General information: Open March through June, Friday through Tuesday, 10:00 am–4:00 pm. August through February, Friday through Monday, 10:00 am–4:00 pm. Closed in July.

Golden Gate Orchids

225 Velasco Avenue, San Francisco 94134
(415) 467-3737, fax (415) 566-8636
Tom Perlite
Wholesale

Plant specialties: Orchids, specializing in intergeneric Odontoglossum hybrids. Also Masdevallia, Dendrobium, and Paphiopedilum, mostly hybrids, some species.

History/description: While a pre-med student at UC Berkeley, Tom Perlite took a botany course, just because he needed the units and could not get into other sciences. This bureaucratic necessity changed his course of action. Graduating with a degree in botany, he went to work at Rod McLellan Co., a well-chosen spot from which to learn the orchid business. He bought an existing azalea nursery with 30,000 square feet of greenhouses in 1981 and opened this orchid nursery. He grows most of his hybrids from seed and sells the seedlings primarily to other nurseries and the flowering plants to florist shops. He has a robust boarding business, retrieving out-of-bloom orchids, lavishing them with care, and then returning them as they just begin to rebloom.

How to get there: Call for directions.

General information: Not open to the public because his business is in a residential area. Open to wholesale customers, by appointment only. Wholesale lists available. Boarding services currently full, but call for opening.

Go Native Nursery

333 Cypress Avenue, Moss Beach
P. O. Box 370103, Montara 94037 (mailing address)
(650) 728-2286, fax (650) 728-3067
e-mail: gonative@coastside.net
David and Nikki Sands
Retail and Wholesale

Plant specialties: California native plants, both inland and coastal varieties, plus selected species from other Mediterranean climates from around the world.

History/description: Shortly after their move to Northern California, the Sands volunteered as docents at Año Nuevo State Reserve. The training included an introduction to coastal native plants, and they got hooked on native plants. They were also involved in the eradication of invasive exotics and grew plants for volunteer native revegetation projects. The nursery opened in May 1996, on a shared site with the Cypress Flower Farm, a retail cut-flower farm and gift store. Fueled by the passion to help heal the earth, the Sands are still involved in many volunteer projects. Their goal is to educate the public about the wonders of the native plants of California and how birds, bees, butterflies, and other fauna use these species in their life cycle.

How to get there: Take Highway 1 to Moss Beach, turn west on Cypress Avenue. The nursery is 1/2 block on the right. Moss Beach is 7 miles north of Half Moon Bay.

General information: Open Friday, 2:00 pm–6:00 pm, weekends, 11:00 am–6:00 pm, and by appointment. Landscaping services and erosion control consultation and installation.

Heritage Garden Growers, Inc.

P. O. Box 7184, Menlo Park 94026
(650) 854-8463, fax (650) 854-0466
Sara and Jim Dreer
Wholesale

Plant specialties: Uncommon perennials, including Salvia (32 species and cultivars), Penstemon (15), and Lavandula (15). Some deer-resistant plants.

History/description: Douglas Neecke, a general contractor, bought this well-established nursery, determined to maintain and increase its collection of interesting perennials. The 1-acre nursery has a large area of mother-stock plants to give customers an idea of the size and habit of mature plants.

How to get there: Call for directions.

General information: Open to wholesale trade, Monday through Friday, 8:00 am–4:30 pm. Retail customers may visit only with their landscaper.

Instant Oasis
P. O. Box 1446, Campbell 95008
(408) 241-6084, fax (408) 247-0521
Ann and Don Kuta
Retail

Plant specialties: Aquatic plants—over 100 varieties of bog and upright plants, 50 types of hardy and
tropical lilies. Complete line of water-garden
components. Custom-built biological filters.

History/description: While living in Colorado
30-some-odd years ago, Ann and Don Kuta started
designing aquatic gardens and selling the plants to
fill them. Don began designing custom filters and
started sharing his many years of expertise building
ponds as a contractor. They can supply you with
everything necessary to put a little splash in your
life, whether it is for a small tub garden or a large
pond installation.

How to get there: The nursery is near the corner of
Winchester Boulevard and Campbell Avenue in
Campbell, tucked away behind other businesses.
Please call for specic directions.

General information: Open Saturday, 11:00 am–
5:00 pm, or during the week by appointment.
On-site pondscape consultation available. Also,
custom fountains for the desk or table.

Rod McLellan Company

"Acres of Orchids"
914 South Claremont Street, San Mateo 94402-1843
(650) 373-3900, fax (650) 373-3913
McLellan Family
Retail, Wholesale, and Mail Order

Plant specialties: Orchids—many genera (thousands of varieties) including Phalaenopsis, Cattleya, Cymbidium, Paphiopedilum, Miltonopsis, Dendrobium, Oncidium. Rod McLellan Co. has introduced many hybrids and the hybrid genus, McLellanara.

History/description: Rod McLellan's grandfather started this business in 1897. Still a family-owned business, Rod McLellan Co. has been growing orchids for over 50 years. MeLellan's headquarters in San Mateo is their primary indoor orchid garden and retail center with "spa" services for out-of-bloom orchids and self-guided tours of their orchid propagation and cloning lab. McLellan's is also open for both retail and wholesale business at the San Francisco Flower Mart, 688 Brannan Street, between Fifth and Sixth Streets, (415) 362-1520, (retail: Monday–Saturday, 9:00 am–3:00 pm; wholesale: early mornings on Monday, Wednesday and Friday). There is also a retail store in South San Francisco at 137 Hickey Blvd, (650) 301-4050, open 9:00 am–6:00 pm daily and Tuesday and Thursday nights until 7:00 pm.

How to get there: To San Mateo store: from Highway 101, take the Third Avenue exit west. Turn left onto Delaware Street, right onto Ninth Avenue, and left onto South Claremont Street. From Highway 92, take the Delaware Street exit north. Turn left onto Ninth Avenue and Left onto South Claremont.

General information: Open for retail customers, every day 9:00 am–6:00 pm. Wholesale customers: Monday through Friday, 8:00 am–4:00 pm. Plant list available for $2. Orders shipped nationwide.

Menlo Growers
11605 New Avenue, Gilroy 95020
(408) 683-4862
Mike Vogel
Wholesale

Plant specialties: Citrus (50 varieties, especially dwarf) and tropical guavas. Also brokers eight kinds of avocado, other subtropical fruits and deciduous fruits.

History/description: Trained in pomology at Cal Poly San Luis Obispo, Mike Vogel figured he had done something right when he found this 20-year-old nursery for sale. Though he bought it just in 1995, he has already established a reputation for innovative work and plans to keep adding new proven varieties. All plants are container grown on 4 acres.

How to get there: Take the San Martin exit off of Highway 101. It becomes New Avenue. Go south 1 mile.

General information: Open by appointment only. Visitors welcome. Catalogue available.

Saso Herb Gardens

14625 Fruitvale Avenue, Saratoga 95070
(408) 867-0307
e-mail: herbgardens@saso.com
website: www.saso.com/herbgardens
Louis and Virginia Saso
Retail

Plant specialties: Medicinal, ornamental, and
unusual culinary herbs. An especially noteworthy
collection of salvias and ornamental oregano species.

History/description: Louis Saso's interest in herbs
stems from his earlier occupation as a wholesale
produce merchandiser. This retirement hobby/
business began in earnest in 1974. Now in addition
to growing herbs, they sell wreaths and other handi-
crafts made from herbs. Though trying (without
much success) to retire, the Sasos have cut back on
their extensive workshop schedule. They still keep the
South Bay herbally aware with classes in herbal
medicine, wreath and garland making, herbal crafts,
and herb garden design. Plan also to visit Hakone
Japanese Gardens and Villa Montalvo, both in
Saratoga.

How to get there: Take Highway 280 south to
Highway 85 exit. Go right for 3 miles to Saratoga.
Continue past stoplight for 1 mile. Left on Fruitvale.
From Highway 101 take Lawrence Expressway,
which ends at Saratoga Avenue. Go right on Saratoga
Avenue for 2 miles. Left on Fruitvale.

General information: Open mid-April through mid-
September (when the gardens are at their best) on
Saturdays, 9:00 am–2:30 pm. Talks to groups may be
arranged. Free tours once a month on a Saturday,
from April through September. Group tours may be
arranged at other times for a fee. Workshops offered.

Shelldance Orchid Nursery

2000 Highway One, Pacifica 94044
(650) 355-4845
Michael Rothenberg, Nancy Davis
Retail and Wholesale

Plant specialties: Orchids—Phalaenopsis, Oncidium, Dendrobium, Paphiopedilum, Odontoglossom, Miltonia, Cattleya. Over 1,000 species and hybrid bromeliads, including two of their introductions, Aechmea 'Shelldancer' and A. 'Pacifica'.

History/description: It really was a case of starting out "selling seashells down by the seashore." Hard to believe this incredible business began on San Francisco's Union Street selling Tillandsias in shells. They moved to Pacifica to expand their bromeliad collection. About the same time they met an orchid grower from Florida and went with him on collecting expeditions to tropical rainforests. Still collecting bromeliads, their attention turned to the propagation of rare and endangered orchid species. A magnificent rainforest display highlights their orchid and bromeliad collections. The nursery operates at Sweeney Ridge, part of the Golden Gate National Recreation Area, under an agricultural use lease with the GGNRA. The National Park Service and Shelldance share a commitment to preserving natural resources for the benefit of future generations.

How to get there: Travel south on Highway 1. Number 2000 is on the left (east) side of road. Make a U-turn at the Reina del Mar stoplight.

General information: Open Saturday and Sunday only, 10:00 am–5:00 pm. Wholesale by appointment only. Tours and special educational programs may be arranged.

Trees of California
P. O. Box 13189, San Jose 95013
(408) 264-3663
Joe Arnaz
Retail and Wholesale

Plant specialties: Huge trees (6- to 14-foot boxes). Over 20 varieties plus most native oak species, all hand dug and collected. Some unusual trees are 50 to 80 years old.

History/description: A bona fide tree hugger, Joe Arnaz actually does something about his passion. Constantly scouting for endangered trees, he arrives to dig just ahead of the bulldozer. He has worked as far away as Saudi Arabia and Chile, and has helped bring shade to important locations in California. Recent projects include the planting of 26,000 trees on a private estate near Woodside quarry, intended eventually to become an arboretum.

How to get there: Located at the corner of Flickering and Falling Tree. Call for directions.

General information: Open by appointment only.

Western Tree Nursery
3873 Hecker Pass Road, Gilroy 95020
(408) 842-4892, fax (408) 848-4260
Wholesale (Retail customers welcome if they know what they want)

Plant specialties: Trees and shrubs, suited to warm coastal and foothill locations, up to 24-inch box. Some California natives.

History/description: Western Tree started in 1970 as a tree farm exclusively. Over time it has added a wide range of shrubs and, most recently, landscape ornamentals—all grown on their 65-acre grounds. While the nursery welcomes retail customers, it is not set up to be able to answer questions and offer individual help. The nursery reminds visitors to check out the specimen trees at the Hecker Pass Specimen Tree Park.

How to get there: In Gilroy go west on Highway 152 towards Watsonville. Nursery is on the right side of highway.

General information: Open Monday through Friday, 8:00 am–4:00 pm, except holidays. Plant list available for SASE. Deliveries from Salinas to Reno on minimum orders of $1,000.

Yerba Buena Nursery

19500 Skyline Boulevard, Woodside 94062
(650) 851-1668, fax (650) 851-5565
Kathy Crane
Retail

Plant specialties: California native plants (more than 500 species), native and exotic ferns.

History/description: This grandmother of all native plant nurseries was established in 1960 by Gerda Isenberg who moved here with her husband in the 1940s to raise cattle. Her fascination with California natives grew from many discoveries of choice plants, especially ferns, found growing on this exquisite 40-acre piece of property in a sheltered coastal canyon in the Santa Cruz Mountains. In 1996, at the age of 94, she sold the nursery to Kathy Crane, who has assembled a top-notch group of horticulturists to keep Gerda's achievements prospering. The 2-acre demonstration garden has been revamped and contains mature specimens of almost all plants sold. Customers can still picnic along the meandering stream.

How to get there: Call for directions or try this: Highway 101 or Highway 280 to Woodside Road exit (Highway 84). Go west to Skyline (Highway 35). Left on Skyline for 4.5 miles. Go right at nursery sign for 2.2 miles. Keep to right for gate of nursery.

General information: Open every day except major holidays, 9:00 am–5:00 pm. Catalogue available for $2. Free self-guided tours; guided group tours available for fee. Internship programs (6- or 12-week) offered. High tea served on the Tea Terrace (reservations required on weekdays).

HORTICULTURAL ATTRACTIONS

Filoli Center
Cañada Road, Woodside 94062
(650) 364-2880 (tour reservations)

History/description: Filoli is one of few remaining grand country estates in California. Now a National Trust for Historic Preservation property, Filoli was created in 1915–1917 by William Bourne who inherited the Empire Mine at age 17. He plowed the same western energy into his garden as he did into the mine, making it the deepest in the country. Filoli's 16-acre garden is distinctly Californian with grand views of the coastal range, although it borrows from European garden tradition. Organized as a series of outdoor rooms, Filoli includes a woodland garden, a rose garden, impeccably maintained formal gardens, and colorful seasonal displays. There are miles of woodland trails on the entire 654-acre estate. Friends of Filoli, the membership support group, organizes lectures and a series of special events (415/366-4640).

Plant sales: Plants propagated at the garden are offered for sale in the garden shop, open at 10:00 am from February through October.

General information: House and garden open February through October, Tuesday through Thursday for tours only, reservations required; open Friday and Saturday, 10:00 am–2:00 pm for self-guided tours.

Gamble Garden Center

1431 Waverly Street, Palo Alto 94301
(650) 329-1356, fax (650) 329-1688
e-mail: admin@gamblegarden.org

History/description: This turn-of-the-century
Colonial/Georgian-Revival-style villa was built by
Edwin Percy Gamble, a banker and son of the
co-founder of Procter and Gamble. The Gamble
family moved to Palo Alto to be near Stanford
University, where their four children were to study.
Today this 2-1/3-acre estate is a community horticultural foundation. Garden highlights include the
wisteria garden, rose garden, cherry allee, herb
garden, and demonstration gardens. Regularly
scheduled classes are held in the historic carriage
house on such topics as soil amending, container
gardening, and flower arranging.

General information: Gardens are open during
daylight hours. The office and reference library are
open from 9:00 am–noon on weekday mornings.
Entrance to the garden is free; docent-led tours for
groups of eight or more are available by reservation
for a fee. Facilities may be rented.

Golden Gate Park

From Stanyan Street to the ocean between
Fulton Street and Lincoln Avenue, San Francisco
(415) 666-7200, (415) 750-5105 (Friends of Recreation
and Parks)

History/description: The transformation of this
strip of wind-whipped, desolate sand dunes into lush
parkland was a horticultural tour de force. Planned
and begun by William Hammond Hall in the 1880s,
credit for most of its development goes to longtime
superintendent, John McLaren. Noted for its
remarkable use of Mediterranean-climate plants to
recreate an English landscape garden setting, Golden

Gate Park is the largest man-made municipal park in
America, host to a myriad of activities. In addition
to Strybing Arboretum, special gardens include the
Japanese Tea Garden, Conservatory of Flowers
(badly damaged during the winter storms of 1996),
Rhododendron Dell, National AIDS Memorial
Grove, Dahlia Garden, and Shakespeare Garden.

General information: The park is open every day.
Visitor centers are being created in the Beach Chalet
at the western end of the park and in McLaren
Lodge at its eastern end. Friends of Recreation and
Parks offers walking tours of the park, school
discovery programs, and various events throughout
the year to help preserve the park. Plan to attend its
major fundraiser, the Preview Party of the San
Francisco Flower and Garden Show in March.

Saratoga Horticultural Research Foundation, Inc.

15185 Murphy Avenue, San Martin 95046
(408) 779-3303, fax (408) 778-9259
e-mail: saratoga@garlic.com
René O. DeLuna

History/description: In response to the post war
building boom's demand for trees and shrubs, Ray
Hartman and a group of nurserymen founded
Saratoga Hort in 1951 to research and develop a
successful flora for California. They brought us fall
with the brightly colored autumnal leaves of Liq-
uidambar styraciflua 'Palo Alto' and Ginkgo biloba
'Autumn Glory'. Continuing emphasis on plant
research here expands the gene pool of California
horticulture; during their first 40 years, they introduced more than 120 plants into the trade, most of
which are cultivars of our native flora. The foundation has a 7-acre testing site in Gilroy and a 2-1/2-
acre property in San Martin which includes a small
demonstration garden.

Plant sales: There are two big plant sales each year—the Fall Festival on the third Saturday in October and the Spring Horticultural Fair in addition to the regular first-Friday nursery openings.

General information: The nursery is open on the first Friday of each month. Membership-supported activities include lectures and field trips. Groups may arrange a visit anytime.

Strybing Arboretum & Botanical Gardens
Ninth Avenue and Lincoln Way, Golden Gate Park,
San Francisco 94122
(415) 661-1316

History/description: Officially opened in 1940, Strybing today has 75 acres containing 7,500 plants from all over the world. Plants are arranged in a series of gardens to educate and delight visitors, including the Garden of Fragrance, Succulent Garden, Conifer Garden, Cape Province Garden, and New World Cloud Forest. Three areas showcase California native plants: the Arthur Menzies garden, Redwood Trail, and John Muir Nature Trail. There are also significant collections of plants from Australia and New Zealand. Strybing Arboretum Society, the Arboretum's membership support group, has a very active education program (ext. 354) with lectures, workshops, tours, gardening clinics, ethnobotany programs, and children's activities (ext. 307). Strybing has a store and horticultural library which houses an impressive 18,000 volumes.

Plant sales: Their big annual plant sale is held the first weekend in May; specialized plant sales take place on occasional Saturdays. For information about plant sales, call the nursery, (415) 661-3090.

General information: Open Monday through
Friday, 8:00 am–4:30 pm; Saturday, Sunday, and
Holidays, 10:00 am–5:00 pm. Library (ext. 303) and
shop (ext. 308) open 10:00 am–4:00 pm. Docent
tours of the gardens (ext. 312) occur every day at
1:30 pm and on the weekends also at 10:30 am.

Allied Arts Guild

75 Arbor Road, Menlo Park
(650) 322-2405

Spanish-style courtyards and gardens in profuse bloom.

Garden for the Environment

7th Avenue at Lawton Street, San Francisco
(415) 285-7584

A demonstration garden about water conservation
and good gardening techniques, a project of SLUG
(see listing under Horticultural Information).

Goldsmith Seeds

2280 Hecker Pass Highway (Highway 152 West),
Gilroy 95020
(408) 847-7333
website: www.goldsmithseeds.com

Goldsmith Seeds, a wholesale producer of flower seeds,
devotes 6 acres of their growing grounds to field-test
new flower selections each year. In bloom from June
through September, this floriferous wallop has been
known to cause traffic jams along the highway.
Interested motorists are now encouraged to stop by
for a closer look at tomorrow's flowers. Goldsmith
has developed many garden favorites, their newest
being 'Fantasy' milliflora petunia, the first and only
miniature petunia. In addition to the seasonal field
trials, a 2-acre public display garden and an interior
courtyard garden are open year-round. Guided tours
may be arranged for groups of 10 or more.

Guadalupe Gardens

715 Spring Street at Taylor Street, San Jose 95161
(408) 298-7657

Part of a 450-acre park project being developed
along the Guadalupe River. Completed gardens
include an Historic Orchard and Heritage Rose
Garden (with 3,400 varieties of roses, it is the
largest collection in the US. and the third largest in
the world).

Hakone Gardens

21000 Big Basin Way, Saratoga 95070
(408) 741-4994

Formerly the private garden of the Stine family,
created by a court gardener of the Emperor of Japan
in 1918 and renovated in 1966. Zen gardens on 15
acres using camellias, shaped trees, wisteria, bamboo, iris, and azaleas. Lectures, demonstrations, and
the meeting place for several plant societies.

Hecker Pass Family Adventure and Bonfante Gardens

3050 Hecker Pass Highway (Highway 152 West),
Gilroy 9502
(408) 842-2121

The horticultural focus here in this emerging family
destination area is on topiary and unusual-shaped
trees. Open Monday through Friday, 8:00 am–5:00
pm. Nursery on-site is open by appointment only.

Overfelt Botanical Gardens

McKee Road at Educational Park Drive, San Jose
(408) 251-3323

Thirty-three-acre botanical garden incorporating an
all-American test garden, fragrance garden, and
Chinese cultural garden.

Prusch Farm Park
647 South King, San Jose 95116
(408) 926-5555

Small farm-style park with animals, fruit orchard,
and community gardens.

San Jose Municipal Rose Garden
Naglee Avenue at Dana, San Jose
(408) 277-5422

Five thousand colorful and fragrant roses with
redwoods and flowering trees.

San Mateo Garden Center
605 Parkside Way, San Mateo 94403
(650) 574-1506

Over 40 horticultural groups hold their meetings,
shows, sales, benefits, classes, and workshops here.

San Mateo Japanese Tea Garden
Central Park, San Mateo
(650) 377-3340, (650) 377-3345

Meandering paths through serene plantings with koi
pond, pagodas, and tea house.

Sunset Publishing Corporation
80 Willow Road, Menlo Park 94025
(650) 321-3600

Imagine a larger-than-life ranch house from the
1950s. Then imagine what its backyard might be in
the hands of these lifestyle experts who have been
defining West Coast living since 1898. A series of
gardens surrounding an immense lawn recreate
distinctive California regions. Included are a Southwest desert garden, a Monterey area coastal garden,
a planting of grapes and oaks to represent Northern

California, and a Northwest woodland garden with firs, dogwoods, and rhododendrons. Self-guided tours offered, Monday through Friday, 8:30 am–4:30 pm.

Villa Montalvo

15400 Montalvo Road, Saratoga 95070
(408) 741-3421

Large country estate of San Francisco Mayor and US Senator James Phelan in the middle of the Santa Cruz Mountains, designed by John McLaren, inspired by European garden tradition.

Monterey Bay Area

Aptos: 211, 225
Aromas: 223, 226, 232
Carmel: 235
Carmel Valley: 234
Hollister: 224
Marina: 228
Monterey: 217
Moss Landing: 220
Santa Cruz: 210, 213, 215, 219, 222, 227, 235
Scotts Valley: 212
Soquel: 214, 218, 230, 233
Watsonville: 216, 221, 229, 231

Antonelli Brothers Begonia Gardens

2545 Capitola Road, Santa Cruz 95062
(831) 475-5222, fax (831) 475-7066
Skip Antonelli, Linda Bobbitt
Retail, Wholesale, and Mail Order

Plant specialties: Tuberous begonias (100 varieties), as well as fibrous (100+ types), Rex and Rieger hybrid begonias. Fuchsias (500 cultivars, varieties, and subspecies). Shade plants such as ferns, Mandevilla, Clerodendrum, Cineraria.

History/description: A family business since its founding by the present owner's father and uncles in 1935, Antonelli's has many begonia hybrids attributed to itself. The current generation, horticulturally educated and trained in the nursery since birth, continues to develop new varieties. Three acres of glass and lath houses provide an enormous selection for their mostly retail customers. The nursery's summer display of tuberous begonias—the largest in America—is decidedly spectacular. They alert you to two special plant sales—one in the fall at UCSC Arboretum and the other on Mother's Day at Cabrillo College.

How to get there: In Santa Cruz, traveling south on Highway 1, go right on 41st Avenue (south). Go right on Capitola Road. Nursery is on the right.

General information: Open every day, 9:00 am–5:00 pm. Mail-order catalogue offering bulbs, tubers, and supplies available in January. Supplemental list of seedlings (fuchsia, begonia) available in late March.

Bamboo Giant, Inc.

5601 Freedom Boulevard, Aptos 95003
(831) 685-1248, fax (831) 662-8320
e-mail: moso@cruzio.com
website: www.bamboogiant.com
Gray and Allison Henry, managers
Retail and Wholesale

Plant specialties: Bamboo, especially Phyllostachys species. The Henrys have introduced P. heterocycla pubescens 'Moso' and P. nigra 'Henon' and have increased the availability of P. nigra 'dikokuchiku'. Also, rhododendron, dogwood, deciduous magnolias, ginkgoes, camellias.

History/description: This nursery business developed when a family group of arborists and horticulturists started to improve a reclaimed 31-acre quarry site. Their weekend hobby of gardening produced a major garden and a fascination with bamboo which, in turn, created the nursery. An 8-acre display garden includes redwood groves, deciduous magnolias, ponds, water plants, and the dense and lofty bamboo, planted among the old, hewn-stone walls.

How to get there: Take the Freedom Boulevard exit off of Highway 1, south of Santa Cruz. Go east for 2 miles. The nursery will be on your right.

General information: Open Saturday, 9:00 am–5:00 pm and by appointment on other days. Pruning, planting, and arboricultural consultations offered. Plant list is available for SASE or by fax or e-mail. Workshops and classes planned for the near future.

Bay Laurel Nursery

P. O. Box 66595, Scotts Valley 95067
(831) 438-3999, fax (831) 438-0779
Peter Moerdyke
Wholesale

Plant specialties: 300 varieties of rhododendrons, including Rhododendron occidentale, Exbury azaleas. Companion plants, including special collections of Kalmia, Pieris, Viburnum, lilac, Hamamelis, dogwood, deciduous Magnolia, Ginkgo, Daphne, Camellia, and maple. Shade plants. Container grown.

History/description: Peter Moerdyke has always been a plant lover. After studies at Cal Poly, he purchased Boulevard Garden Rhododendron Nursery in Palo Alto in 1977 and moved it to Scotts Valley. A display garden is in the works on his 12 acres in the coastal hills. He suggests you combine your visit with a trip to see the redwoods at Henry Cowell Park and the arboretum on the UCSC campus.

How to get there: Call for directions.

General information: Open house held for retail clients on spring weekends. Call for invitation. Tours available at that time. Plant list available. Deliveries to San Francisco and Monterey Bay Area on minimum order of $250.

Bay West Nurseries, LLC
2669 Mattison Lane, Santa Cruz 95062
(831) 476-8865, fax (831) 476-4867
Mike Coxwell, John Gargiulo
Retail and Wholesale

Plant specialties: Trees and shrubs with many available in larger sizes (15 gallon and 24-inch boxes).

History/description: Under new ownership since February 1998, Bay West Nurseries (formerly Far West) has undergone extensive revitalization. The new owners bring 25 years of horticultural and business experience to the venture. They met in the early 1980s when John, who was managing a vegetable business and 70-acre tree farm, hired Mike to help with a humongous golf course and resort community landscaping project. They have been involved in several ventures since, including a strawberry farm that was recently sold to Monsanto. This joint venture combines retail and wholesale sections on a 3-acre site. It is organized simply for the novice but has enough depth and diversity for the expert. There is also a 4-acre growing ground in Watsonville where plants grow faster, and larger specimens are nurtured for customers interested in instant gratification.

How to get there: Take Highway 17 to Highway 1 south. Take Soquel Avenue exit. Turn left at end of ramp. Continue 1/2 mile to Mattison and turn right.

General information: Open weekdays, 8:00 am–4:30 pm; Saturday, 9:00 am–4:30 pm, Sunday, 10:00 am–4:30 pm. Deliveries within Santa Cruz County. Wholesale availability list. Landscape design and installations services available.

Central Coast Wilds

Old San Jose Road, Soquel
114 Liberty Street, Santa Cruz 95060 (office address)
(408) 459-0656, fax (831) 457-1606
e-mail: jtfodor@centralcoastwilds.com
website: www.centralcoastwilds.com
Joshua Fodor, Kirk Dakis
Retail and Wholesale

Plant specialties: California native plants suited to
Monterey and San Francisco Bay Areas, featuring
grasses, coastal prairie wildflowers and shrubs.
Small selection of named varieties.

History/description: Josh Fodor studied botany
and environmental studies at UC Santa Cruz and at
its Center for Agroecology which led to a job
managing a 10-acre organic farm. Increasingly his
focus went wild, literally, and his attention shifted to
a fascination with native vegetation. When asked to
propagate grasses for a restoration project, he saw
the opportunity to start a new pursuit. Today he and
his business partner oversee a 2-acre nursery and
120 acres of native wonderland.

How to get there: Directions provided when
appointment is made.

General information: Open by appointment only.
Their website offers information about tours and
workshops. Site specific consultations for restoration
projects remain an important part of the business.
Plant list available for SASE. Local deliveries.

Dancing Crane Fine Bonsai Nursery/ Bonsai Courtyard

1001 Center Street, Santa Cruz 95003
(831) 479-1343
Jay Caron
Retail

Plant specialties: Bonsai, large specimens, some over 100 years old, using a wide variety of plant material, pots, and tools.

History/description: Jay Caron's interest in bonsai started from necessity. He inherited a collection of venerable old specimens, shortly after moving to California in the late 1970s. To keep them alive, he quickly started studying on his own and then with several bonsai masters. What started as a crisis developed into a hobby, and then a business in 1988. Schooled as a sculptor, he considers each plant a living sculpture. The nursery includes many bonsai displays populating a 1/2-acre plot of California countryside. Large garden pottery pieces are also for sale.

How to get there: Call for directions.

General information: Open every day from 11:00 am–6:00 pm. Tours and classes offered at the nursery. Consultations given. Pruning and re-potting services. Corporate rentals of selected bonsai plants may be arranged.

Desert Theatre

17 Behler Road, Watsonville 95076
(831) 728-5513, fax (831) 728-4091
Kate Jackson
Retail, Wholesale, and Mail Order

Plant specialties: Cacti and succulents, with special
collections of Euphorbia (145 varieties), Notocactus,
Mammillaria, Haworthia, Echeveria, Gymno–
calycium, Rebutia.

History/description: On vacation from her work as
midwife and delivery nurse, Kate Jackson visited the
Southwest and fell in love with the desert. She began
collecting a few plants. By 1982, she was selling her
growing collection part-time and by 1987 she had a
full-scale business. Worth a visit for the artistic
arrangement of display beds, the nursery really is a
re-created desert "theatre." She passes along her
love of plants by giving talks or group tours of the
nursery.

How to get there: From Highway 101, take
Highway 17 west to Highway 1 south. Drive 14
miles to Watsonville. Take Airport Boulevard exit to
Green Valley Road. Go left. Entrance to nursery is
1/2 mile on right.

General information: Hours vary with the season.
Call for exact times. Closed Monday. Mail-order
catalogue is available for $2.

Drought Resistant Nurseries
850 Park Avenue, Monterey 93940
(831) 327-2120, fax (831) 375-2973
Thom Crow, Steve Halvorson
Retail and Wholesale

Plant specialties: Specializing in plants for coastal gardens—drought-tolerant, Mediterranean (special collections of Lavandula, Cistus), Australian, South African, and California native plants, including Ceanothus (16 varieties) and Arctostaphylos (8). Trees up to 15-gallon.

History/description: These two gentlemen have been good friends for 25 years, ever since they resolved their differences from vying for the attention of the same childhood sweetheart. Both were contractors on the San Francisco Peninsula and got the itch to launch second careers. Thom had 5 acres of family property with water on flatland in the Carmel Valley—conditions ripe for a nursery, which they opened as a wholesale business in 1987. They bought the retail venue in Monterey in 1996, but continue to propagate and grow their stock in Carmel Valley. They have developed good connections with local botanical gardens, plant lovers, and hobbyists who provide them with a steady stream of unusual things to propagate.

How to get there: Call for directions.

General information: Open Monday through Saturday, 8:00 am–4:30 pm. Availability list for wholesale buyers.

Dynasty Gardens, Inc.
3621-A Main Street, Soquel 95073
(831) 475-5296 (let ring), fax (831) 475-7083
Robert Herse; Carol Herse, manager
Retail and Wholesale

Plant specialties: 600 varieties of unusual small-flowering perennials and alpines, especially Campanula, Salvia, Lavandula, Dianthus, Phlox, Thymus. Also succulents, aquatic plants, ornamental grasses, bulbs, annuals, and ground covers.

History/description: After he retired as an elementary school principal in 1982, Robert Herse started a nursery specializing in ground covers; over time his interests switched to perennials. The nursery is now managed by his daughter. Trained as a molecular biologist, she advocates the importance of good soil and can offer propagation assistance.

How to get there: From Highway 1, take Bay Avenue/Porter Street exit. Go north to stoplight at Main Street. Go up Main Street for a mile.

General information: Open Monday through Friday, 9:00 am–5:00 pm, Saturday, 9:00 am–3:00 pm. November to March not open Saturdays. Plant list available for SASE.

Ecoscape

424 National Street, Santa Cruz 95060
(831) 459-8106
e-mail: ecoscape@scruznet.com
website: www.scruz.net/~ecoscape
Alan and Joan Beverly
Retail, Wholesale, and Mail Order

Plant specialties: The succulent Aloe polyphylla and other aloes for landscapes of Northern California.

History/description: When Alan Beverly was a Peace Corps volunteer in Lesotho, South Africa, in 1974–77, he discovered a wild population of the spectacularly sculptural Aloe polyphylla and gathered some seed. This plant proved exceptionally slow to flower and hence to propagate. He had to wait 18 years before he was able to introduce it at a Cactus and Succulent Society gathering in Pasadena. Since then, he has perfected his propagation technique to keep up with the demand for this unusual plant. Alan Beverly is a landscape contractor who operates this backyard nursery with his wife.

How to get there: Call for directions.

General information: Open by appointment only. Mail orders accepted for bare-root plants. Deliveries possible throughout the Bay Area on minimum order of 10 plants.

Elkhorn Native Plant Nursery
Off Highway 1, north of Moss Landing
P. O. Box 270, Moss Landing 95039 (mailing address)
(831) 763-1207, fax (831) 763-1659
Robert Stephens; Jean Ferreira, manager
Retail and Wholesale

Plant specialties: California native plants suited to
the Central Coast and coastal ranges, including
native grasses, riparian plants, and succulents.

History/description: The Packard Ranch, on the
edge of Elkhorn Slough, had been growing native
grasses for their own use for several years when they
realized there was a commercial demand for the
seeds. In 1989, Mr. Packard started a native-seed
business which diversified in the early 90s to include
plants sales as well, both for habitat restoration and
landscape use. Jean Ferreira, a trained botanist and
ecologist, has transferred her talents from the
California State Park system. From their demonstration garden of bunch grasses and native flowering
plants, there are great views of oak woodlands and
the nearby wetlands area of Elkhorn Slough National Estuarine Research Reserve, (831) 728-2822,
an important bird-watching site in the Pacific Flyway.

How to get there: North of Moss Landing, at the
junction of Struve Road and Highway 1 (a Beacon
gas station helps mark the spot), go east on an
unnamed ranch road for 1 mile.

General information: Open for retail sales,
Wednesday, 10:00 am–4:00 pm. Wholesale sales,
Monday through Friday, 8:00 am–4:00 pm. Big
open house and sale held on a Saturday in April and
October. Brochure available. Local deliveries for
orders over $100.

John Ewing Orchids

487 White Road, Watsonville 95076
P. O. Box 1318, Soquel 95073 (mailing address)
(831) 684-2222
Loraine and John Ewing
Retail and Mail Order

Plant specialties: Orchids, exclusively the flasks and small seedlings of novelty Phalaenopsis and species Cattleyas. Introduced hybrids include Phalaenopsis 'Mahalo' and P. 'Fire Water'. Also, small carnivorous plants.

History/description: John Ewing started growing orchids at age nine, tending his first plant, which was a gift from his father. With degrees in botany and biology and joined by an equally interested wife, he founded the nursery in 1969, located first in Southern California and, since 1975, in Watsonville. Well-known hybridizers, they seek to extend the color range of Phalaenopsis to include shades of pastels, peach, and stripes. Recently the Ewings opened their plant tissue lab to propagate seed from retail customers.

How to get there: From Highway 1, take the Larkin Valley exit. Go east for 1 mile. Turn left onto White Road.

General information: Open by appointment only. Closed Sunday. Free catalogue. Plants shipped throughout the country.

The Garden Company
2218 Mission Street, Santa Cruz
(831) 429-8424, fax (831) 429-8477
Charles and Maria Keutmann
Retail and Wholesale

Plant specialties: Unusual perennials, shrubs and trees, palms and cycads, bamboo (14 varieties), English primula hybrids, large selection of house-made topiary. Variegated plants and plants with colored foliage.

History/description: Graduating with a degree in landscape architecture in 1986, Charles Keutmann started his professional life in the corporate business world. After moving to Santa Cruz and realizing the error of his ways (and the possibilities of growing almost anything in Santa Cruz), he returned to his primary interests—plants and design. Maria is also active in the business. The nursery is always on the lookout for new introductions. On a collecting trip to Japan in the spring of 1999, Lance Reiners, The Garden Company's respected plantsmith and propagator, was able to pursue his fascination with colored and variegated foliage; he thinks that variegation in plants, so prized by the samurai, is still underappreciated in this country. Just wait.

How to get there: Mission Street is Highway 1. Traveling south on Highway 1, the nursery is on the left in about 3 blocks after the first stoplight in Santa Cruz.

General information: Open Monday through Saturday, 8:30 am–5:30 pm; Sunday, 9:00 am–4:30 pm. Occasional demonstrations of topiary and dried wreath making.

Kimura International, Inc.

18435 Rea Avenue, Aromas 95004
(831) 726-3223
Fumi Kimura
Wholesale

Plant specialties: Cacti and succulents, specializing in crested and variegated forms.

History/description: The Kimura family's cacti and succulent collection dates back to Fumi's father, Makoto Kimura, and his childhood fascination with these plants in Japan. He started selling his private collection, opened a nursery in Japan, and began grafting in earnest. In 1978, on a collecting trip to Mexico and California, he heard about a nursery for sale in Aromas. Given the stiffening competition in Japan, he quickly bought it and shipped over his collection of children and plants. Though Makoto died in 1997, the family continues his lifelong interest. Working on 8 rural acres, they maintain 10 greenhouses and more than 3 acres of field-grown cactus, in addition to a fair number of chickens.

How to get there: From Highway 101 south, go right towards Aromas on San Juan Road. Go right on Carpinteria Road for 2 miles. Rea Avenue is on the left, opposite the fire station.

General information: Open Tuesday and Wednesday, 9:00 am–5:00 pm by appointment only.

Meadowlark Nursery

824 Las Viboras Road, Hollister 95023
(831) 636-5912, fax same
Claire Steede-Butler
Retail and Wholesale

Plant specialties: Salvias and unusual drought-tolerant plants, California native perennials, hardy and heat-tolerant perennials.

History/description: As a landscape contractor, Claire Steede-Butler was frustrated by the short supply of perennials for her drought-resistant gardens. In 1986 she started this nursery in a beautiful valley at the southern extension of the Diablo Range because its climate was relatively cooler than that of the surrounding areas. This picturesque 5-acre property is home to her family, home to the nursery, home to her garden filled with old-fashioned roses and perennials, and home to her 11 Peruvian paso horses. She will give slide talks for small groups, can custom-grow for special projects, and continues to build gardens in San Mateo, Santa Clara, and San Benito counties.

How to get there: From intersection of Highway 152 (Pacheco Pass Highway) and Highway 156, go south on Highway 156. Turn left on Fairview Road. Take second road on left which is Las Viboras Road (called Churchill on the right). After about a mile, nursery will be on unnamed side road to the left.

General information: Open by appointment only. Deliveries to San Francisco, Peninsula, East Bay, Santa Clara, Monterey, and Santa Cruz Counties. Minimum order $250. Free 4-page plant list of hardy perennials is available.

Native Revival Nursery

8022 Soquel Drive, Aptos 95003
(831) 684-1811, fax (831) 984-2151
Erin O'Doherty
Retail and Wholesale

Plant specialties: California native plants from central California; deer-resistant, drought-, heat-, and salt-tolerant plants. Ferns, perennials, and ornamental grasses.

History/description: For several years the O'Dohertys supplied homegrown plants to a landscape contractor friend. These plants were so well received that a full-fledged nursery business was started in 1992. Trained in ornamental horticulture at Foothill College and by Yerba Buena Nursery, the O'Dohertys contract-grow for water districts, parks, individuals, and, of course, their friends. They collect much of their seed from the Santa Cruz Mountains and Mt. Hamilton Range, believing that well-acclimatized plants are good garden choices both for their ease of maintenance and for the habitat they provide for wildlife.

How to get there: From Highway 1 in Aptos, take Aptos/Seacliff Road east to Soquel Drive. Right on Soquel.

General information: Open Wednesday through Sunday, weekdays, 9:00 am–5:00 pm; weekends, 10:00 am–4:00 pm. Wholesale customers by appointment. Catalogue available for $5. Free plant list. Deliveries throughout the Bay Area. Classes offered in spring. Nursery tours and lectures can be arranged for fee. Design and maintenance services and site-specific consultations offered.

Plant Horizons
P. O. Box 57, Aromas 95004
fax (831) 726-2018
Joe Solomone
Wholesale

Plant specialties: Clivia.

History/description: Californians should know
about and be thankful for longtime plant breeder
Joe Solomone—which is why we include him here
even though he does not sell his plants directly. He
opened Prunedale Nursery in 1960, moving it in
1966 to Watsonville and changing its name to
Monterey Bay Nursery. Over time he has introduced
many plants into the trade, such as Ceanothus
'Snow Flurry' and Grevillea 'Aromas', propagated
from imported plants and his own hybrids. He sold
the nursery in 1987, then went to work as research
director at Saratoga Horticultural Research Institute
where he continues today as a volunteer. In 1968 he
discovered a clivia seedling with a small, pale-yellow
flower instead of the usual orange; since then he has
expanded the flower and improved its color range.
He is still experimenting, working with reds,
apricots, and variegated forms of this plant. Clivia
seeds take about four years to flower from seed,
making clivia hybridization a sport only for the
patient.

General information: Distributing rights for Joe
Solomone's clivias were given to Monterey Bay
Nursery when he sold the nursery to them.
Monterey Bay is a large, strictly wholesale nursery
(and therefore not included in this book), but it
distributes to a great number of retail outlets. The
very interested may contact Joe for an appointment;
if he has time, he would be happy to show you around.

Redwood Nursery
2800 El Rancho Drive, Santa Cruz 95060
(831) 438-2844
Flora Schweizer
Retail and Wholesale

Plant specialties: California native plants primarily. Vaccinium ovatum, Sambucus, Torreya californica. Trees, shrubs, perennials, and bonsai starters.

History/description: Flora Schweizer's parents moved to this pretty hillside property in the coastal forest in 1959. Enamored with the native vegetation and wanting to be able to stay home with her children, her mother began propagating from her woodland and creekside backyard. The 1-acre nursery now occupies about a third of their homesite where mother and daughter still live and still collect cuttings and seed.

How to get there: From Highway 17 take the Mt. Herman Road exit at Scotts Valley. Go left at the stoplight on Mt. Herman Road. Go left on El Rancho Drive.

General information: Open every day, 9:00 am– 7:00 pm. Deliveries to Santa Cruz County.

Shein's Cactus

3360 Drew Street, Marina 93933
(408) 384-7765
Anne and Rubin Shein
Retail and Mail Order

Plant specialties: Cacti and succulents, especially Mammillaria, Copiapoa, Neochilenia, Neoporteria, Rebutia. Also Haworthia specialties and others.

History/description: Anne Shein began collecting cacti and succulents as a child growing up in Germany. Arriving in this country in 1951, her excitement at seeing these plants growing in their natural habitat caused her to collect in earnest. Twenty-six years of plant collecting produced quite a start-up inventory for this business, which officially opened in 1977. Now there are seven greenhouses and an outdoor display garden of cold-tolerant cactus.

How to get there: Call for directions.

General information: Open by appointment only. Plant list is available for $1. Mail orders accepted. Talks offered to groups.

Sierra Azul Nursery
2660 East Lake Avenue, Watsonville 95076
(831) 763-0939, fax (831) 728-2537
e-mail: sierrarosendale@compuserve.com
website: www.gardenliving.com/sierraazul.html
Jeff and Lisa Rosendale
Retail (Wholesale dba Rosendale Nursery)

Plant specialties: Plants for California's Mediterranean climate—California natives, Australian and South African plants. Perennials, drought-tolerant plants. Large collections of Protea and Grevillea.

History/description: In 1989 the Rosendales had the opportunity to buy an existing nursery business after having been involved professionally with plants for 15 years. Their 6-acre site, located at the base of the coastal foothills east of Pajaro Valley near Hecker Pass, has a temperate, coastal climate conducive to growing a great variety of plant material. The gardens at Sierra Azul cover 2 acres, demonstrating the myriad possibilities of year-round gardening in California. Generous of spirit and knowledge, Jeff is on the Board of Directors of the UC Santa Cruz Arboretum.

How to get there: East from Highway 1 or west from Highway 101 to Highway 152 (Hecker Pass). Nursery located 2 miles east of Watsonville on Highway 152 across from the Santa Cruz County Fairgrounds.

General information: Retail at Sierra Azul, every day, 9:00 am–5:30 pm. Wholesale at Rosendale, Monday through Friday, 8:00 am–5:00 pm. Retail deliveries within local area. Wholesale deliveries to Bay Area on minimum order of $250. Hundred-page descriptive catalogue available for $5.50. Guided garden tours first Saturday of each month at 10:00 am. Design services and site-specific consultations available. Newsletter.

Soquel Nursery Growers

3645 North Main Street, Soquel 95073
(800) 552-0802, (831) 475-3533, fax (831) 475-1608
Wholesale

Plant specialties: Perennials; California native plants for the coastal area; ornamental grasses; heat-, shade-, and drought-tolerant plants; trees and shrubs; ferns and rock garden plants.

History/description: Soquel Nursery Growers started life as a bedding-plant nursery in Mountain View called the Flower Garden. A group of five businessmen bought it and moved it to Soquel in the late 1960s, changing its name and some of the partners in the early 1980s. It has grown into a sizable (13-acre) institution, noted for an interesting plant selection propagated from a wide variety of sources including botanical gardens and home gardeners. The nursery occupies a beautiful site along Soquel Creek near Santa Cruz.

How to get there: From the south, take the Bay/Porter exit off Highway 1. Go right on Porter and take the next, immediate right on Main Street. Nursery is on the right, up the hill. From the north, take the Capitola/Soquel exit from Highway 1. Turn left on Porter (under the freeway) and the next right on Main.

General information: Emphatically not open to the public, but landscapers are welcome. Wholesale hours: Monday through Friday, 8:00 am–5:00 pm (4:30 pm in winter); Saturday, 8:00 am–noon (closed on Saturdays in winter). Monthly availability list. Deliveries from Napa to Carmel on minimum orders of $250.

Suncrest Nurseries, Inc.

400 Casserly Road, Watsonville 95076
(800) 949-5064, (831) 728-2595, fax (831) 728-3146
Stan Iversen, president; Jim Marshall, nursery manager;
Nevin Smith, horticultural director
Wholesale

Plant specialties: Plants from all five Mediterranean-climate zones, California native plants (mostly
for coastal areas, especially large Arctostaphylos
collection), perennials, bamboo (60 varieties), vines,
ferns, ornamental grasses, shrubs, and trees. Two
thousand plant varieties in stock.

History/description: Although Suncrest started in
1991, it is a synthesis of revered California horticultural enterprises. On the 40-acre site of the former
Leonard Coates nursery, in business since 1876, it
combines the historical expertise of this institution
with the enviable stock of the former Wintergreen
Nursery, established by Nevin Smith. Nevin, better
known as Mike, continues to experiment and
introduce exciting plants. Located on prime agricultural land with views of the Santa Cruz Mountains,
it is one of the biggest concerns in this specialty area
with a solid 35 acres covered with landscape plants.

How to get there: From Highway 101, go west on
Highway 152 to bottom of hill. Go right (north) on
Casserly Road. From Highway 1, exit at Green
Valley Road. Go 3 miles northwest to Casserly.

General information: Open to wholesale trade
only, Monday through Friday, 8:00 am–4:30 pm.
Retail customers may visit only with a landscape
professional. They deliver statewide (minimum
order $300–$500). Plant list available upon request.
Catalogue available for $8. Nursery tours may be
arranged.

Sunset Coast Nursery
2745 Tierra Way, Aromas 95004
(831) 726-1672, fax same
Patti Kreiberg
Retail and Wholesale

Plant specialties: California native plants suited to the coastal dunes and five other coastal habitats. Salt-marsh revegetation plants. Their collections are growing to include species suited to bluff, prairie, and oak woodland areas. Good collections of Abronia, Arctostaphylos, Eriogonum, Eriophyllum, Lupinus, and many others. Limited quantities of Castilleja latifolia (Monterey paintbrush).

History/description: Trained as a biologist, Patti Kreiberg was a home gardener with an enviable crop of winter flowers and vegetables. Her hobby got serious when she learned from a friend about the lack of native plant material available for revegetation projects underway to repair the coastline damaged by winter storms in 1983. Her first sale was to the Monterey Bay Aquarium. Mother Nature's new best friend, she now also does habitat restoration for vertebrate and invertebrate animals' use. Plan to visit nearby Manzanita Park (home of the Pajaro manzanita) and Elkhorn Slough National Estuarine Reserve.

How to get there: Call for directions.

General information: Open anytime, by appointment only. Plant list available for SASE. Contract growing and site-specific consultations offered. A first-rate slide show available for interested groups.

Tiedemann Nursery
4835 Cherryvale Avenue, Soquel 95073
P. O. Box 926, Soquel 95073 (mailing address)
(831) 475-5163, fax (831) 475-4067
Dick Hartman; Jon Beard, general manager
Wholesale

Plant specialties: California native plants (more than 100 varieties, including large Ceanothus and Romneya collections). Perennials (more than 100 var.), fuchsias, cyclamen (grown outdoors), poinsettias.

History/description: Tiedemann's has been in business since 1942—quite an accomplishment given the vagaries of the nursery business and the public's continually shifting taste in plants. Under the present ownership since 1975, the nursery keeps ahead of the game, focusing on first-rate natives and perennials. Nearby horticultural attractions include the UCSC Botanic Garden and Butano State Park.

How to get there: Call for directions.

General information: Open to wholesale customers, Monday through Friday, 7:30 am–4:00 pm. General public may visit only with landscape professional. Deliveries from Santa Rosa to Carmel. Slide talks offered to groups.

William R. P. Welch

264 West Carmel Valley Road (growing fields)
P. O. Box 1736, Carmel Valley 93924 (mailing address)
(831) 659-3830
William R. P. Welch
Retail, Wholesale, and Mail Order

Plant specialties: Bulbs—Amaryllis family, especially old varieties of the bunch-flowered Narcissus tazetta ("the world's most diverse collection"). Also Amaryllis belladonna hybrids.

History/description: As a young lepidopterist, William Welch began to grow plants as food for his caterpillar collections. Still in his late teens, he got into the nursery business in 1979, selecting narcissus as his specialty because they were well suited to his area, deer- and gopher-resistant, and reasonably drought-tolerant. Located in the upper bench area of the Carmel Valley, he welcomes visitors to his 3-acre growing fields to enliven his somewhat solitary horticultural pursuits. This Bulb Baron has introduced Amaryllis Belladonna 'Welch Hybrids', Narcissus tazetta 'Autumn Colors Strain', and N. t. 'Welch's Paper White'. During flowering season, he will gladly sell cut flowers and will give talks anytime.

How to get there: Directions given when appointment is made.

General information: Open by appointment only. Flower season: Narcissus and daffodils—November to April; Amaryllis—July to September. Bulb season (field digging): June through October. Bulbs may be ordered from mailing address. Free catalogue available.

HORTICULTURAL ATTRACTIONS

UC Santa Cruz Arboretum
Santa Cruz 95064
(831) 427-2998

History/description: UC Santa Cruz Arboretum specializes in Southern Hemisphere drought-tolerant plants and has the largest collection of Australian, New Zealand, and South African proteas outside each of these countries. Of their 200 acres, 50 are planted. Arboretum Associates, the membership support group, organizes lectures and slide shows. Group tours may be arranged.

Plant sales: Major plant sales occur in April and the second Saturday in October. Friends of the Arboretum (831/423-4977) operates Norrie's Plant and Gift Shop, Tuesday through Saturday, 10:00 am–4:00 pm; Sunday, 1:00 pm–4:00 pm.

General information: The arboretum is open from 9:00 am–5:00 pm every day. The Jean and Bill Lane Horticultural Library is open Wednesday through Sunday, 1:00 pm–4:00 pm.

Lester Rowntree Native Plant Garden
25800 Hatton Road, Carmel
(831) 624-3543

Native garden honoring California naturalist; part of Mission Trail Park.

Central Coast

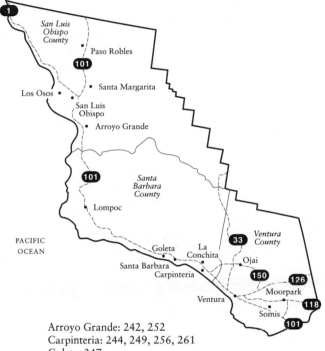

Australian Native Plants Nursery

Nye Road, Casitas Springs (between Ventura and Ojai)
9040 N. Ventura Ave., Ventura 93001 (mailing address)
(805) 649-3362, fax (805) 649-4080
Jo O'Connell, Byron Cox
Retail and Wholesale

Plant specialties: Australian and South African plants, including Banksia (20 species), Leuco–dendron, Grevillea (15), Acacia (10), Hakea (15, including hard-to-find H. multilineata, H. salicifolia, H. trineura, H. coriaceae, H. cucullata, and H. bucculenta).

History/description: Jo O'Connell is an Australian horticulturist who came to Ojai in 1989 to design the Australian garden at the Center for Earth Concerns (see listing). She returned to Australia but came back to California on holiday in 1993. As one would expect in this land of milk and honey, she soon found both a landscape design business and husband. Realizing that there was an inadequate supply of plants to spec for her clients, she opened this nursery in 1995 in a lovely, small, rural town a few miles east of Ventura.

How to get there: From Highway 101, take Highway 33 towards Ojai. Pass through Casitas Springs, take first right onto Nye Road. Nursery is in 1/2 mile, opposite Baptist Church. Call first, owners not always there.

General information: Open most weekends and weekdays by appointment only. Plant list available for SASE. Deliveries to local area. Design services offered.

Berylwood Tree Farm

1048 La Loma Avenue, Somis 93066
(805) 485-7601, fax (805) 485-8268
Rolla J. Wilhite
Wholesale

Plant specialties: Trees, especially large specimens, including many species of Quercus (oak), an 80-foot Pinus canariensis, and a 30-foot Ficus. Also bonsai for landscape use and espaliered magnolias on 10-by-10-foot trellises.

History/description: Rolla Wilhite is the 836th registered landscape architect in California, having obtained his license in the 1940s. Since then some of the landmark projects he has worked on have been for the May Company, the Annenberg Estate, and Levi Plaza in San Francisco. This amazing, arboretum-like nursery originated from the need to supply his landscape projects with quality large trees. Managing its 25 acres now occupies most of his time. No newcomer to the nursery business, however, he worked at his family nursery in Missouri learning to bud and graft trees at 10 years of age.

How to get there: Directions given when appointment is made.

General information: Open to wholesale customers Monday through Friday, 7:30 am–3:30 pm, by appointment only. Plant catalogue is available. The nursery delivers plants and gives nursery tours to schoolchildren.

Bio-Quest International

1781 Glen Oaks Drive, Santa Barbara 93108-2111
(805) 969-4072
e-mail: bioquest@silcom.com
website: www.silcom.com/~bioquest
Dr. Richard Doutt
Retail and Mail Order

Plant specialties: Bulbs, almost exclusively Amaryllis belladonna (naked ladies) and its intergeneric hybrid cultivars. Also yellow Clivia miniata.

History/description: Another lucky victim of a rampaging hobby, Dr. Doutt discovered bulbs by way of a 30-year career as a UC Berkeley entomologist and environmental lawyer. In the bulb business since 1980, he has written a book on Cape bulbs, published in 1993. Currently he has returned to entomology and is studying the fauna of the Channel Islands. Just recently, he sold his South African bulb business to Jim Duggan so he could concentrate on the hybridizing of the monotypic genus Amaryllis, crossing it with other related genera to produce multiflowered plants in a wide range of colors which reliably bloom each year.

How to get there: Call for directions.

General information: Open by appointment only. Free mail-order catalogue.

Cal-Orchid, Inc.

1251 Orchid Drive, Santa Barbara 93111
(805) 967-1312, fax (805) 967-6882
James and Lauris Rose, Makoto Hanajima
Retail and Wholesale

Plant specialties: Orchids, 150 genera. Specializing in orchid plants suitable for Southern Californian gardens (cold-hardy to 27°), especially Cymbidium hybrids.

History/description: Following the advice of her mother, an orchid collector, and after attending what must have been an inspirational meeting of the Orchid Society, Lauris Rose plunged headlong into the commercial orchid business. She met her husband while working in one orchid enterprise and together they bought this nursery in 1987. They offer decades of experience in orchid hybridizing, having had particular success with Neofinetia falcata, Brassia, and Paphiopedilum hybrids. Their business continues to grow, now occupying 2 acres of greenhouses.

How to get there: Take the Patterson exit off of Highway 101. Travel west. Two blocks from the ocean, Patterson becomes Orchid Drive. The nursery is on the right after the third speed bump.

General information: Open Monday through Saturday, 9:00 am–4:00 pm, except for major holidays. Mail-order catalogue available for $1.

Central Coast Growers
275 Pacific Pine Drive, Arroyo Grande 93420
(805) 489-1802, fax (805) 481-8999
Dorthy and Roger Bunch
Wholesale

Plant specialties: Herbaceous perennials (1,400 varieties), in 5-1/2-inch square pots, including Salvia (200+), Artemisia (19), Campanula (40), Penstemon (30), Lavandula (33), Geranium (55), Heuchera (32). Also, ornamental grasses, ground covers, and old-fashioned roses.

History/description: Self-described as "a little guy with a huge inventory," Roger Bunch taught horticulture and agricultural mechanics while his children started a nursery to earn money during high school. In 1982 when the children wanted to move on to new ventures, the Bunches bought them out. They now have a mother stock of 7,000 plants in 5-gallon cans. They rotate their selections each year, testing new plants for one to two years before their official introduction. They recommend you visit the Cal Poly San Luis Obispo Arboretum while in the area.

How to get there: Take Highway 101 to Oak Park Road exit (Arroyo Grande). Drive east 1 mile on Oak Park Road, turn left on Old Oak Park Road. In 1-1/2 miles turn left on Pacific Pine Drive.

General information: Open to wholesale trade only, Monday through Friday, 8:00 am–5:00 pm. Retail customers may visit with landscape professional. They deliver locally or can send a whole truckload almost anywhere. Catalogue available upon request.

Jeff Chemnick Nursery
114 Conejo Road, Santa Barbara 93103
(805) 965-0895, fax (805) 564-0895
Jeff Chemnick
Retail and Wholesale

Plant specialties: Cycads (40 of the 300 known species are offered here), members of the Cycadaceae, Zamiaceae, and Stangericaeae families, including very rare species of Encephalartos, Dioon, and Ceratozamia.

History/description: During his collegiate studies in botany, Jeff became fascinated with cycads, the prehistoric, cone-bearing gymnosperm, a favorite food of the dinosaurs. He has traveled all over the world to locate choice and rare cycad specimens for his collection. None is collected in the wild; Jeff is a staunch supporter of CITES, the law protecting wild plant habitat. Selling his seed-propagated plants for over 20 years as a sideline to his landscape contractor business, he opened this nursery full-time in 1990. Located at the top of a 2-acre residential site, the nursery looks out over the ocean and a hillside dotted with cycads. There is an eclectic and exotic demonstration garden in front of the house.

How to get there: From Highway 101, take the Salinas Street exit. Go right on Salinas Street; continue for 1 mile. At the roundabout, take a 90° turn to the right onto Sycamore Canyon Road. Continue for 1 mile to a Y. Go left onto Stanwood, then left onto Conejo Road and follow to the top.

General information: Open by appointment only. Plant list is available. Deliveries possible for large orders. Plants guaranteed for one year. Jeff also has an informative slide show about cycads.

Chia Nursery
6380 Via Real, Carpinteria 93013
(805) 684-3382, fax (805) 684-4993
Robert Abe
Retail and Wholesale

Plant specialties: Perennials (more than 500 varieties), ornamental grasses, bamboos, California native plants, succulents, drought-tolerant plants. Big collections of hardy Geranium, Canna, Salvia, Achillea, and Buddleia.

History/description: Robert Abe's lifelong involvement with nurseries (his father's is nearby) has made him an irrepressible collector. He bought this business in 1992 from Daryll Combs and with it got Daryll's supply of plant exotica. His basic instincts and inability to resist the unusual have added many new and wondrous things, especially perennials. This 2-acre location includes a drought-tolerant demonstration garden, complete with a carp pond and "casitas de lizardos."

How to get there: From Highway 101, take the Bailard Avenue exit in Carpinteria. Go east towards the mountains. Turn right on Via Real and continue for 1/2 mile.

General information: Open for retail customers, Thursday through Saturday, 8:00 am–4:30 pm. Plant list available for SASE. Talks and nursery tours may be arranged.

Conway's Classic Clivias
2324 Santa Barbara Street, Santa Barbara 93105
(805) 682-7651
David J. Conway
Retail and Mail Order

Plant specialties: Clivias, more than 60 named cultivars, including 30 different yellows (also bicolors, pale creams, lavenders, reds, and greens), sized tiny to 4 feet tall.

History/description: David Conway has reinvented himself many times during his distinguished career in the broad field of landscape. During landscape architectural studies at Cal Poly Pomona, he raised and sold tropical fruits to supplement his student income. After graduation he moved north to Palo Alto, designing many landscape projects in northern and central California. Then he turned to public service, serving as superintendent of parks in Burbank during the "beautiful downtown Burbank" days immortalized by Laugh-In, and later for the city of Santa Barbara. Returning to the work he liked best, he opened a nursery of unusual plants which evolved into an exclusive preoccupation with Clivia. He has been hybridizing clivias since the late 1970s, still fascinated by the schizoid nature of this rhizomatous corm with bulblike leaves and still searching for a pure white or purple.

How to get there: Take the Mission Street exit off of Highway 101 and follow the brown signs to the mission. Santa Barbara Street is a block before the mission. The nursery is located at the very top of the street.

General information: Open every day, 9:00 am–5:00 pm. Free catalogues while they last.

Desert Images
11140 North Ventura Avenue, Ojai 93023
(805) 649-4479
Richard L. and Nancy Bogart
Retail

Plant specialties: Cacti and succulents for indoor use, for the landscape, and for the collector. 2-inch to 15-gallon pots.

History/description: Desert Images began in 1972 as a part-time diversion from Richard Bogart's full-time occupation with engineering/survey work. No doubt encouraged by his botanist-trained wife, he developed an interest in succulents. A full-time business since 1982, the nursery covers 3/4 acre with additional growing grounds in the Ojai Valley. The Bogarts alert groups to make a reservation to see the gardens at the Center for Earth Concerns in Ojai.

How to get there: From Highway 101 take Highway 33 towards Ojai. Highway 33 becomes Ventura Avenue. Nursery is on the right, 1 mile north of the town of Oak View.

General information: Open weekdays, 10:00 am–4:00 pm; weekends, 9:00 am–5:00 pm. Lectures and demonstrations can be arranged for visiting groups.

Dos Pueblos Orchid Co.

Off Highway 101, north of Santa Barbara and Goleta
P. O. Box 158, Goleta 93116
(805) 968-3535, fax same
Margaret Mosher
Retail, Wholesale, and Mail Order

Plant specialties: Orchids—Phalaenopsis, Cymbidium.

History/description: Started in the 1950s as a hobby of successful oilman Samuel Mosher, Dos Pueblos quickly prospered. Encouraged by the Beverly Hills Garden Club and Roy Wilcox, Mosher transferred his business talents to the breeding and division of orchids, until Dos Pueblos covered 50 acres of lath houses and greenhouses on the ocean, 16 miles north of Santa Barbara (part of this has been recently leased out). Since her husband's death in 1974, Mrs. Mosher has ably carried on, though she's thinking now of winding down just a bit. These are family genes you want, to say nothing of their plants.

How to get there: From Highway 101 north of Santa Barbara and Goleta, take the Dos Pueblos Canyon Road exit. Continue under bridge towards the ocean to a stop sign. Nursery is right across the road.

General information: Open Monday through Friday, 7:00 am–3:30 pm. Plant list available for SASE. Mail orders shipped six plants per case.

Turk Hessellund Nursery

1255 Coast Village Road, Santa Barbara 93108-2793
(805) 969-5871
Raymond Sodomka
Retail

Plant specialties: California native plants suited to
coastal and foothill regions, heat- and drought-
tolerant plants, perennials, Mediterranean plants,
exotic subtropical flowering trees, hard-to-find items.

History/description: Ray Sodomka worked with
the distinguished Danish plantsman Turk Hessellund
at his nursery for almost 20 years before taking it
over when Turk died in 1983. Though Hessellund's
propagates only a small portion of its meritorious
stock of plants, it has a network of small growers
who grow specifically for the nursery. Sodomka
arrived at Hessellund's quite by happenstance,
taking the nursery job as a part-time emergency
measure upon arrival in the area as a young Stanford
graduate. He has kept the smallish nursery (2/3 acre)
brimming with treasures for over 30 years.

How to get there: From Highway 101 heading
south past the Milpas exit in Santa Barbara, take the
Hot Springs/Coast Village Road exit. Keep right on
Coast Village Road. Nursery is on the right.

General information: Open Monday through
Saturday, 8:00 am–5:00 pm. Closed holidays.

Hi-Mark Nursery, Inc.
1635 Cravens Lane, Carpinteria 93013
(805) 684-4462, fax (805) 684-8132
Mark Bartholomew
Wholesale

Plant specialties: Herbaceous, hardy perennials, some general ornamentals, Primrose, Cyclamen, Begonia species and ferns. Sizes range from 4-inch pots to 10 gallons.

History/description: We would like to think this nursery, founded by Mark's father, R. C. Bartholo–mew, was named for the words of joy uttered at his son's birth. Not so. Founded in 1951, the nursery predates Mark. Originally located in Orange County, the nursery moved to this 7-acre site in 1976. Originally specializing in bedding plants, Hi-Mark made the big shift to perennials in 1984.

How to get there: From the south, exit Highway 101 at Santa Monica Road. Go left on frontage road (Via Real) for 1 mile. Turn right on Cravens Lane. Nursery is in 1/2 mile on left. From the north, exit Highway 101 at Santa Claus Lane. Go left at bottom of off-ramp and right on Via Real for 1 mile. Turn left on Cravens Lane. Nursery is in 1/2 mile on left.

General information: Open Monday through Friday, 7:30 am–4:00 pm; Saturday, 7:00 am–noon. No minimums on will-calls. Delivery by our truck to greater Los Angeles area only.

Las Pilitas Nursery

3232 Las Pilitas Road, Santa Margarita 93453
(805) 438-5992, fax (805) 438-5993
e-mail: bawilson@slonet.org
website: www.laspilitas.com
Bert and Celeste Wilson
Retail, Wholesale, and Mail Order

Plant specialties: California native plants (more than 200 genera; 500-1,000 species on hand) including site-specific mitigation material. Penstemon 'Margarita BOP', Salvia 'Pozo Blue', and Arctostaphylos 'Ghostly' were introduced by Bert Wilson at Las Pilitas.

History/description: Fascinated with the indigenous plants of California and aware of their unavailability, Bert Wilson created Las Pilitas Nursery in 1975. In 1979, he moved the nursery to its present site, because of the perfect growing conditions. The nursery includes a one-acre garden designed around five massive, 60-foot coast live oaks. Many nursery plants are sold for ecological restoration projects, yet there is an abundant variety of native garden perennials. The nursery has expanded to offer biological services and ecological restoration consultation—work that takes the Wilsons throughout California.

How to get there: Take Highway 101 to Santa Margarita. Go east on Highway 58, which becomes Pozo Road after about a mile. Continue for 3 1/2 miles. Left on Las Pilitas; drive 6 miles. Do not give up. Las Pilitas means "hole in the rock filled with water," which describes a spring on the road, not the nursery.

General information: Open on Saturday, 9:00 am–5:00 pm. Wholesale only, weekdays, 8:00 am–6:00 pm. Closed Sunday. Free plant list. Catalogue $8; software version available soon. Site-specific consultations. Mail orders throughout the continental US.

Matilija Nursery

8225 Waters Road, Moorpark 93021
P. O. Box 429, Moorpark 93021 (mailing address)
(805) 523-8604
Robert Sussman
Retail and Wholesale

Plant specialties: Mostly California native plants, especially those suited to coastal, chaparral, and montane regions. Some natives from Southwestern states. Large collections of Arctostaphylos, Ceanothus, Rhamnus, Rhus.

History/description: After analyzing prospective businesses, this former banker decided that the nursery business offered the most amount of opportunity for the least amount of capital and offered the most rewards for personal initiative. To say nothing of the fact that he had been successfully growing natives for some time in Santa Monica. The Santa Barbara Botanic Garden and the California Native Plant Society encouraged his interest and supplied much of his early stock. In business only since 1992, the nursery has already developed a reputation for fine plant selection.

How to get there: The nursery is located between Moorpark and Somis. Complete directions given when appointment is made.

General information: Open by appointment to retail customers, Friday and Saturday, 8:30 am–4:00 pm; wholesale hours are every day, 6:30 am–3:30 pm, also by appointment. Local deliveries may be arranged.

Native Sons Wholesale Nursery, Inc.
379 West El Campo Road, Arroyo Grande 93420
(805) 481-5996, fax (805) 489-1991
e-mail: native.son@nativeson.com
Dave Fross, Robert Keefe
Wholesale

Plant specialties: California native plants especially
suited to coastal areas, including Arctostaphylos
'Austin Griffiths' and Ceanothus maritimus 'Pt.
Sierra' both introduced here. Australian plants,
Mediterranean plants, drought-tolerant plants,
perennials, ornamental grasses, herbs, ground
covers, rock garden plants.

History/description: With a M.S. in agriculture,
Dave Fross and partner Bob Keefe decided to open a
nursery in 1979. Since Fross and Keefe are both
fourth-generation Californians, they were bound to
have an inborn fascination with California native
plants. Inspiration for its name came from their
favorite Loggins and Messina song, "Native Sons."
The 6-acre site includes a mostly native garden
containing a wide variety of grasses. Also plan to
visit the Cal Poly Experimental Gardens, Nipomo
Dunes, and the Montana de Oro State Beach.

How to get there: Highway 101 south to El
Campo Road exit. Go 1-1/2 miles to stop sign. Left
on Los Berros. After 10 yards, go right on El
Campo. Nursery in 1 mile.

General information: Wholesale customers only.
Monday through Friday, 7:30 am–4:30 pm; Saturday, 8:00 am–noon. Retail customers may visit only
with a landscape professional. Demonstration
garden open to the public. Plants delivered San
Francisco to San Diego on minimum order of $350.
Catalogue available. Availability lists issued weekly.

The Orchid House

1699 Sage Avenue, Los Osos 93402
(800) 235-4139, fax (805) 528-7966
e-mail: orchid@orchidhouse.com
website: www.orchidhouse.com/orchid
N. H. Powell
Retail, Wholesale, and Mail Order

Plant specialties: Orchids—many genera with large selections of Paphiopedilum, Phalaenopsis, Odontoglossum.

History/description: Trading bad habits for good, N. H. Powell started growing orchids when he gave up smoking 50 years ago. A Cal Tech–trained engineer, he found orchid raising to be a superb stress management technique. His scientific background has well served the orchid world and his efforts have received many awards. He claims the orchid of the future will be petite, easy to care for, long-lasting, and a sure bet to flower every year. We are waiting. Largely wholesale, he welcomes seriously interested retail customers only.

How to get there: Call for directions.

General information: Open by appointment only, Monday through Saturday, 8:00 am–5:00 pm. Mail-order catalogue with directions for orchid culture available for $5, refundable on first order over $100. Plants shipped worldwide.

Orchids of Los Osos

1614 Sage Avenue, Los Osos 93402
(800) 55-ORCHID, (805) 528-0181, fax (805) 528-7466
Michael Glikbarg
Retail, Wholesale, and Mail Order

Plant specialties: Mostly orchids for indoor and outdoor use, especially cool-growing types. Cymbidium, Paphiopedilum, Pleione, Masdevallia, Zygopetalum, and species orchids. Also, bonsai, cacti, Mediterranean plants, Protea.

History/description: After graduating in ornamental horticulture from Cal Poly San Luis Obispo, Michael Glikbarg bought George Moran's orchid and cut-flower business. The nursery has been located here since 1964 and has introduced Cymbidium goldmine 'Osso-Sunset' (GA/CSA AM/AOS), Paphiopedilum dollgoldii, among many others. It will custom-grow plants for customers. The native plant study area in Montana de Oro State Beach and the Cuesta College Botanical Gardens are of particular local interest for plant lovers.

How to get there: From Highway 101 just south of San Luis Obispo, take Los Osos-Baywood Park exit. Follow Los Osos Valley Road for about 10 miles. Go right on South Bay Boulevard. Go right on Nipomo. Go left on Sage to end.

General information: Open Tuesday through Saturday, 10:00 am–3:00 pm. Retail catalogue available for $3 which includes coupon for $5, credited to first purchase. Local deliveries on minimum order of $50. Workshops and design services offered. Orchid show held in November.

Perry's Panorama

P. O. Box 540, Somis 93066
(805) 987-1257, fax (805) 484-3249
Dennis Perry
Retail and Wholesale

Plant specialties: South African proteas and other uncommon members of the Proteaceae family, Anigozanthus, South African Ericaceae, Mediterranean plants.

History/description: For years Dennis Perry's father had a nursery called Perry's Plants. He got hooked on proteas in retirement and passed along this passion to Dennis, who joined him in the nursery business in 1982. The original Perry's Panorama was so called because of the fantastic views from the nursery. This expanded 2-acre location offers a panorama of an ever increasing expanse of plants.

How to get there: Directions will be given when appointment is made.

General information: Open by appointment only. Plant list available. Shipping on minimum orders of $200. Contract propagation.

Pianta Bella
5154 Foothill Road, Carpinteria 93013
(805) 684-8380, fax (805) 684-9540
Bernard Acquistapace
Wholesale

Plant specialties: Perennials and ferns.

History/description: Thinking he might just earn a little extra money by selling plants to supplement his high school English teacher's salary, Bernard Acquistapace suddenly found himself in the nursery business. The nursery relocated in 1997 to a 3-acre parcel.

How to get there: Call for directions.

General information: Open Monday through Friday, 8:00 am–4:30 pm; Saturday, 8:00 am–noon. Call first. Catalogue available upon request. Local deliveries.

San Marcos Growers

P. O. Box 6827, Santa Barbara 93160
(805) 683-1561, fax (805) 964-1329
website: www.smgrowers.com
Randy Baldwin, Manager
Wholesale

Plant specialties: Drought-tolerant plants, perennials, California native plants, Mediterranean plants, Australian plants, South African plants, aquatic and bog plants, bulbs, ferns, ornamental grasses, ground covers, succulents, vines. New Zealand flax (Phormium). More than 1,500 varieties of plants.

History/description: Since 1980 San Marcos has been actively introducing water-conserving plants from Mediterranean areas around the world. They seek out plants which have horticultural merit, ornamental value, and are appropriate to the microclimates of California. Much of the credit for the lush look now possible in drought-tolerant gardens belongs here. They have exclusively propagated the new color hybrids of New Zealand flax. The nursery's 21 acres includes demonstration gardens using grasses and Mediterranean-climate plants and a full acre of propagation greenhouses.

How to get there: Call for directions.

General information: Open to wholesale customers only, Monday through Friday, 7:30 am–4:30 pm; Saturday, 8:00 am–noon. Deliveries from Santa Rosa to San Diego on minimum order. Catalogue available and plant information offered on their website. Group tours may be arranged.

San Simeon Nursery

10190 Los Osos Valley Road, San Luis Obispo
P. O. Box 7149, Los Osos 93412
(805) 549-9150
John Goetz
Wholesale

Plant specialties: Low-water-use plants. Australian plants (including Melaleuca, Casuarina stricta), South American plants (Luma, Azara dentata), Mediterranean plants, California native plants, perennials, palms, cacti, and succulents (including a large variety of Aloes, Dudleyas, Euphorbias and Agaves). Up to 24-inch box.

History/description: This owner-contractor specializes in low-water-use landscapes and in plants suited to arid and cold situations. With a degree in horticulture and years of practice in the field, he opened the nursery in 1980 to make more plants available for his landscapes and yours. Seeds and cuttings brought back from travels to Australia and Mexico have enriched his collections. Seeing how plants grow in their native habitats has taught him where to plant them. The nursery moved to its present location from Cayucos in 1996. John offers site-specific consultations and will give talks about his specialties.

How to get there: Call for directions. The nursery is located in an agricultural area near the corner of Foothill Boulevard.

General information: Open to wholesale customers and serious collectors, by appointment only. General public may come with landscaper. Plant list available for SASE.

Santa Barbara Heirloom Seedling Nursery

P. O. Box 4235, Santa Barbara 93140
(805) 968-5444
Russ Waldrop, Joanna LeForce, Michael Ommaha
Retail, Wholesale, and Mail Order

Plant specialties: Organic herbs and vegetables in 3-inch pots. Tomatoes (34 kinds), peppers (34), lettuces (15).

History/description: In 1993 these three interesting folks combined their diverse backgrounds to form a partnership to grow heirloom species of vegetables and herbs. Archaeologist/anthropologist Russ taught high school history and organic gardening to adult education classes. Joanna is a registered pharmacist who has studied medicinal plants in Chiapas and does consultation work with long-term care facilities on nutrition and natural pharmaceuticals. With her sister she developed "Gardener's Balm," a salve for overworked hands. Michael is an organic grower who helped develop Burbank's Gourmet Gardens in Sebastopol which started the mesclun craze. This trio will keep California cuisine on its forks.

How to get there: Call for directions.

General information: Twice a year the nursery throws a garden party for the public, complete with wine and music. Call for exact dates. Open to wholesale trade by appointment only, Monday through Friday, 9:00 am–noon. The nursery's "Heirloom Guarantee" promises to replace any plant which has died or not produced for any reason. A retail catalogue is available for mail orders. Plant list sent to wholesale customers. Local wholesale deliveries.

Santa Barbara Orchid Estate
1250 Orchid Drive, Santa Barbara 93111
(805) 967-1284, fax (805) 683-3405
Alice and Parry Gripp
Retail, Wholesale, and Mail Order

Plant specialties: Orchids—Cymbidium species,
outdoor orchids for coastal California.

History/description: Santa Barbara Orchid Estate,
founded in 1957, was bought in 1967 by the Gripp
family from the original owner for whom they
worked. Trained horticulturists, they have been
expanding and refining the business ever since. The
nursery caters to the whole spectrum of orchid
fanciers, from beginning growers to the most
discriminating hobbyists. Even non-orchid enthusiasts enjoy walking around the 2 acres of vintage
nursery and grounds. The Santa Barbara International Orchid Fair, which brings together orchid
vendors from around the world, is held on their
grounds the third weekend of July. The Santa
Barbara International Orchid Show, which is the
West Coast's oldest, is held every spring at Earl
Warren Showgrounds.

How to get there: Just north of Santa Barbara on
Highway 101, take Patterson exit towards ocean.
Follow the center yellow divider line until it runs out
as you turn right up Orchid Drive. Turn left into the
long driveway immediately after the third speed bump.

General information: Open Monday through
Saturday, 8:00 am–4:30 pm; Sunday, 11:00 am–4:00
pm. Free catalogue upon request. Orchid flowers
and plants shipped Federal Express. Visitors always
welcome for self-guided tour. Orchid gifts.

Stewart Orchids

3376 Foothill Road, Carpinteria 93013
(805) 684-5448, fax (805) 566-6609
AgriStar
Steve McNerney, general manager
Retail, Wholesale, and Mail Order

Plant specialties: Orchids—Cattleya, Phalaenopsis, Paphiopedilum, Miltonia.

History/description: Stewart Orchids has had a long (90-year) and distinguished history. Starting out as Armacost & Royston, the present company was formed in 1985 by the merger of three orchid growers, including the Stewart family, who had been growing orchids since 1908. The 2 acres of green-houses in Carpinteria have been part of the picture since 1977. Bought in 1993 by AgriStar, a Texas-based company specializing in agricultural tissue culture, the nursery has dressed up its showrooms and is putting more emphasis on visitor services. Their on-site lab continues to develop new varieties, patenting their very best award winners, such as Laeliocattleya 'Puppy Love' and L. 'Prism Palette'.

How to get there: From Highway 101 south, take Padaro Lane exit. Go back over freeway, then right (south) on frontage road. Go left at Polo Field on Nidever, which runs into Foothill.

General information: Open Monday through Friday, 8:00 am–5:00 pm; Saturday, 9:00 am–5:00 pm; Sunday, 10:00 am–5:00 pm. Mail-order catalogue is free. Gift baskets planted with live orchids are available.

Sycamore Farm

2485 Highway 46 West, Paso Robles 93446
(800) 576-5288, (805) 238-2187
website: www.sycamorefarm.com
Bruce and Sandy Shomler
Retail and Mail Order

Plant specialties: Herbs, 300 varieties of medicinal and culinary herbs, 3-inch pots to 5-gallon cans. Some oreganos and thymes for landscape use. Many cultivars of Ocimum basilicum (sweet basil), including 'African Blue', 'Cinnamon', 'Citriodorum', 'Lettuce Leaf', 'Minima', and 'Thai'.

History/description: Bruce Shomler attributes a lifelong interest in horticulture to his having grown up across from Descanso Gardens. When he retired, he brought property in Paso Robles and planted a vineyard of Rhone varietal grapes. An herb hobbyist from way back, he decided to grow them as well. He now has 10,000 square feet of greenhouse and a display garden which shows how herbs grow in a range of climates. (The temperature here ranges from 10° to 100°). The Shomlers also offer information about the installation of an herb garden. A wine-tasting room and a gift shop featuring locally made food items, crafts, and books are on premises. They suggest you visit the Elfin Forest Natural Area and the San Luis Obispo Botanical Garden.

How to get there: Take Highway 101 to Highway 46 west towards Cambria. The nursery is in 3 miles.

General information: Open every day, 10:30 am–5:30 pm. Their Basil Festival usually takes place on the first Saturday in August. Catalogue is available. Mail orders accepted. Site-specific consultations offered. The nursery offers herb walks and classes on cooking with herbs, medicinal uses of herbs, and making herbal cheeses, soaps, baskets, and wreaths.

Valley Heart Gardens

545 Toro Canyon, Santa Barbara 93108
(805) 969-3701, fax (805) 565-5561
Brian Tappeiner
Wholesale

Plant specialties: Pelargoniums—P. hortorum, P. domesticum, and P. peltatum hybrids. Zonal geraniums.

History/description: Valley Heart specializes in well-grown, virus-free pelargoniums sold mainly to retail nurseries and growers. This longtime family business was started by Brian Tappeiner's father in 1931 as a retail business growing perennials in the San Fernando Valley. In 1951, the family moved to Santa Barbara and started specializing in field-grown pelargoniums. After studies in ornamental horticulture and business at UC Davis, Brian started working at the nursery in the 1960s. Today the pelargoniums are grown in greenhouses on the 5-acre nursery site.

How to get there: Call for directions.

General information: Open to landscapers with resale number only. Plant list is available. Will ship cuttings to other growers.

Rudolf Ziesenhenne

1130 North Milpas Street, Santa Barbara 93103
(805) 966-6956
Rudolf Ziesenhenne
Retail

Plant specialties: Begonia (900 species, including 50 from Mexico), for example, B. boliviensis, B. piercei, B. cinnabarina. He has introduced 75 cultivars and named 36 new species. Staghorn ferns.

History/description: Rudolf Ziesenhenne is a founding father of the California Begonia Society (1932—later the American Begonia Society). He got started in the nursery business only because other jobs were scarce during the Depression. He chose begonias because this plant was not widely available at that time. Since then, he has studied taxonomy and botany, pioneered the importation of foreign species, and helped finance a plant expedition of Frank Kingdon-Ward. His collection is huge and his reputation equally so. Many of his plants are type-specimens, meaning that they come from the original collection from which the species was named. These will be donated to the California Academy of Sciences.

How to get there: Going south on Highway 101, take the Milpas exit. Continue on Milpas to its end in the hills. Turn into County Bowl. Nursery is on the left.

General information: Open by appointment only.

HORTICULTURAL ATTRACTIONS

Lotusland

Santa Barbara
(805) 969-9990 (reservations: call Monday–Friday,
9:00 am–noon); (805) 969-3767 (office)

History/description: In the twilight of her erratic
career as operatic diva, Mme. Ganna Walska turned
her full energies and attention to the garden. Living
here since 1941, for a brief while with husband
number six, she focused on the gardens until her
death at age 97 in 1984. Her flair for theatricality is
evident everywhere. Over 2,000 species of tropical
and subtropical Mediterranean-climate plants fill the
garden's 37 acres with spines, whorls, hairy tufts,
and fanciful forms. The Lotusland Foundation and
its membership support group, Friends of Lotusland,
opened the garden to the public in 1993.

General information: Reservations are required.
The garden may be visited only on scheduled tours,
Wednesday through Saturday at 10:00 am and 1:30
pm. Due to county restrictions, only a very limited
number of visitors can be accommodated. Reservations are taken one year in advance of the date
requested. Admission fee is $10.

Santa Barbara Botanic Garden

1212 Mission Canyon Road, Santa Barbara 93105
(805) 682-4726

History/description: The 65-acre grounds of the
Santa Barbara Botanic Garden are dedicated to the
display, propagation, and conservation of California's
native flora. Featured areas include a Demonstration
Garden showing landscape use of native plants, and
meadow, redwood forest, desert, chaparral, oak
woodland, and Channel Island sections.

Plant sales: The nursery, managed by volunteer
Garden Growers to raise income for the garden, is
open Tuesday and Thursday through Sunday, 10:00
am–3:00 pm, (closed Monday and Wednesday).
Plants are also sold at the shop and in big spring and
fall plant sales.

General information: Garden, library, and office
open weekdays, 9:00 am–5:00 pm, weekends 9:00
am–6:00 pm. Admission fee. Docent tours of the
garden are held every day at 2:00 pm and Thursdays
and weekends at 10:30 am.

Center for Earth Concerns

2162 Baldwin Road, Ojai 93023
P. O. Box 978 Oak View 93022 (mailing address)
(805) 649-3535, fax (805) 649-1757
e-mail: info@earthconcerns.org

The Center for Earth Concerns is located on 275
acres of land with 15 acres of botanical gardens
featuring South African, Australian, and California
natives. The property, part of the Taft Ranch which
was dedicated to advance the cause of conservation
in the 1980s, is surrounded by the Los Padres
National Forest. The Center's mission is to inspire
and involve people with nature in order to
strengthen their ability to act on its behalf.

Dallidet Adobe

1185 Pacific Street, San Luis Obispo
(805) 543-6762

One-acre garden surrounding an 1860s adobe,
imaginatively planted by Cal Poly students.

Elfin Forest Natural Area

Los Osos
(805) 781-5930

One hundred seventy-five species of plants on the
coastal strand, including stunted (10-foot-tall) trees,
still a mystery to botanists. Hard to locate. Call
Chamber of Commerce in Los Osos or Morro Bay
for a map. Jointly run by the state and the city of
Los Osos.

Firescape Garden

Stanwood Drive at Mission Ridge Road (across from fire
station), Santa Barbara
(805) 564-5720

A demonstration garden showing what to plant in
the four basic fire zones surrounding your home to
eliminate a continuous fuel system. Created by a
local committee of civic-minded garden experts,
maintained by city of Santa Barbara.

Franceschi Park

1510 Mission Ridge Road (at Franceschi), Santa Barbara

Former grounds of a turn-of-the-century, premier
plant collector. Fifteen acres of mature exotic plants,
offering great ocean views.

Alice Keck Memorial Garden

1300 Micheltorena Street (across the street from
Alameda Park), Santa Barbara
(805) 564-5418

The site of the old Mirasol Hotel, relandscaped in 1980 to include a wide variety of plants in a natural setting along streams and ponds, courtesy of philanthropist Keck.

Leaning Pine Arboretum
California Polytechnic State University,
San Luis Obispo 93407
(805) 756-2888

Part of the Environmental Horticultural Science Department, this 5-acre site includes gardens with extensive displays of plants from California, Australia, the Mediterranean basin, and New Zealand. Parking fee but no entrance fee. Up the hill past the Campus Market.

Pan American Seed
703 Floradale, Lompoc 93436
(805) 525-3348

This major grower of flower seeds is open to the trade only, but its 200 acres in bloom from early May through October are well worth a drive by. Tours are offered during the Flower Festival, held the third week in June. Pan American has a controlling interest in Burpee, their retail partner.

Richardson's Seaside Banana Plantation
6823 Santa Barbara Avenue, La Conchita 93067
(tiny town south of Summerland, east of Highway 101)

A 10-acre garden of exotic bananas, palms, and other fruit trees. Fruits and plants for sale. Mail orders accepted.

San Luis Obispo Botanical Garden

El Chorro Regional Park on Highway One
(805) 546-3501

A preview garden opened in 1996 on this 150-acre site to serve as a model for future gardens which will feature Mediterranean plant communities from around the world. The gardens are open April to November, second Saturday of the month. The nonprofit Friends of SLO Botanical Garden organizes lectures, docent tours, children's activities and can use your support (P. O. Box 4957, San Luis Obispo 93403). Special garden festival on the first weekend in May.

Los Angeles Basin/
Inland Empire

Burkard Nurseries, Inc.

690 North Orange Grove Boulevard, Pasadena 91103
(626) 796-4355
Frank Burkard, Jr.
Retail

Plant specialties: General nursery stock with an
emphasis on citrus (80 varieties), unusual perennials
(500 sps., incl. 130 salvias), Japanese maples (60
varieties), South African bulbs, over 500 varieties of
roses, including antique and David Austins.

History/description: Started by Frank Burkard Jr.'s
grandparents in 1937, this nursery has been providing unusual perennials and uncommon nursery stock
ever since. Though it propagates only 20% of its
offerings, we include it here because its selection has
rewarded nurserygoers for 60 years and has made
an impact on the horticulture of the Pasadena area.
Frank Burkard, Jr. started work here for his father in
1974. An Eagle Scout with merit badges in horticulture and a Cal Poly graduate, Frank is well trained
to keep up Burkard's good work.

How to get there: The nursery is located on the
corner of Lincoln Avenue and Orange Grove
Boulevard across from the post office, 2 blocks from
the Rose Bowl.

General information: Open Monday through
Saturday, 8:30 am–5:00 pm; Sunday, 9:00 am–4:00
pm. Services of landscape architect available.

Coastal Zone Nursery

31427 Pacific Coast Highway, Malibu 90265
(310) 457-3343
Richard Howlett, Bill Long
Retail and Wholesale

Plant specialties: Over 150 varieties of trees, palms, ferns, and shrubs, including hard-to-find and coastal varieties. Examples include Arbutus, Bischofia, Cassia, Erythrina (6 varieties), Ficus (9 varieties), Harpephyllum, Howca, Leptospermum, Livistonia, Markhamia, Maytenus, Melaleuca (10 varieties), Metrosideros, Myoporum, Otatea, Podocarpus, Psidium, Quillaja, Schinus, Stenocarpus, Tabebuia, and Vitex.

History/description: Mr. and Mrs. Richard Howlett bought this property in 1978, the former site of La Herran Nursery which was started in the 1940s. The 21-acre site has half of the area under production with a current inventory of just under 14,000 plants, growing in 1-gallon containers through 60-inch boxes. Cranes are available to assist in off-loading and plant placement. They recommend combining your visit with a trip to Zuma Beach, the Adamson House and gardens at Malibu Lagoon State Beach, the Santa Monica Pier, and the Will Rogers Historic Park.

How to get there: The nursery is located 3/4 mile north of the intersection of Trancas Canyon Road and Pacific Coast Highway, on La Herran Road which is on the north side of the Highway.

General information: Open Monday through Friday, 7:30 am–4:00 pm. Descriptive catalogue available. Plant availability lists upon request. Deliveries and nursery tours may be arranged.

Cycad Gardens
4524 Toland Way, Los Angeles 90041
(323) 255-6651
Loran Whitelock
Retail and Mail Order

Plant specialties: Cycads, including 150 of the 250 existing species, all propagated by seed. First offered here are Encephalartos horridus x E. longifolius 'Gray Form' and E. eugene-maraisii x E. concinnus.

History/description: Forty years ago, Loran Whitelock got inspired by the famous, old—unfortunately now gone—California Jungle Gardens in West Los Angeles. He wrote to every area where cycads grow and tracked down the nurseries which would send him plants. Soon he had surplus of some and others he desperately wanted, so he started selling his extras to finance his growing collection. He developed a landscape consulting business and has created cycad displays for hotels, wild-animal parks, and arboreta. The nursery's rolling 1-1/2 acres includes a garden of cycads and palms mixed with other tropical foliage. This acknowledged cycad expert travels all over the world still adding to his collection. He is writing a book on the 11 genera of the Cycadaceae and suggests you visit the nice palm collection in Elysian Park in Los Angeles.

How to get there: The nursery is located in the Eagle Rock residential area. Directions given when appointment is made.

General information: Open by appointment only. Plant list available for SASE. Plants shipped within the country on minimum orders of $30.

Desert to Jungle Nursery

3211 West Beverly Boulevard, Montebello 90640
(323) 722-3976, fax (818) 890-2776
Gary Hammer, owner; Del Pace, manager
Retail and Wholesale

Plant specialties: Perennials for Mediterranean climates, drought-tolerant plants from Australia and South Africa, and subtropicals.

History/description: Soon after graduating from Cal Poly San Luis Obispo, Gary Hammer hit the road—prodded by his relentless desire to see and find the new and unusual. Plants brought back from many exploration trips to Australia, South Africa, South and Central America, and the American Southwest formed the backbone of Glendale Paradise Nursery which he opened as a wholesale only business in the 1970s in Glendale. In the mid-1980s he moved the wholesale nursery onto property leased from Southern California Edison in Lakeview Terrace. In the late 1980s he joined forces with Del Pace to make his plant introductions available to retail customers and opened Desert to Jungle. Gary is a prime mover in the new horticulture of California.

How to get there: Take I-5, to Highway 60 east. Take the Atlantic Boulevard exit and go right. After two stoplights, go left on West Beverly for a mile.

General information: Open Wednesday through Saturday, 10:00 am–4:00 pm. Gary's plants are also available at Worldwide Exotics (open Saturdays and by appointment) next door to his growing grounds, 11157 Orcas Avenue, Lakeview Terrace 91342, (818) 890 1915. The wholesale nursery is open by appointment only.

Forever Green

1312 Cambrin Road, Pomona 91768 (mailing address)
(909) 629-9591
Dave Ellis
Retail and Wholesale

Plant specialties: Cacti, succulents, desert plants, heat-tolerant plants. Agave (20 varieties), Euphorbia (more than 30 varieties), Yucca (7), Cereus, cycads. Very large specimens.

History/description: Dave Ellis has been tilling the same garden soil in an old walnut grove since the early 1970s when he first moved into this house during his Cal Poly Pomona days. Armed with training in horticulture and landscape architecture, he continues to divide his time between garden design and plant propagation. Many of the plants in his 1-1/2-acre garden nursery are truly huge, rescued from sites where they outgrew their space. The growing grounds are located nearby.

How to get there: Directions given when appointment is made.

General information: Open by appointment only. Local deliveries possible for minimum orders of $1,000.

Greenlee Nursery

257 East Franklin Avenue, Pomona 91766
(909) 629-9045, fax (909) 620-9283
John Greenlee
Primarily Wholesale, some Retail and Mail Order

Plant specialties: Ornamental grasses and grasslike plants, drought-tolerant plants, ground covers, coastal California natives.

History/description: Probably more than anyone, John Greenlee is responsible for the increased interest in ornamental grasses in the west. Known as The Grassman, he is an articulate believer in the "natural" lawn, using low-growing native tufted grasses instead of mowed turf. He travels widely in search of tough and suitable native species. His book, *The Encyclopedia of Ornamental Grasses* (Rodale Press, 1992), offers color photographs and comprehensive descriptions of over 300 ornamental grasses. An articulate spokesman for the splendors of grass, John has hosted many episodes of the PBS television series, "The New Garden". The 4-acre nursery includes a display of lawn substitutes using grasses and roses. He oversees several growing grounds, in Malibu and elsewhere.

How to get there: Call for directions.

General information: Open Monday through Friday, 9:00 am–5:00 pm, closed from noon–1:00 pm for lunch. Open to visitors by appointment only. Wholesale and retail orders have $100 minimum for shipping and $50 minimum for walk-in. Design and installation services.

Greenwood Daylily and Iris Garden

4601-C Pierce Avenue, Riverside (growing grounds)
5595 E. 7th St. #490, Long Beach 90804 (mailing address)
(562) 494-8944, fax (562) 494-0486
Cynthia and John Schoustra
Retail, Wholesale, and Mail Order

Plant specialties: Daylilies—nearly 2,000 different cultivars, field- and container-grown. Iris—tall bearded and heritage.

History/description: UC Berkeley-educated landscape architect John Schoustra was a landscape contractor for 10 years. He started a soil business and then this nursery when he discovered no one was selling quality, named daylilies well suited to Southern California. The Schoustras bought their initial stock of daylilies from the Greenwood Nursery in Goleta when it switched its specialty to palms. John is on the new All-American Daylily Selection Council which will field test daylilies and thus get them into the general nursery trade. Recently they bought Blooming Fields' extensive iris collection, doubling their specialties. The growing grounds include 20 acres of daylilies, 5 acres of iris, and a 5-acre retail area with labeled plants and accessible walkways.

How to get there: From I-15 take I-91 east towards Riverside. Take the Pierce Avenue off-ramp and travel north. The nursery is located on the grounds of La Sierra University behind the Child Development Center.

General information: Open March through June, every Sunday and Monday, 9:30 am–4:00 pm. July through November, second and fourth Sundays, 9:30 am–4:00 pm. Free plant list. Mail orders shipped. Nursery tours, talks, and lectures for groups may be arranged. Contract growing offered.

HORTUS

284 East Orange Grove Boulevard, Pasadena 91104
(626) 792-8255, fax (626) 792-4687
e-mail: HORTUS@mindspring.net
Gary Jones
Retail

Plant specialties: Unusual perennials, California native plants suited to the interior valley, drought-tolerant plants, heat-tolerant plants. Roses (recent introductions and antiques).

History/description: Gary Jones has been growing and selling plants since he was a teenager in northern Utah. He studied landscape architecture at Utah State and UCLA, but ended up as a music theory major. Pursuing a musical career in Pasadena, he found supplemental work at Burkard Nurseries. Over time, he became increasingly intrigued with the nursery operation and the prospect of starting his own. Music remains a major fascination; happily he is playing our tune. The nursery has many demonstration gardens including a sunken herb garden, water garden, potager, espaliered apple fence and pear tunnel. They are the exclusive distributor for Blooms of Bressingham.

How to get there: The nursery is located north of Highway 210, east of Marengo Avenue in Pasadena.

General information: Open Monday through Saturday, 8:00 am–5:00 pm; Sunday, 10:00 am–5:00 pm. Quarterly newsletter, *Dig;* annual rose catalogue. Scheduled workshops and lectures at the nursery. Local deliveries on minimum orders of $35,

Katie's Scenteds and Other Greens

6236 Bellflower Boulevard, Lakewood
820 East 5th Street, Long Beach 90802 (mailing address)
(562) 619-6266, fax (562) 437-4419
website: www.katiesgeraniums.com
Kathyrn Jennings
Retail and Wholesale

Plant specialties: Geraniums—scented (100 varieties), angels and pansy-faces (40 varieties), hard-to-find zonals, ivies, and very hardy varieties adapted to the climate of Southern California. Pelargoniums. Scented topiaries.

History/description: This English teacher is having a grand time propagating uncommon varieties of geraniums and pelargoniums. A friend involved with Heard's in the San Diego area, told her that scented geraniums were hard to come by and suggested she grow them. Responding to the power of suggestion, Kathryn sought the expert knowledge of Annebelle Rice and John Schoustra, went back to school, and got certified as a nurserywoman. Business has been booming ever since it began in 1993. This small nursery has a large greenhouse and display garden.

How to get there: From the north, take Highway 91 and continue east to Bellflower Blvd. Go right onto Bellflower for 1/2 mile. Go left through gate with small sign for geraniums. Continue to the last greenhouse on the right.

General information: Open Saturday, 10:00 am–3:00 pm; Monday and Wednesday, 10:00 am–4:00 pm. Tours are welcomed, workshops occasionally given, and plant consultations available. Plant list available for SASE (two stamps). Plants delivered to Los Angeles, Orange, and San Diego counties.

Limberlost Roses
7304 Forbes Avenue, Van Nuys 91406 (mailing address)
(818) 901-7798
Kathy and Bob Edberg
Retail

Plant specialties: Roses (425 varieties, including many antique roses).

History/description: During World War II, young Bob Edberg was sent to live with his grandmother in San Mateo. Charged with the care of her American Beauty roses, he has been a dedicated rosarian ever since. Happily, Kathy shares this interest. They started a nursery in 1981—opened only on the weekends, mainly for friends. The nursery has been a full-time business since 1993 and the Edbergs are working harder than ever in their alleged retirement. Their introductions include 'Montecito', 'Souvenir de Pierre Notting', 'Dr. Grill'. They recommend you visit the exquisite Japanese garden in the Sepulveda Dam Basin Recreation Area.

How to get there: Call for directions since their nursery and home display garden are in separate locations.

General information: Open Wednesday through Saturday, 10:00 am–4:30 pm. The nursery will do custom propagation.

Magic Growers

2800 Eaton Canyon Drive, Pasadena 91107
(626) 797-6511, fax (626) 564-8928
e-mail: b-ptibbet@msn.com
Lance Tibbet, Joe Brosius, Bert Tibbet
Wholesale

Plant specialties: Herbaceous perennials, herbs, Mediterranean plants. 171 genera, including special collections of Achillea, Cistus, Geranium, Iris, Lavandula, Penstemon, Rosa, Salvia, Thymus. The dwarf Pennisetum 'Eaton Canyon' introduced here.

History/description: Occupying 9 acres at the base of Eaton Canyon along the San Gabriel Mountains, Magic Growers produces container-grown perennials for the retail market and landscape trade. Started in 1980 to take advantage of a growing interest in perennials, the nursery soon expanded into flowering Mediterranean shrubs and herbs. Close relationships with local botanic gardens and garden designers help create an inventory of useful and desirable subjects. Visitors may wander through their display garden.

How to get there: Call for directions.

General information: Open to wholesale trade only, Monday through Friday, 7:30 am–4:30 pm. General public may visit only with landscape professional. Deliveries within Southern California. Catalogue available to the trade, as are a series of lists providing information about specific plants and use-lists valuable for designers. Nursery tours may be arranged. Will contract-grow for landscape projects.

Northridge Gardens

9821 White Oak Avenue, Northridge 91325
(818) 349-9798, fax same
e-mail: NorGardens@aol.com
Arnie and Susan Mitchnick
Retail, Wholesale, and Mail Order

Plant specialties: Succulents—large collections of
Euphorbia, Pelargonium, Sarcocaulon, and
Pachypodium. Plants which lend themselves to the
bonsai form, such as Ficus, Brachychiton, Adenium
obesum, all unusual and hard to obtain. California
native plants.

History/description: A hobbyist for many years,
Arnie Mitchnick bought plants from Manny and
Bert Singer of Singer's Growing Things. When the
Singers retired in 1992, Arnie bought their incredible stock. Suddenly this writer/editor and former
chemistry and biology teacher found himself in the
nursery business. He is working on creating additional display areas demonstrating the combination
of California native and succulent plants, as he will
soon be stocking California natives. Plan to visit the
Huntington Library in Pasadena and Descanso
Gardens in La Canada Flintridge as well.

How to get there: From Highway 118 (Simi Valley
Freeway), take Balboa exit. Go south on Balboa to
Lassen. Go right on Lassen. Go left on White Oak.
From Highway 101, take Balboa exit north, then
left on Lassen.

General information: Open by appointment only.
Mail-order catalogue available for $1 credited to
your first purchase. Catalogue includes cultural
information and plant's native location. Workshops
offered through local garden clubs and cactus and
succulent clubs.

Nuccio's Nurseries, Inc.
3555 Chaney Trail, Altadena 91001
P. O. Box 6160, Altadena 91003 (mailing address)
(626) 794-3383
Julius, Tom, and Jim Nuccio
Retail, Wholesale, and Mail Order

Plant specialties: Camellias (600 species and
special hybrids), including 'Guilio Nuccio', 'Nuccio's
Cameo', 'Nuccio's Carousel', 'Spring Festival'.
Azaleas (more than 500 varieties), with more than
100 varieties of Satsuki azaleas.

History/description: Brothers Joe and Julius
Nuccio started this nursery in 1935. Their sons now
run the business, just as fascinated by the scientific
possibilities of hybridizing and just as thirsty for
new introductions as were their fathers. They strive
to remain small enough to remain focused on being
knowledgeable and exceptional. Plants displayed
during blooming season offer a major springtime
spectacle.

How to get there: Take the Ventura Freeway
(Highway 134) into Pasadena. It becomes the
Foothill Freeway (Highway 210). Go north off of
210 onto Fair Oaks Avenue. After 4 miles, go west
on Loma Alta. Go north on Chaney Trail. Nursery
is at end of road.

General information: Open Friday through
Tuesday, 8:00 am–4:30 pm, year-round except June
1 through December 31, closed Sundays. May close
early if raining; call first. Plants shipped all over the
world. Free catalogue available. Nursery tours
offered.

Papaya Tree Nursery
12422 El Oro Way, Granada Hills 91344
(818) 363-3680, fax same
David and Tina Silber
Retail

Plant specialties: Tropical and exotic fruit trees and spice plants, many unusual varieties including lychee, sapote, jackfruit, and jujube. Mostly grafted (clonal) plants.

History/description: This home nursery is the result of a rampant hobby. Since the early 1980s, while still an electrical engineer, Dave Silber began tracking down and collecting rare tropical fruit trees. He and wife, Tina, started experimenting with the limits of hardiness and learned to propagate by grafting. By the mid-1980s their backyard was bursting with excess trees and they opened the nursery. This same backyard is today a demonstration orchard.

How to get there: From Highway 118, take Balboa exit in Granada Hills. Go north on Balboa, then left on Midwood. Right on El Oro Way. Pull into driveway.

General information: Open every day, 8:00 am–5:00 pm, but please call before you come. Samples of fruits in season and nursery tours offered. Plant list available. Deliveries on orders above $500.

Theodore Payne Foundation
10459 Tuxford Street, Sun Valley 91352
(818) 768-1802
Retail and Mail Order

Plant specialties: California native plants and seeds
(700 species, 100 of which are endangered), large
collections of Arctostaphylos, Ceanothus. Mahonia
nevinii saved from extinction.

History/description: Named in honor of Theodore
Payne (1872–1963), this nonprofit foundation was
established in 1961 to preserve native vegetation
through propagation and to teach the public about
its value. Theodore Payne's impact on the California
landscape was immense, occurring at a critical time
when underappreciated native vegetation was being
lost to farming and progress. As a nurseryman and
designer, his hand helped shape Rancho Santa Ana
Botanic Garden, Los Angeles State and County
Botanic Gardens, and Torrey Pines State Park. He
popularized California natives in his native England,
even before they caught on at home. In addition to
the nursery and mail-order seed business, the
foundation has classes, field trips, library, horticultural consultants, and the Wildflower Hotline, (818)
768-3533. Their 21-acre site includes a 5-acre
wildflower hill, trails, and picnic facilities.

How to get there: From Highway 210 (Foothill
Freeway), take La Tuna Canyon exit. Go west for 4
miles, then right at signal onto Wheatland. Go right
on Tuxford. Nursery in 1/2 block on left.

General information: Open Wednesday through
Sunday, 8:30 am–4:30 pm. Summer hours: Friday
through Sunday (Wednesday and Thursday by
appointment). Catalogue and plant list available for
$3.50. Mail orders only on books and seed.

Rainforest Flora, Inc.

1927 West Rosecrans, Gardena 90249
(310) 515-5200, fax (310) 515-1177
e-mail: bromtilly@aol.com
Jerry Robinson; Paul Isley, president
Retail, Wholesale, and Mail Order

Plant specialties: Tillandsias, Staghorn ferns, Cycads, Bromeliads, Neoregelias.

History/description: That little Tillandsia plant glued on wood that you picked up at Home Depot probably got its start here. Although their business is now big and mostly wholesale, it started as a hobby. In 1974 these two bromeliad collectors went to Mexico and Guatemala to explore and collect, and the partnership was born. The nursery occupies 2 acres, and there are additional growing grounds in San Diego. Featured on "The Victory Garden," their immense Lord & Burnham greenhouse (built in Maine in 1925 and somehow moved here) recreates a rainforest for visitors. Waterfalls, brick pathways, specimen plants over 25 years old, and a massive stump festooned with epiphytes exude a distinctly tropical atmosphere.

How to get there: From Los Angeles airport, go south on Highway 405 for 3 miles to Rosecrans. Go east on Rosecrans for 3-1/2 miles past Van Ness Avenue. Their driveway is between Nissin Foods and the Southern California Edison substation on the left.

General information: Open Monday through Saturday, 8:00 am–4:30 pm. Plant list is available for SASE. Mail orders shipped.

San Gabriel Nursery

632 South San Gabriel Boulevard, San Gabriel 91776
(626) 286-3782, (626) 286-0787, fax (626) 286-0047
website: www.sgnursery.com
Yoshimura family; Saburo Ishihara and Henrick Mar
Retail and Wholesale

Plant specialties: Bonsai, bulbs, citrus, fruit trees, herbs, houseplants, perennials, subtropical plants, aquatic plants, over 500 varieties of bare-root roses, Asiatic shrubs and trees, including Michelia champaca alba, Pachira aquatica (the good luck money tree), azaleas, camellias, hydrangeas, and gardenias. Hallmark is variety and the hard to find.

History/description: Founded in 1923 by Fred Yoshimura, his family has been involved ever since. This long history accounts for their extensive knowledge about each and every plant. Everyone's recommendation for an all-around nursery in the Los Angeles area, San Gabriel propagates many of its own plants on 60-acre wholesale growing grounds located elsewhere. This 2-acre retail location includes a large bonsai display and florist and gift shop.

How to get there: Thirteen miles east of Los Angeles on I-10, exit at San Gabriel Boulevard. Go 2 miles north.

General information: Open every day, 8:00 am–5:00 pm. Retail nursery tours available for groups by arrangement. Rose list available. Deliveries possible.

Serra Gardens

Malibu
(310) 456-1572, fax same
e-mail: aloe@nwc.net
website: www.cacti.com
Don Newcomer
Wholesale and Mail Order

Plant specialties: Cacti and succulents from all parts of the world, including Pedilanthus macrocarpus, Geradanthus macrorhizus, Ruschia lineolata, Aloe, Agave, Sedum, Euphorbia. Large plants for landscape use.

History/description: In 1986 Don Newcomer made a business out of his father's 30-year-old cacti and succulent habit. A 10-acre growing facility located in the Serra Retreat area of Malibu offers exotic landscape solutions to the problems of drought and fire, to say nothing of a gorgeous view. They propagate by tissue culture and seek to preserve species in endangered habitats. For those who cannot visit the nursery's extensive botanical gardens, check out their descriptive website. A nearby sight of interest is the Malibu Lagoon Museum.

How to get there: Call for directions.

General information: Open to the wholesale trade, Monday through Friday, by appointment only. Catalogue on website. Mail orders accepted over website only.

Sunnyslope Gardens

8638 Huntington Drive, San Gabriel 91775
(626) 287 4071, fax (626) 287-4120
Phil Ishizu
Retail, Wholesale, and Mail Order

Plant specialties: Chrysanthemums (1,200 varieties
on site—more than half are of his own introduction,
hybrids of C. indicum and C. morifolium), 400
noncommercial varieties for sale. Cut specimens of
chrysanthemum and carnation.

History/description: Phil Ishizu is the cousin of
Mamoru Tashima (see Sunnyslope Mum Gardens),
the son of the other brother who helped launch
California's chrysanthemum business in the early
1930s. The original nursery had Sunnyslope in its
name and both cousins have kept it in theirs, though
no one knows why for sure. Perhaps it had to do
with there being a Sunnyslope Avenue near the
original nursery in San Gabriel. Perhaps it has to do
with the golden fields which appear each fall during
the blooming season.

How to get there: Take the San Gabriel exit off of
Highway 10. Go north for 4 miles. Right on Huntington Drive.

General information: Open every day but New
Year's. Blooming plants available in the fall, rooted
cuttings in the spring. Catalogue is available. Mail
orders accepted in the spring. Cut flowers all year long.

Sunnyslope Mum Gardens

11819 Kagel Canyon Street, Lakeview Terrace 91342
(818) 899-1020
Mamoru Tashima
Retail and Wholesale

Plant specialties: Chrysanthemums (500 varieties—
a little bit of everything, including older varieties
C. 'Muto's Crimson', a sport of 'Armistice Day',
C. 'Country Gentlemen', and C. 'Country Maiden').
In 4-inch and 1-gallon pots in the fall; rooted
cuttings available in 2-inch pots from mid-April
through June.

History/description: Mamoru's father and uncle
started a chrysanthemum business in the early 1930s
in San Gabriel. When the San Marino School
District took the nursery's property under eminent
domain, the brothers went their separate ways.
Mamoru's father started again at this location and
his son, equipped with an O.H. degree from UCLA,
took over in 1959. The nursery puts on a chrysanthemum show from late October through November. Its 5 acres of growing grounds and shade houses
are on slightly sloping ground within the city limits
of Los Angeles.

How to get there: Take the Osborne exit off of the
Foothill Freeway (Highway 210) which puts you
onto Foothill Boulevard. Go west on Foothill
Boulevard to Kagel Canyon Street. Turn right. The
nursery is across from Hanson Dam.

General information: Open "just about all the
time," but it is best to call ahead. Plant list available
for SASE.

Van Ness Water Gardens, Inc.

2460 North Euclid Avenue, Upland 91784
(800) 205-2425, fax (909) 949-7217
website: www.vnwg.com
William C. Uber
Retail and Mail Order

Plant specialties: Aquatic plants, aquatic ecosystem components, bog plants, small flowering aquatics, and tropical water lilies. Newest introduction is a hardy water lily which changes color from pale pink to fiery crimson, named after his daughter, 'Amanda Uber'.

History/description: There have been a lot of changes in Upland since this family business was launched in 1922. The lemon grove, which then surrounded the nursery, is today a residential area. Three generations have run the business; the original Mr. Van Ness was a cousin of Bill Uber's father. Bill's father took over in 1952. It was Bill's turn in 1976. They must have the kinks out of their hoses by now. Their 1-acre-plus growing area makes a noteworthy display.

How to get there: From Highway 10, take Euclid exit in Upland. Go 4-1/2 miles north. When the double lane ends, Euclid forks; take the left fork for 1/4 mile to base of Mt. Baldy. Nursery is on the right.

General information: Open Tuesday through Saturday, 9:00 am–4:00 pm. 56-page catalogue is available for $3. Mail orders shipped worldwide (minimum order $15). Tours and talks may be arranged for groups. Design and garden planning services.

Michael Vassar

14155 Le May Street, Van Nuys 91405-4168 (mailing address)
(818) 908-8867
Michael Vassar
Retail

Plant specialties: Winter-growing bulbs of the North Cape of South Africa. 220 species of field-collected Oxalis, including 19 forms of Oxalis obtusa. Pelargonium (80 species).

History/description: Always interested in plants, especially Oxalis, Michael Vassar earned a degree in ornamental horticulture from OSU. A pivotal trip to South Africa in 1985 opened his eyes to the possibilities of plant collecting. He continued his training as a staff member at the Huntington Botanical Gardens and returned to South Africa, this time in winter. There he found more Oxalis species in bloom, many of which were still unidentified. Along the way he became intrigued with the possibilities of pelargoniums. His backyard nursery has many unusual varieties, including the woodsy-scented Pelargonium 'Poquito' and the dwarf P. panduriforme. Who knows where his interests will take him next.

How to get there: Directions given when appointment is made.

General information: Open by appointment only. Plants shipped for minimum order of $25.

HORTICULTURAL ATTRACTIONS

The Arboretum of Los Angeles County
301 North Baldwin Avenue, Arcadia 91007-2697
(626) 821-3222
website: www.parks.co.la.ca.us

History/description: Jointly administered by the
County Parks and Recreation Department and the
California Arboretum Foundation, the Arboretum's
127 acres include more than 4,000 species of plants
from around the world. The grounds include several
historical buildings, vestiges of the former estate of
mining magnate Lucky Baldwin, and a 3-1/2-acre
lake. The faint-footed can get around by shuttle for
a fee. Sights include the Herb Garden, Tropical
Greenhouse, Demonstration Garden, Jungle Garden,
and Water Conservation Garden. Founded in 1947,
the arboretum has introduced more than 100 plants
for Southern California landscapes.

Plant sales: Their big plant sale, the Baldwin
Bonanza, takes place in early May. Plants are also
available at the many plant-society shows held at the
arboretum. A few are sold at the gift shop.

General information: Arboretum is open every day
but Christmas, 9:00 am–5:00 pm. Gift shop is open
from 10:00 am–5:00 pm. Entry fee. The California
Arboretum Foundation, a membership support
group, organizes trips, lectures, events, and can get
you a discount on purchases at participating nurseries. Annual garden show takes place in October on
the premises.

Descanso Gardens

1418 Descanso Drive, La Canada Flintridge 91011
(818) 952-4400, (818) 952-4408 (Gardens Guild)

History/description: Manchester Boddy lived the good life of a Los Angeles newspaper publisher in a 22-room house built for him in 1939 on this 165-acre piece of the old Rancho San Rafael. Although bought by the county in 1953, the gardens' future was secure only when a group of concerned neighbors formed the Gardens Guild, a membership support group. Their efforts got the property placed under the jurisdiction of the Los Angeles County Department of Arboreta. Boddy's huge Rose and Camellia Gardens remain highlights in this oak-woodland canyon setting. Also featured are the Japanese Garden, Lake Bird Sanctuary, Fern Canyon, Iris Garden, and Native Plant Garden.

Plant sales: Big plant sales are held in April and October. Plants also sold at the gift shop.

General information: Garden open every day 9:00 am–4:30 pm. Closed Christmas. Gift shop open 10:00 am–4:00 pm. Admission fee; half-price on third Tuesday of each month. Plant societies regularly hold shows here and the guild offers lectures, a Christmas show, docent tours, and events.

Huntington Library, Art Collection, and Botanical Gardens

1151 Oxford Road, San Marino 91108
(626) 405-2160 (gardens), (626) 405-2100 (main)

History/description: Moving his railroad and real estate empire south, Henry Huntington bought the San Marino Ranch in 1904. He spent the rest of his life creating this estate to house his art and book collections. In 1919 Henry and his wife Arabella deeded the property to a nonprofit trust to ensure its perpetuity. His pleasure garden is today's 130-acre botanical garden. Fifteen specialized gardens include the world-renowned Desert Garden, Japanese Garden, Rose Garden, and Camellia Collection. Primarily a display garden, the Huntington also has an herbarium, mounts plant expeditions, and issues botanical publications.

Plant sales: Plants are sold on the second Thursday of each month during the Garden Talk and at their plant sales in May and November.

General information: Open Tuesday through Friday, noon–4:30 pm; Saturday and Sunday, 10:30 am–4:30 pm. Entrance fee. The Huntington Library's many public services include docent tours, classes, workshops, and lectures.

Rancho Santa Ana Botanic Garden
1500 North College Avenue, Claremont 91711
(909) 625-8767

History/description: Rancho Santa Ana was the first botanical garden in California devoted to scientific study of its native flora. Founded in the 1920s on the Orange County ranch of its benefactor, Susanna Bixby Bryant, the garden served as a catalyst for the efforts of native plant pioneers. In its present location since 1951 and affiliated with the Claremont Colleges, the garden offers wildflower walks in season and public classes. A leading research center, it has an herbarium and a library. Half of the 86-acre garden is devoted to research projects; half is public, organized by plant communities—desert, coastal, woodland, riparian, with special manzanita, ceanothus, conifer, and wildflower display areas. The new California Cultivar Garden highlights cultivated forms of native flora.

Plant sales: Plants are sold at the gift shop and at their big plant sale the first weekend in November (9,000 plants for sale).

General information: Open every day, 8:00 am–
5:00 pm. Closed Christmas, New Year's, July 4, and
Thanksgiving. The gift shop is open weekdays, 9:00
am–4:30 pm; weekends, 11:00 am–4:00 pm. The
Friends of Rancho Santa Ana Botanic Garden, a
membership support group, offers guided tours,
March through May, Saturday and Sunday at 2:00 pm.

South Coast Botanic Garden
26300 Crenshaw Blvd., Palos Verdes Peninsula 90274
(310) 544-1847, on weekends (310) 544-6815

History/description: The South Coast Botanic
Garden is California's first major successful reclama-
tion project. Formerly a landfill, its natural setting
gives no clue to its past. Specialized gardens on its
87 acres include the Waterwise Garden; Rose,
Cactus, Fuchsia, and Palm Gardens; pine, ficus, and
flower areas; and a Garden for the Senses. Everything from weddings and concerts to flower shows
takes place here.

Plant sales: The South Coast Botanic Garden
Foundation, a membership support group, operates
a gift shop which also sells plants and food for the
resident ducks. Big plant sales take place on the first
weekend in October.

General information: Garden is open every day
except Christmas, 9:00 am–5:00 pm. Admission fee.
Gift shop admission free.

Antelope Valley California Poppy Reserve
Lancaster Road, 15 miles west of Highway 14, Lancaster
(805) 724-1180

More than 7 miles of trails through the wildflowers.
Open mid-March through mid-May.

Hannah Carter Japanese Garden

University of California, Los Angeles,
10619 Bellagio Road, Bel Air
(310) 825-4574 (reservations through UCLA)

Bel Air garden (1961) of Gordon Guiberson, with
authentic Japanese details, symbolically pruned and
artfully maintained plantings. Reservations required.

La Casita del Arroyo

177 South Arroyo Boulevard, Pasadena 91105
(626) 744-7275

Charming old casita with original garden from the
1930s, redesigned in 1988 by Isabelle Greene to
illustrate waterwise and low-maintenance plantings.
Managed by the Pasadena Department of Parks and
Natural Resources. Reservations required.

Gamble House

4 Westmoreland Place, Pasadena 91103
(626) 793-3334

Early California garden with Greene & Greene
designed house.

J. Paul Getty Museum Gardens

1200 Getty Center Drive, Los Angeles 90049
(310) 440-7300
website: www.getty.edu

Central gardens designed by Robert Irwin provide
an artistic complement to the large Getty Center and
offer a serene setting overlooking the city of Los
Angeles. Reservations required. The gardens and
museum in Malibu are being restored and will re-
open in 2001.

Charles F. Lummis House ("El Alisal")

200 East Avenue 43, Highland Park 90031 (area of LA)
(323) 222-0546

Almost 2-acre garden redesigned in 1986 by Robert
Perry using waterwise plantings and gardening
techniques. Current home of Historical Society of
Southern California.

Malibu Lagoon State Beach

23200 Pacific Coast Highway, Malibu 90265
(310) 456-8432

The old Rancho Malibu, this preserved chunk of
Southern California's coast includes the 1929
Adamson House and Malibu Lagoon Museum. For
information about nature walks, (818) 880-0363.

Mildred E. Mathias Botanical Garden

University of California, southwest corner of campus,
Los Angeles 90024
(310) 825-3620

Rare trees, landscaped displays of Mediterranean
and subtropical plants.

"El Molino Viejo" (Old Mill)

1120 Old Mill Road, San Marino 91108
(626) 449-5450

Walled mission garden with old citrus and fruit trees
and Spanish tub-mill. Pomegranate patio and
plantings display plants used by the padres.

Franklin Murphy Sculpture Garden

University of California, northeast corner of campus,
Los Angeles 90024
(310) 825-9345

Sculpture garden with trees and earthwork, designed
by Ralph D. Cornell.

Placerita Canyon Park

Placerita Canyon Road off Highway 14 near Santa Clarita
(805) 259-7721

350 acres of mountainous chaparral and oak woodland on the northern slope of the San Gabriel Mountains at an elevation of 1,500 feet; featuring a nature center and trails of various lengths and difficulties.

Palomares Adobe

491 East Arrow Highway, Pomona
(909) 623-2198

Period restoration of an 1854 garden, now managed by the Historical Society of Pomona Valley.

Pomona College

550 North College Avenue, Claremont 91711
(909) 621-8000

Collegiate landscape and small gardens by Ralph D. Cornell.

Rancho Los Alamitos

6400 Bixby Hill Road, Long Beach 90815
(562) 431-3541

Large rancho with adobe and garden of the 1920s designed by Florence Yoch, the Olmsted Brothers, and others. Considered a fine example of historic garden preservation and restoration.

Rancho Los Cerritos

4600 Virginia Road, Long Beach 90807
(562) 570-1755

Established as part of John Temple's rancho in 1844, several large old trees exist from the original garden. In 1931, the Bixby family commissioned Ralph D.

Cornell to create a private estate garden on 4-3/4 acres surrounding the old adobe house. Currently being restored to its 1930s design, the gardens boast many interesting, historical varieties of plants. Now a state and national landmark owned by the city of Long Beach, it is the only private estate garden designed by Cornell that is open to the public.

Virginia Robinson Gardens
1008 Elden Way, Beverly Hills 90210
(310) 276-5367

Italianate estate garden on terraced hillside with palm grove, citrus garden, and exotic trees. Docent tours.

Soka University Botanical Research Center and Nursery
26800 West Mulholland Highway (corner of Las Virgenes), Calabasas 91302
(818) 880-6400

The estate of King Camp Gillette (who brought us the disposable razor), dating from the late 1920s, is being returned to a more natural state. Though the center of campus still consists of sweeping lawns and ponds, there is a new demonstration garden of native plants surrounding an old guest house and areas dedicated to oak woodland, coastal scrub, chaparral, and riparian habitats. The Botanical Research Center is open every day, 9:00 am–5:00 pm. Scheduled historical and garden tours.

South Coast Plaza's Noguchi Garden
San Diego Freeway at Bristol Street, Costa Mesa 92626
(949) 241-1700

Sculptor Isamu Noguchi has created "California Scenario", a 1-1/2-acre reflective environment portraying elements of the California landscape, such as a forest walk, the desert land, water use, water source, land use, and the spirit of the lima bean.

UC Riverside Botanical Garden
University of California, Riverside 92521
(909) 787-4650

Founded in 1963 on 39 acres of rugged terrain on the east side of campus. A broad spectrum garden featuring water-efficient, Mediterranean-climate and California native plants. Also a subtropical orchard with 40 species of citrus, a rose garden, and huge palm and cycad collections.

Walnut Creek Nature Park
Baldwin Park
(626) 813-5245

California native garden. Gated, but walk in.

Wisteria Vine
Sierra Madre 91021
(626) 355-5111 (Chamber of Commerce)

World's largest wisteria vine gone rampant over two private backyards; call for notification of peak bloom visiting days in March.

Wrigley Memorial Botanic Garden
1400 Avalon Canyon Road, Avalon, Catalina Island 90704
(310) 510-2288

Cactus and succulent garden; California native plant garden, emphasizing flora of the Channel Islands.

From the desk of

SANDRA SPODEN

San Diego & Orange Counties

Carlsbad: 305
Chula Vista: 318
Clairemont: 333
Corona del Mar: 332, 333
Del Mar: 333
Encinitas: 307, 325, 328, 331, 332
Escondido: 320, 329, 332
Fallbrook: 311, 326
Fullerton: 330
Irvine: 331
La Mesa: 321
Lakeside: 323
Rancho Santa Fe: 312, 324
San Diego: 304, 314, 333
San Juan Capistrano: 327
San Marcos: 306, 313
Spring Valley: 319
Valley Center: 317
Vista: 308, 309, 315, 316, 322
Westminster: 310

Walter Andersen Nursery

3642 Enterprise Street, San Diego 92110
(619) 224-8271
Walter Andersen, Jr., Ken Andersen
Retail (courtesy discount to landscape professionals)

Plant specialties: Unusual bedding and perennial plants. Palms, cycads, cacti, vines, including Bougainvillaea (30 varieties), Hibiscus (20).

History/description: This family business started in 1928 at this location, though the family has roots deep into pioneer farming in Nebraska. Walter Andersen began work for a cousin in his wholesale indoor foliage business in 1922. At the start, this enterprise was part landscaping and part plant supply. Now the nursery is a prime time occupation, with the second and third generation Andersen family already on staff. The family hosts a once-a-week radio program for call-in gardening questions and tends a 2-acre demonstration garden.

How to get there: From I-5 south, take Rosecrans exit. At the second stop, go left on Kurtz to its end at Pacific Coast Highway. Go right on Pacific Coast Highway for 1 block. Nursery is on right side at foot bridge.

General information: Open every day, 8:00 am–5:00 pm. Saturday garden classes offered at the San Diego nursery. The Andersen family recently opened a 5-acre nursery at 12755 Danielson Court, Powry, 92064, (619) 513-4900.

Bird Rock Tropicals

6523 El Camino Real, Carlsbad 92009 (subject to change, call ahead)
(760) 438-9393, fax (760) 438-1316
e-mail: pam@birdrocktropicals.com
website: www.birdrocktropicals.com
Wayne Schuster, Pamela Koide
Retail, Wholesale, and Mail Order

Plant specialties: Bromeliads (2,000 types, including 500 species and hybrids of Tillandsia). Orchids (800 species—for retail only), palms, and cycads. This partnership has discovered 15 species of Tillandsia in Mexico and Peru.

History/description: Wayne Schuster had been living in Puerto Vallarta on and off for five years when Pamela Koide came for a visit in the late 1970s. Seeing her first bromeliad got them both excited and started their odyssey of collecting (bromeliads and orchids) all over Central and South America. They opened for business in the Bird Rock area of La Jolla in 1980 selling bromeliads exclusively, especially tillandsias which at that time were hard to find. This successful operation moved to Carlsbad in 1986 for more space and began selling orchids, as well. Their "little" collection has now grown to over a million plants, located on two sites, covering 2-1/2 acres on top of a hill overlooking the sea.

How to get there: Call for directions.

General information: Open Monday through Saturday, 9:00 am–4:00 pm. Plant list available for SASE and on the internet. Nursery tours and slide programs about bromeliads and orchids may be arranged. Deliveries to the Los Angeles area on wholesale orders of $250 or more.

Buena Creek Gardens

418 Buena Creek Road, San Marcos 92069
(760) 744-2810
Steve Brigham
Retail (Mail Order dba Cordon Bleu Daylilies, P. O.
Box 2033, San Marcos 92079, (760) 744-8367)

Plant specialties: New and uncommon flowering
perennials, shrubs and vines. 2,000 varieties of
reblooming daylilies and reblooming iris.
Suptropicals and drought-tolerant plants.

History/description: Horticulturist Steve Brigham,
trained at UCSC, Kartuz Greenhouses, and Quail
Botanical Gardens, developed Buena Creek Gardens
in 1988 and bought the business and property in
1996. Featured gardens on the 4-acre site are the
Sun Perennial Garden, the Drought-Tolerant Garden, the Shade Garden, and Palm Canyon, plus
nearly 2 acres of daylily and iris flower fields. This is
a true horticultural mecca for plant enthusiasts,
containing over 5,000 outstanding varieties of
flowering plants from temperate and tropical regions
around the world. Buena Creek is justly proud of its
knack to collect and grow new plant discoveries.

How to get there: From I-5 at Oceanside, take
Highway 78 to Twin Oaks Valley Road. Go left for
3 miles through valley. Turn left on Buena Creek
Road for 1/4 mile. From Interstate 15, take Deer
Springs Road exit west for 3 miles to the stoplight at
Buena Creek Road and turn right.

General information: Open Wednesday through
Saturday, 9:00 am–5:00 pm; Sunday (March
through November), 11:00 am–4:00 pm. Regularly
scheduled garden talks. Plant demonstrations and
garden tours offered. Cordon Bleu Daylilies catalogue available for $2 for daylily mail orders.

Encinitas Gardens

1452 Santa Fe Drive, Encinitas 92024
(760) 753-2852
Jim Duggan
Retail (Mail Order dba Jim Duggan Flower Nursery—
bulbs only)

Plant specialties: Mediterranean-climate plants—
shrubs, trees, and perennials. Australian plants.
Uniquely offered here: Babiana 'Jim's Choice',
Tritonia 'Jim's Choice'. Potted South African bulbs
in spring season.

History/description: Jim Duggan has always loved
plants. His career as a tile contractor, then general
contractor, helped support his passionate acquisition
of plant goodies. The 1/2-acre nursery was started as
a "spare time" project; it has been full-time since
1995 and the concept of "spare time" has vapor-
ized. He does find time for landscape design and
horticultural consultations, such as his present
involvement in the central garden at the Getty
Center in Los Angeles, in collaboration with artist
Bob Irwin.

How to get there: Take the Santa Fe Drive exit off
I-5. Go 1 mile east.

General information: Open Wednesday through
Saturday, 9:00 am–4:00 pm. Catalogue is available
for $2. Mail orders accepted for his South African
bulb business, Jim Duggan Flower Nursery.

Exotica Rare Fruit Nursery & Seed Co.

2508B East Vista Way, Vista 92083
P. O. Box 133, Vista 92085 (mailing address)
(760) 724-9093, fax (760) 724-7724
Jessica Leaf, Steven Spangler
Retail, Wholesale, and Mail Order

Plant specialties: Edible landscape plants, especially tropical fruits. Subtropical and Mediterranean shrubs; Asian and South American fruiting, flowering, and fragrant plants (longan, lychee, jujube); bamboo, palms. All plants organically and biodynamically grown. Figs (30 varieties), old guavas, mulberries, tropical cherries, sweet pomegranates, bananas (18 types), and Buddha's Tree of Enlightenment, Ficus religiosa. Compost occasionally available. Seeds for wholesale only.

History/description: Steven Spangler supplemented his oceanographic studies in Hawaii with picking pineapples. He discovered a unique Tahitian squash and advertised its seeds in *Organic Gardening*. English seed company Thompson and Morgan ordered a huge amount and the Exotica Seed Company was born. Jessica Leaf joined the partnership in 1984, establishing the nursery as a miniature botanical garden on about 3 acres. She now runs their wholesale business. With a large pond and fruiting trees from all over the world growing in the ground, this place has become a haven for birds and butterflies.

How to get there: From I-5 about three-quarters of an hour north of San Diego, go east for 6-1/2 miles on Highway 78. Exit on Escondido Avenue. At the sixth stoplight, go right on East Vista Way for 2-1/2 miles.

General information: Open every day, 10:00 am–4:00 pm. Mail-order catalogue available for SASE. Lectures, design consultations, and contract growing offered. Local deliveries. Fruit tasting in season.

Grigsby Cactus Gardens

2326–2354 Bella Vista Drive, Vista 92084-7836
(760) 727-1323, fax (760) 727-1578
Madelyn Lee
Retail, Wholesale, and Mail Order

Plant specialties: Cacti and succulents, including Euphorbia, Sansevieria, large specimen plants for collectors and landscape use.

History/description: Madelyn Lee, Grigsby's longtime manager and avid collector of cacti and succulents in her own right, recently bought this business from David Grigsby who started planting out his "hobby plants" in 1965 as a retirement activity. What started out as a hobby run amok, is now a 3-acre nursery interspersed with special display gardens. All plants are propagated; none is collected in the wild.

How to get there: Call for directions.

General information: Open by appointment Tuesday through Thursday; open Friday and Saturday, 8:00 am–3:30 pm. Closed Sunday and Monday. No wholesale on Saturdays. Catalogue available for $2. Minimum mail order is $20. Group tours of the nursery can be arranged.

Heard's Country Gardens

14391 Edwards Street, Westminster 92683
(714) 894 2444, fax (714) 799-0265
Mary Lou Heard
Retail

Plant specialties: Cottage-garden type plants, including flowering trees, scented pelargoniums, old and unusual annuals, perennials, and everlastings. Campanula (25 species) and Ranunculus (12).

History/description: It took a lot of imagination for Mary Lou Heard to have envisioned her present cottage-garden nursery on the empty site of an old chinchilla farm. She started in 1984 propagating and selling herbs. Propelled by a strong childhood memory of a profusion of flowers surrounding her home, Mary Lou started to research and acquire old and unusual annuals and perennials. She now offers a one-stop shop for down-home country living, selling plants, tools, furniture, and other artifacts. She also offers classes in naturopathy, floral design, and herbal gardening.

How to get there: Going south on I-405, take the Westminster East exit onto Westminster Boulevard. Go right on Edwards Street up and over I-405. Edwards runs into an industrial park. Follow road with double yellow line.

General information: Open Monday through Saturday, 9:00 am–5:00 pm; Sunday, 10:00 am–5:00 pm. The nursery will track down and order customer requests for unusual plants.

Herban Garden

136 Ranger Road, Fallbrook 92028
(800) 407-5268, fax (760) 723-6169
Jeanne and Chris Dunn
Retail and Wholesale

Plant specialties: Over 200 varieties of herbs. Spring and winter vegetables.

History/description: A graphic artist from a farming family, Jeanne Dunn has reverted to her roots. She quit the arts to work in a nursery where she developed a passion for herbs. Wanting to go into business for themselves, the Dunns opened their nursery in Encinitas in 1983, moving it to Rainbow in 1990. In 1997, the Dunns bought 6 acres in Fallbrook and made their final move. With so much room, the Dunns have plans for gardens, a retail shop with a classroom, and much more.

How to get there: From Riverside take I-5 south to Mission Road exit. Turn right at end of ramp. Bear right onto Mission Road. Go 3/4 mile to Ranger Road. Turn left onto Ranger Road. Nursery entrance is second drive on left.

General information: Open every day from 10:00 am–4:00 pm.

Hubbard Farms
P. O. Box 3446, Rancho Santa Fe 92067
(619) 756-1000, fax (619) 756-9559
Bruce Hubbard
Retail and Wholesale

Plant specialties: Australian and South African
plants, especially Acacia (15 sps. from South Africa,
5 sps. from Australia). Uniquely offered here are
A. abyssinica, A. albida, A. ataxacantha,
A. drepanaliobum, A. karoo, A. nilotica, A. seyal,
A. xanthophloea. Species orchids.

History/description: As a forensic psychiatrist,
Bruce Hubbard developed an appetite for unusual
things. His interest in collecting Acacia began when
he first saw Acacia xanthophloea at the Wild
Animal Park in San Diego. Subsequent trips to
South Africa introduced him to other species and
horticultural madness began. His 30-year habit of
acquiring plants is well manifest in his more-than-2-
acre garden containing over 3,000 species—an
unruly thicket, complicated a bit by his wife's
collection of tropical birds. The nursery is nearby,
officially opened in 1993.

How to get there: Directions will be given when
appointment is made.

General information: Open on weekends only, by
appointment. Nursery tours and lectures may be
arranged. Site-specific consultations offered. Plant
list available.

Judy's Perennials
436 Buena Creek Road, San Marcos 92069
(760) 471-8850, (760) 744-4343
Judy Wigand
Retail

Plant specialties: Perennials, including Salvia, Penstemon, Alstroemeria (Meyer hybrids), and Australian and Mediterranean plants. Although she specializes in perennials suited to the South and Central Coast, over half her stock is cold-hardy. Also, bulbs, ornamental herbs, ground covers, and shrub roses.

History/description: This refreshingly obsessed perennial grower raised her kids, shed her apron, and stepped outdoors to garden. Taking over the job from her son, she went to work for Bob Brooks at Buena Creek Gardens next-door for five years. With his good training, she was soon growing things at home. Customers of Buena Creek, noticing her well-grown and unusual plants, wanted to buy. Business just grew. She has turned her 1/2-acre front yard into a profusely blooming flower garden.

How to get there: From I-5 at Oceanside, go east on Highway 78. Continue for 15 miles to San Marcos and exit at Twin Oaks Valley Road. Go north on Twin Oaks Valley Road for 3 miles. Go west on Buena Creek Road for 1/2 mile.

General information: Open Wednesdays through Fridays and first and third Saturdays, 10:00 am–4:00 pm. Judy makes lively presentations to arboretums, plant societies, and other interested groups; call for more information.

Jungle Music Palms and Cycads

3233 Brant Street, San Diego 92103 (mailing address)
(619) 291-4605, fax (619) 574-1595
e-mail: palmncycad@aol.com
Phil Bergman
Retail

Plant specialties: Palms (600 types) and cycads
(190), including rare species unavailable elsewhere,
such as the cycads Encephalartos schmitzii,
E. dolomiticas, Zamia herrerae, and Ceratozamia
miqueliana; and the palms Trithrinax biflabellata,
Licuala elegans, Basselinia favaerii.

History/description: This San Diego hospital
emergency-room physician grew up in a gardening
family in Southern California and majored in
biology at Stanford. He got interested in palms
while a student in medical school in San Francisco
and started collecting them during his residency in
San Diego in the early 1970s. Pretty soon Phil
Bergman was collecting and trading seed with palm
specialists all over the world. He opened the nursery
in 1976 and now has over 50,000 plants and his
own personal rainforest in Southern California.
Next door to the Encinitas site is the Monarch
Program, a breeding program for this butterfly.

How to get there: The nursery is in two locations;
growing grounds are in San Diego and greenhouses in
Encinitas. Directions given when appointment is made.

General information: Open by appointment only.
Plant list available for SASE. Plants shipped on
minimum order of $200.

Kartuz Greenhouses

1408 Sunset Drive, Vista 92083-6531
(760) 941-3613, fax (760) 941-1123
e-mail: mikekartuz@aol.com
Michael Kartuz
Retail and Mail Order

Plant specialties: Begonias (cane-type, Rex, rhizomatous, shrubby), gesneriads, hoyas, passionflowers, flowering subtropicals, flowering vines.

History/description: In 1979, Michael Kartuz brought his business west from Wilmington, Massachusetts, attracted by the infinitely nicer weather and lower heating costs. Although most plants are still grown in greenhouses, they summer (April to October) outside in shade houses. He will custom grow for clients.

How to get there: Call for directions.

General information: Open Wednesday through Saturday, 9:00 am–4:00 pm. Best to call first. Mail orders shipped. Catalogue available for $2.

Nature's Curiosity Shop
1388 Sunset Drive, Vista 92083
(760) 726-1488
Rick Nowakowski
Retail, Wholesale, and Mail Order

Plant specialties: Bamboo, Canna, Agave, Haworthia, Gasteria, Aloe, Crinum, and other liliaceous plants. 3,500 plant varieties, reflecting a fondness for variegation.

History/description: Once a collector, always a collector, and Rick has been amassing plant favorites since the age of 10, starting with ferns, begonias, and orchids. While in school he worked for Talmadge Fern Gardens in Chula Vista, then became a landscaper. During 15 years spent creating gardens for clients, he gradually started selling plants wholesale. In 1970, he started a mail-order business and also opened Nature's Curiosity Shop in the San Diego area, moving to Vista in 1986. Over the years he has introduced many succulents from Japanese growers and several of his own succulent hybrids as well.

How to get there: From I-5 south, take Highway 78 east into Vista. Take the Melrose exit and go right. Continue through four stoplights. At the fifth stoplight, go right onto Sunset Drive for 1/2 block.

General information: Open Saturday, 9:00 am–4:00 pm; Monday through Friday, by appointment only. Plants shipped throughout the US. Plant list and garden design services available.

Obra Verde Growers

10916 Mystery Mountain Road, Valley Center 92082
(760) 749-2050
Joe and Julie Walker
Mostly Wholesale, some Retail

Plant specialties: Australian plants, few South African plants, perennials, featuring Ericaceae, Myrtaceae (e.g., Chamelaucium), and Proteaceae (e.g., Leucodendron). Also cut flowers.

History/description: Trained as an archaeologist, Joe Walker happened upon a little Australian plant, a chamelaucium, growing in a field of a neighboring farm. Intrigued, he discovered that it was a tough survivor of a cut-flower plantation that had flourished there 30 years before. About this time, the Walkers decided to follow his family's farming tradition, bought some wide-open acreage and planted a citrus and avocado orchard. They included a few chamelauciums in deference to this plant's ruggedness. Seeing how well this Australian plant prospered, they shifted gears, replacing their orchards with an increasingly varied selection of Australian plants. Self-taught, dedicated, and admittedly insane at the start, they are now respected Australian plant experts. About a third of their business is in wholesale cut flowers, and they continue to develop and test-market new varieties. Their large growing grounds way out on Mystery Mountain are in peak blossom November through April.

How to get there: Call for directions.

General information: Open by appointment only for retail customers. Open for wholesalers, Monday through Friday, 6:00 am–3:30 pm; Saturday, 8:00 am–noon. Photographs of all their plants in bloom available at the nursery.

Pacific Tree Farms

4301 Lynwood Drive, Chula Vista 91910
(619) 422-2400, fax (619) 426-6759
Bill Nelson, Kurt Peacock
Retail, Wholesale, and Mail Order

Plant specialties: Unique trees (15,000 varieties), shrubs, and vines, especially fruit and nut trees, berries, conifers (60 varieties of pines, Cupressus cashmeriana) and cold-hardy plants. Citrus (80 varieties). Uniquely offered here: Eugenia aggregata, E. uniflora 'Bountiful Beauty', Passiflora edulis x P. laevicarpa 'Bountiful Beauty', Macadamia tetraphylla 'Fenton'.

History/description: In the mid-1960s Mr. Nelson, an optometrist, got involved in a Boy Scout plant project through his volunteer efforts with Kiwanis. We don't know what this did for the Scouts, but it sparked his lifelong fascination with growing things. He started to collect plants, studied horticulture, and traveled in pursuit of interesting specimens. His first commercial project, a living Christmas tree farm, opened in 1970. As priorities shifted he became a certified arborist and a part-time optometrist. He now oversees 4-1/2 acres of rare and unusual fruit trees full-time. The people of Chula Vista must go elsewhere for vision assistance. All pest control is done with soap and water making the prospect of eating some of his exotic fruits even tastier.

How to get there: From San Diego take Highway 805 south to Chula Vista. Take the Bonita/E Street exit. Go left on Bonita Road for 1 block. Go right on Lynwood.

General information: Open every day but Tuesday. A catalogue describing plants, books, tools for sale, propagation clinics, and nursery tours is available for $2. Mail orders shipped worldwide.

Palms Nursery

2676 Helix Street, Spring Valley 91977
(619) 463-2225
Rudy LaSogga
Retail and Wholesale

Plant specialties: Palms.

History/description: Already at four years old, Rudy LaSogga was mucking about in a cutting bed behind his home in northern Germany. Coming to the United States in 1929, he started a wholesale growing business while serving in the navy. For the next 30 years he brought back seeds to try at the nursery from his far-flung travels for the navy. Palms became an absorbing interest. Over time he has collected most all of them. Now in his eighties and still doing all the work, he has "cut back" his palm stock to 100 different types. This is one fascinating and knowledgeable man whose nursery is really a tropical jungle.

How to get there: Take the El Cajon Boulevard exit off of I-8 to Highway 125, then to Highway 94 east. Take the Bancroft exit south to La Mar. Go left on La Mar. Go right on Helix.

General information: Open by appointment only.

Pecoff Bros. Nursery and Seed

20220 Elfin Forest Road, Escondido 92029
(760) 744-3120
Ronald Pecoff
Retail and Wholesale

Plant specialties: Over 350 species of trees, shrubs, ground covers, and their seeds. Specializing in plants grown for use in adverse conditions—dunes, cut-and-fill slopes, erosion/bank stabilization, salinity, drought, and fire. Though stock is constantly changing, he often carries Acacia 'Pecoff Verde', Acacia 'Onderup', Atriplex glauca, Galvezia speciosa, as well as many other natives and exotics.

History/description: Horticulturist Ronald Pecoff started this business in 1963, selling native plants and seeds exclusively. He developed a hydroseeding technology which enabled disturbed areas to be planted with plants as well as with seeds. He specializes in contract growing for large-scale projects; the remainder sold at his retail nursery accounts for only 10% of his business. He has worked on sand-stabilization projects in Qatar, Iran, and Dubai and is presently restoring a mine-tailings site in New Guinea.

How to get there: Call for directions.

General information: Open Monday through Friday, 6:30 am–5:00 pm. Call first. He will ship native plants and exotic seed.

Perennial Adventure
10548 Anaheim Drive, La Mesa 91941
(619) 660-9631
Christine Wotruba
Retail

Plant specialties: Perennials, vines, small shrubs, heat-tolerant plants, Mediterranean plants, and subtropicals, emphasizing foliage color. Uncommon selections include 4 varieties of Glaucium and Dianthus japonicus.

History/description: Christine Wotruba's emphasis on artistry is the hallmark of this small cottage garden and nursery surrounding her hilltop home. Equipped with an M.A. in Fine Arts and with Master Gardener credentials, her garden and plant selections reflect her interest in foliage color. Chartreuses, bronze and gold tones, and silver grays mingle with various other shades of green and provide the full-color complement to the garden. In the course of creating her own garden from seeds obtained from the Hardy Plant Society and other organizations, she discovered she had a surplus and decided to sell them. Her garden has so many admirers that she now finds herself in the business of helping customers design theirs.

How to get there: From downtown San Diego, take Highway 94 east for 10 miles to the Avocado Boulevard exit. Continue north for eight blocks uphill to Anaheim Drive.

General information: Open Thursday through Saturday, 10:00 am–4:00 pm. Newsletter available for stamped business-sized envelope. Design services offered.

Rainbow Gardens Nursery & Bookshop

1444 East Taylor Street, Vista 92084
(760) 758-4290, fax (760) 945-8934
e-mail: rbgdns@aol.com
Chuck Everson
Retail and Mail Order

Plant specialties: Tropical cacti from the jungle, including Epiphyllum (200 varieties), Rhipsalis, Hoya, Schlumbergera. Rhipsalidopsis.

History/description: Who knows how you develop jungle fever? Chuck Everson caught the bug when a business opportunity presented itself. In 1980 he bought out a nursery and merged it with his existing bookstore which specialized in books about horticulture and cactus culture. He claims he now has every book in print about cacti and succulents, bromeliads, epiphyllums, palms, and cycads to help you make an educated purchase. This nursery, the largest mail-order, flowering-jungle-cacti nursery in the country, has both cactus and succulent display gardens.

How to get there: From Highway 78, take the Escondido Avenue exit and head north to East Vista Way, then right on Taylor Street.

General information: Open Tuesday through Saturday, 9:30 am–4:00 pm, by appointment. 48-page catalogue with 200 color photos is available for $2. Mail orders shipped on minimum order of $21.50. Bookshop catalogue free upon request. Nursery tours offered to interested groups.

Rancho Jojoba Nursery
11935 Highway 67, Lakeside 92040
(619) 561-0751
Ed and Linda Reindl
Retail and Wholesale

Plant specialties: Mostly Australian trees and shrubs, including Eucalyptus (60 kinds), Melaleuca (15), Acacia (12), Callistemon (10), Calothamnus. Some California natives suited to coastal and foothill climates. Mediterranean plants.

History/description: Ed Reindl's career went from earthworms to eucalypts, and then to the rest of Australian flora. Equipped with an agricultural degree, Ed began as an earthworm farmer in the 1970s. As market demand shifted, he switched first to growing the Southwestern native jojoba (Simmondsia chinensis), prized for its valuable oil, and then to eucalyptus, valued for its firewood. Meanwhile, Linda, an emergency room nurse, began to notice and became fascinated by other eucalypts and melaleucas and started ordering their seed as well. By 1978 they had a well-developed collection of Australian plants and opened the 2-acre nursery. Their stock plants are now fully mature and give visitors an idea of their size and habit.

How to get there: From San Diego take I-8 east to El Cajon. The nursery is 10 miles north of El Cajon on Highway 67. From the north, take I-15 south to Poway exit. Follow this road to Highway 67; then go right (south) on 67.

General information: Open every day but Wednesdays and holidays, but call first. Local deliveries possible on minimum orders of $250.

Rancho Soledad Nursery

18539 Aliso Canyon Road, Rancho Santa Fe 92067
(619) 756-3717, fax (619) 756-4597
Donald Jerry Hunter
Retail and Wholesale

Plant specialties: Tropical and subtropical foliage plants, drought-tolerant plants, palms.

History/description: Donald Hunter, following the footsteps of his parents, started in the nursery business in 1954 by buying old Soledad Gardens nursery near Mt. Soledad in La Jolla. The nursery has been at its present location since the mid-1960s. In its early days, the nursery focused on water-conserving plants, with only a small section devoted to tropical foliage. With the acquisition of a 25-acre growing ground in Hawaii (in addition to his 25 acres here), the nursery's emphasis switched to tropicals. Now, the pendulum is starting to swing back and a lot more space and effort is centered on xerophytes. The nursery includes a huge, 3-story palmarium.

How to get there: The nursery is located east of I-5, west of I-15, and south of Highway 78. Call for more specific directions.

General information: Open Monday through Saturday, 8:00 am–4:30 pm. The retail area is small but the wholesale area is open to knowledgeable customers. Availability list for wholesale trade. Tours can be arranged. Limited deliveries on orders over $350.

Samia Rose Topiary

1236 Urania, Encinitas 92024
(760) 436-0460 or (800) IV TOPIARY
fax (760) 436-6869
website: www.srtopiary.com
Pat Hammer
Retail, Wholesale, and Mail Order

Plant specialties: Topiary plants: Hedera helix (more than 200 cultivars), Leptospermum, Myrtus communis, Buxus, flowering vines, herbs, ground covers, and woody plants. Pat Hammer's ivy introductions include Hedera helix 'Tussie Mussie' and H. h. 'Calico'.

History/description: A professional gardener, Pat Hammer spent 15 years at Longwood Gardens developing her topiary techniques and writing *The New Topiary*. She moved west in 1992 and selected this location because there were people in the area who would grow on her large collection of ivies. Working together they produce the plants for her topiaries. The nursery is named after her mother and the mother of a close friend. Pat is also the president of the American Ivy Society. The 1/4-acre nursery has a topiary display garden, the Court of Lions.

How to get there: From San Diego go north on I-5 for 25 miles to the Leucadia Boulevard exit. Go east for 1 block on Leucadia Boulevard. Go left on Urania. The nursery is in 3 blocks on your left.

General information: Open Tuesday through Saturday, 9:00 am–5:00 pm. Sunday, noon–4:00 pm. Price sheets available for SASE. Mail orders accepted. The nursery will custom-grow for clients. Classes and workshops offered on making topiary.

South Coast Palms
960 El Caminito, Fallbrook 92028
(760) 723-1354, fax (760) 723-1256
e-mail: palmnut@tfb.com
Gary Wood
Retail and Wholesale

Plant specialties: Palms (75 varieties) and cycads (30 types), seedlings to 15-gallons.

History/description: A Southern California native, Gary Wood got interested in palms while living for 10 years in the San Jose area. In 1986 he chose Fallbrook as the perfect site to house his growing collection. This area is within Zone 23, described in *Sunset Western Garden Book* as "one of the most favored areas in North America for growing sub-tropical plants." Still a teacher by trade, he runs this 1-1/2-acre oasis in his supposed spare time. To date there are 185 species of palms in his garden.

How to get there: Directions given when appointment is made.

General information: Open by appointment, Monday through Saturday. Plant list available. Cultural instructions included with purchase. Deliveries on minimum order of $250. Nursery tours may be arranged.

Tree of Life Nursery

33201 Ortega Highway, San Juan Capistrano 92693
P. O. Box 635, San Juan Capistrano 92693 (mailing address)
(949) 728-0685, fax (949) 728-0509
e-mail: toln@flash.net
Mike Evans, Jeff Bohn
Retail and Wholesale

Plant specialties: California native plants for all regions of the state, especially plants of the coastal mountains. Over 400 species and varieties.

History/description: These former landscape contractors and native plant enthusiasts knew from their garden installation experience that California natives made first-rate garden plants. Now the largest native supplier in California, they had taken a gamble in 1978 by starting a nursery devoted exclusively to California natives. Presently 20 of its 40 acres are under cultivation, including a display garden and bookstore made out of plastered straw bale. Tree of Life brings longtime experience to ecological restoration, habitat enhancement, and authentic landscaping.

How to get there: Take Ortega Highway exit off of I-5. Go east for 7-3/4 miles. Nursery is on the left.

General information: Open for retail customers on Fridays, 9:00 am–4:00 pm. Nursery tours may be arranged for groups. Catalogue and planting guide available for $7.50. Local deliveries on wholesale orders.

Weidners' Gardens

695 Normandy Road, Encinitas 92024
(760) 436-5326, fax (760) 436-3681
e-mail: weidner@weidners-gardens.com
website: www.weidners-gardens.com
Evelyn Weidner; Mary Witesman, manager
Retail and Wholesale

Plant specialties: Subtropical plants, including
tuberous Begonia, Fuchsia, Mandevilla (Dipladenia),
Scaevola, Brunfelsia.

History/description: Mr. Weidner retired from many
years in the foliage business, moved to Encinitas, and
set up one greenhouse to grow plants for friends.
Never intending to retire really, he bought 25,000
tuberous begonia seedlings, and created a garden of
raised beds and shade houses. In 1973 he opened for
business, as Weidner's Begonia Gardens. Then as
now, customers dig their own begonias and pansies
in season. The nursery no longer confines its offerings to begonias and over the years has introduced
Scaevola 'Blue Wonder', Dipladenia 'My Fair Lady'
and D. 'Scarlet Pimpernel', and Verbena 'Temari'.
Their greenhouses are ablaze with Ecke poinsettias
and cyclamen in November and December. You
might combine your visit here with the nearby Quail
Botanical Garden, Torrey Pines State Reserve, and
the butterfly preserve in Encinitas.

How to get there: The nursery is located on I-5
between Leucadia and La Costa exits on the frontage road (Piraeus road), east of the freeway. Corner
of Piraeus and Normandy Roads.

General information: Open every day but Tuesday,
April 1 to September 15, 9:30 am–5:00 pm; November 1 to December 22, 9:30 am–4:30 pm. Wholesale
plant list available. Deliveries on wholesale orders of
$300 or more. Printed cultural information available
for each plant.

Zorro Protea Farm

P. O. Box 462487, Escondido 92046
(760) 723-2450
Peter Sacks, managing partner
Wholesale and Mail Order

Plant specialties: Proteaceae—some sold as plants, most sold as cut flowers. Protea (100 kinds, mostly South African), Chamelaucium, Leptospermum.

History/description: As you might expect, South African Peter Sacks had a natural affinity for proteas and started growing them as a hobby. He lined up several partners and launched the nursery in 1979 to produce proteas for the cut-flower trade. The nursery has exclusive rights from the Fynbos Agricultural Research Council of South Africa to market all new cultivars developed by that group. Located on 40 acres of gently rolling hills sparsely studded with eucalyptus, row upon row of nursery cans march over the dry mounded landscape. It is well worth your effort to arrange a tour.

How to get there: Directions given when tours arranged. The nursery is in the Fallbrook area.

General information: Not open to the public, but nursery tours are offered. Call for schedule. Catalogue available. Plant and cut flowers shipped worldwide.

HORTICULTURAL ATTRACTIONS

Fullerton Arboretum
California State University, 1900 Associated Road (corner of Yorba Linda Boulevard), Fullerton 92631 (714) 278-3579, Friends (714) 278-3404

History/description: This 26-acre arboretum was opened in 1979 through the joint efforts of the California State University Fullerton, the city of Fullerton, and community resources. The arboretum includes plants from all parts of the world which can grow well in Southern California and organizes them according to their cultural requirements. Hence moisture-loving plants grow alongside streams and ponds, dryland plants are found in the chaparral section. Other areas include the Palm Garden, Subtropical Fruit Grove, Conifer Area, Cactus and Succulent Garden, and Historic Area, a re-creation of an 1890s garden surrounding a Victorian house. The Friends of Fullerton Arboretum, a membership support group, organizes events, a newsletter, and the shop.

Plant sales: Specializing in unusual, drought-tolerant plants propagated on site. Selected plants also available in the Gift and Garden Shop. Open October through June, Saturday, 10:00 am–4:00 pm, and Sunday, 1:00 pm–4:00 pm.

General information: Arboretum is open every day, 8:00 am–4:45 pm, except Thanksgiving, Christmas, and New Year's. Admission free, donations accepted.

Quail Botanical Gardens

230 Quail Gardens Drive, Encinitas 92024
(760) 436-3036

History/description: In 1957 Ruth Baird Larabee donated her home and 26-acre garden of drought-tolerant plants to the county. An additional 4 acres were given by poinsettia grower Paul Ecke in 1971. A foundation was formed in 1961 to provide support for the garden and enable it to grow botanically. The gardens are known throughout the country for having the most diverse collection of bamboo; they maintain a bamboo-quarantine house for imports. Other special collections are of native plants, pan-tropical plants, hibiscus, palms, and cycads. There is also the Fruit Demonstration Garden, Desert Garden, Overlook Pavilion, and waterfall with subtropical plants.

Plant sales: Plants sold at the nursery, open Tuesday–Sunday, 11:00 am–3:00 pm and at the gift shop.

General information: Open daily, 9:00 am–5:00 pm. Admission fee. Docent tours are given every Saturday at 10:00 am; children's tours are on the first Tuesday of each month.

UC Irvine Arboretum

University of California, Irvine 92697
(949) 824-5833

History/description: Specializing in plants of the five Mediterranean ecosystems, the arboretum began as the holding area for plants used to landscape the campus in 1964. Noted for its collection of South African bulbs and perennials and African aloes, the arboretum is involved in the conservation of endangered species. The Friends of UCI Arboretum, a membership support group, publishes a quarterly newsletter, gives lectures, and supports conservation activities.

Plant sales: Large bulb and plant sale is held in August. Spring and fall perennial plant sale. Smaller sales accompany monthly events.

General information: Open Monday through Saturday, 9:00 am–3:00 pm. Closed university holidays.

Paul Ecke Ranch
441 Saxony Road, Encinitas

In 1920, Paul Ecke started the tradition of using poinsettias as a holiday plant. This premier purveyor of poinsettias is open only one day a year, during the Chamber of Commerce's Fall Flower Tour at the beginning of the holiday season. Call the Chamber for reservations (760) 753-6041. The growing fields along Saxony Road are spectacular in December.

Rogers Gardens
2301 San Joaquin Hills Road, Corona del Mar
(949) 640-5800

A horticultural extravaganza on 7 acres, also a garden center. Huge Christmas display.

San Diego Wild Animal Park Botanical Gardens
1550 San Pasqual Valley Road, Escondido 92027
(760) 747-8702
website: www.sandiegozoo.org

Under the auspices of the San Diego Zoological Society, the Park has a botanical garden containing 4,000 plant species, including 260 endangered species such as the North African cypress. Plant collections, most maintained by local plant societies, include a Conifer Forest, Herb Garden, Baja Garden, Bonsai House, California Nativescapes Garden,

Epiphyllum Garden, Protea Garden, and Old World Succulent Garden. Special educational programs, group tours, and events. Plants available all year at the Plant Trader, and at scheduled plant sales.

San Diego Zoo
2920 Zoo Drive, San Diego 92103
(619) 231-1515

The 125 acres include interesting plantings and an orchid house. Annual plant sale.

Sherman Library and Gardens
2647 East Pacific Coast Highway, Corona del Mar 92625
(949) 673-2261

Horticultural display garden, with rose garden, tropical greenhouse, large annual flower beds, and hanging basket displays.

Torrey Pines State Reserve
North Torrey Pines Road, a mile south of Del Mar
(619) 755-2063

The only natural torrey pine forest in California, on 1,100 acres of beach, bluff, and coastal mountain terrain.

Jim Wright's "Private Palm Paradise"
Clairmont, near San Diego
(619) 276-5295

A small oasis containing hundreds of palms, bromeliads, and other tropical plants. This is a private garden. Reservations required.

OTHER
SOURCES

BULBS
all mail order only

Davids & Royston Bulb Co.
550 West 135th Street, Gardena 90248
(310) 532-2313
Wholesale

Since 1938, a source for spring and summer flowering bulbs, mostly from South Africa. Their growing grounds off I-5 in Carlsbad next to the Anderson Pea Soup Company are well worth a drive by in March and April.

Jim Duggan Flower Nursery
1452 Santa Fe Drive, Encinitas 92024
(760) 943-1658

South African bulbs. Available June through September only. Catalogue $2.

Robinett Bulb Farm
P. O. Box 1306, Sebastopol 95473
(707) 829-2729, fax (707) 823-1954
e-mail: jarobinett@att.net.com
Wholesale and Retail

West Coast native bulbs, including Allium, Brodiaea, Calochortus. Most are exclusively theirs. This part-time, labor-of-love business alternates between wholesale and retail sales each year. Next retail list available August 1999, though inquiries welcomed all year. Dormant bulbs shipped from September to mid-October.

Skittone Wholesale Bulb Co.
Greenlady Retail Gardens
1415 Eucalyptus, San Francisco 94132
(415) 753-3332
Retail and Wholesale

Five hundred uncommon kinds of bulbs and bulbous plants. Specializing in bulbs from South Africa, but including bulbs from many parts of the world. Terrestrial bulbous orchids. Catalogue available for $1.

(For other bulb sources, refer to William R. P. Welch and Nancy Wilson in the Growers section.)

SEEDS

Albright Seed Company
487 Dawson Drive, Bay 5S, Camarillo 93012
(800) 423-8112
website: www.albrightseed.com
Wholesale, some Retail (minimum order $25)
Walk-in sales, phone, or internet orders

Seeds of California native wildflowers, grasses, legumes, pasture grasses, turf grasses for erosion control, revegetation plants, and cover crops. Hand- and custom-harvested seeds. Free catalogue.

Bountiful Gardens
18001 Shafer Ranch Road, Willits 95490
(707) 459-6410
 e-mail: bountiful@zapcom.net
Retail
Mail order only

Untreated, open-pollinated seeds for vegetables, grains, cover crops, herbs, and some flowers. Primarily heirloom plants. Also complete Biointensive literature and organic gardening supplies. Operated by nonprofit Ecology Action of the Mid-Peninsula in Palo Alto. Free catalogue. Bulk prices available.

Carter Seeds
475 Mar Vista Drive, Vista 92083
(760) 724-5931
website: www.carterseeds.com
Retail, Wholesale, and Mail Order
Limited walk-in, by arrangement

Seeds for flowers, trees, shrubs, ornamental grasses, palms. Free catalogue. Minimum order $30 cash or $40 credit.

Clyde Robin Seed Company
P. O. Box 2366, Castro Valley 94545 (mailing address)
(510) 785-0425, fax (510) 785-6463
e-mail: sales@clyderobin.com
website: www.clyderobin.com
Mail and internet orders
Limited walk-in

Collectors and producers of over 600 kinds of wildflowers. Also ornamental grass, legume, and shrub seed. Grown, combined, and cleaned on location. Free full-color catalogue available on request.

ConservaSeed
P. O. Box 455, Rio Vista 94571
(916) 775-1676
website: www.conservaseed.com
Wholesale primarily (bulk sales), some Retail
Mail, internet, and phone orders with consultation

Largest producer of California native grass seed. Also legume and forb seeds for erosion control, revegetation, and cover crops. A genetic collector and increaser. Free catalogue on their website. Spring open house held for public visits to their 300+ acres of native grasses.

Environmental Seed Producers
P. O. Box 2709, Lompoc 93438
(805) 735-8888
Wholesale

Seeds for California native wildflowers, ornamental
grasses, wildflower mixes, herbs. Free catalogue. No
retail mail orders.

Forest Seeds of California
1100 Indian Hill Road, Placerville 95667
(530) 621-1551, fax (530) 621-1040
e-mail: Graton@Directron.net
Retail and Wholesale
Mail, phone, and fax orders

Forest tree and shrub seeds primarily. Also do
custom seed collecting and cleaning. Catalogue $1.

Hedgerow Farms
21740 County Road 88, Winters 95694
(530) 662-4570, fax (530) 668-8369
e-mail: hedgefarm@aol.com
Retail and Wholesale
Mostly mail order; walk-in by appointment

California native grass seed, some wildflowers,
focusing on habitat restoration of lower-elevation
Northern California.

Heirloom Garden Seeds
P. O. Box 138, Guerneville 95446
(707) 887-9129
Retail and Wholesale

Herb and flower seeds—more than 400 varieties of
open-pollinated (nonhybrid) seeds. Retail catalogue
available for $2.50.

J. L. Hudson
Star Route 2, Box 337, La Honda 94020
Retail mail order only
No telephone orders

Offbeat seed from around the world. Bulbs, vegetables, cyclamen. Catalogue available for $1.

Kamprath Seed Company
205 Stockton Street, Manteca 95337
(209) 823-6242, fax (209) 823-2582
Wholesale
Phone or fax orders

Native grasses, clovers, corn, alfalfa, and special mixes. Free catalogue.

Kitazawa Seed Company
1111 Chapman Street, San Jose 95126
(408) 243-1330
Retail and Wholesale
Mail order only; no walk-in

Primarily Asian vegetable seed, including burpless cucumber and Japanese hybrid spinach, which grows year-round in hot or cool climates. All seed guaranteed. Free brochure.

Lockhart Seeds, Inc.
P. O. Box 1361, Stockton 95201
(209) 466-4401
Retail and Wholesale
Mail and phone orders, walk-in

Field-grown occidental and oriental vegetable seeds, including many types of onions. Some flowers. Retail shop at 3 North Wilson Way in Stockton also sells small garden equipment and other gardening products. Free catalogue.

Moon Mountain Wildflowers
P. O. Box 725, Carpinteria 93014
(805) 684-2565, fax (805) 684-2798
e-mail: ssseeds@silcom.com
Retail
Mail order

Seeds of North American wildflowers and ornamental grasses. Specialty and regional mixes. Informative catalogue contains sun exposure and moisture requirements, available for $3.

Ornamental Edibles
3622 Weedin Court, San Jose 95132
(408) 946-7333, fax (408) 946-0181
e-mail: orned@pacbell.net
website: www.ornamentaledibles.com
Wholesale (bulk sales)
Mail order only

International vegetable, herb, edible-flower seeds, and hydroponics specialties. Large selection of salad and braising greens. Wholesale catalogue $2 USD, $5 international.

Pacific Coast Seed Company
6144 Building A—Industrial Way, Livermore 94550
(925) 373-4417, fax (925) 373-6855
Wholesale

Seeds for turf grasses, native grasses, wildflowers. Free catalogue.

Peaceful Valley Farm Supply
110 Spring Hill Drive, Grass Valley
P. O. Box 2209, Grass Valley 95945 (mailing address)
(530) 272-4769 or toll free (888) 784-1722
Retail
Mail and phone orders, walk-in

Wildflower, vegetable, lawn, and native-grass seeds, cover-crop seeds, fall-flower bulbs, garlic, onions, potatoes, bare-root strawberries, fruit trees and berries. Free catalogue available.

Redwood City Seed Company
P. O. Box 361, Redwood City 94064
(650) 325-7333
website: www.ecoseeds.com
Retail and Wholesale
Mail order only; no walk-in

Open-pollinated and very old-fashioned seed varieties of vegetables and herbs. Many unique to the trade. Retail catalogue, *Endangered Cultivated Plants,* available free; wholesale and retail list is on the internet.

S and S Seeds
P. O. Box 1275, Carpinteria 93014
(805) 684-0436, fax (805) 684-2798
Wholesale
Mail and phone orders

Seeds for California native wildflowers, grasses, trees, and shrubs. Catalogue available for $6. The wholesale arm of Moon Mountain Wildflowers.

Seed Savers Exchange
3076 North Winn Road, Deborah, IA 52101
(319) 382-5990, fax (319) 382-5872
Retail
By subscription

A membership organization that supports genetic preservation of heirloom vegetables and fruits. Their publications, *Winter Yearbook, Summer Edition,* and *Harvest Edition,* include a list of member-grown seeds of heirloom vegetable varieties and are offered for sale nowhere else. They also have a directory of commercial mail-order seed sources. Lists of seeds which can be ordered directly from the exchange are available each January.

Seedhunt
P. O. Box 96, Freedom 95019
(831) 763-1523
e-mail: seedhunt@aol.com
Retail
Seed sales by mail order; plant sales by appointment only

Ginny Hunt, formerly of Western Hills Nursery, offers seed collected from her garden in Watsonville and from the gardens of a host of other avid gardeners and friends. She specializes in seeds of uncommon plants for Mediterranean climates, California natives, and unusual annuals. Seed catalogue $1.

MAIL ORDER ONLY NURSERIES

This list is admittedly arbitrary and by no means exhaustive. However, it does include old friends who have retired from walk-in sales, and growers of plants which are available only at certain times of the year.

Abbey Garden Cactus
P. O. Box 2249, La Habra 90632
(562) 905-3520, fax (562) 905-3522

Lem and Pat Higgs have been collecting cacti and succulents for 25 years, propagating many endangered species whose natural habitat is being lost to agriculture and suburban encroachment. They closed their respected retail nursery in Carpinteria in 1995 and are currently doing domestic mail order only.

Babette's Gardens
40975 North 172 Street East, Lancaster 93535
(805) 264-3781

Daylilies and perennials. Catalogue available for $1, deductible from first order.

Cal-Dixie Iris Gardens
14115 Pear Street, Riverside 92508
(909) 780-0335

Bearded iris (2,500 varieties), including rebloomers. Catalogues requested before March 1 are free, after that, include $1. Rhizomes shipped July through September. Two acres of growing grounds are open during peak bloomtime, mid-April through mid-May, 9:00 am–6:00 pm.

Cordon Bleu Farms
P. O. Box 2033, San Marcos 92079

Daylilies. Catalogue available for $2. (Refer to Buena Creek Gardens in Grower section.)

Dietter's Water Gardens
21 Ralston Street, San Francisco 94132
(415) 586-6384

Craig Dietter can design and install most any kind of water feature or provide kits for you to do it yourself. He grows a good selection of aquatic plants, for clients, local customers, and mail order. Free catalogue.

Iris Hill Farm
7280 Tassajara Creek Road, Santa Margarita 93453
(805) 438-3070

Iris germanica, standard dwarf bearded iris. Iris sold in 1-gallon cans for walk-in trade only. Take Tassajara Creek Road exit (small road sign) off of Highway 101.

The Iris Pathway
3785 Oaktree Lane, Loomis 95650
(916) 652-6437

350 varieties of iris, a collection-in-progress for 30
years. Catalogue available.

Maryott's Iris Garden
P. O. Box 1177, Freedom 95019
(831) 722-1810, fax (831) 722-2217
e-mail: billmaryott@irisgarden.com

550 varieties of bearded iris—bloom-sized rhizomes,
talls, intermediates, and rebloomers. The Maryotts
have introduced 90 bearded iris, many of which have
won awards: I. 'Octoberfest', 'Almaden', 'En Garde',
'Cherry Glen', and 'It's Magic'. Color catalogue
available for $5, refundable with purchase. Mail
orders accepted until September 1.

Mendocino Heirloom Roses
P. O. Box 670, Mendocino 95460
(707) 937-0963, fax (707) 937-3744
e-mail: gdaly@mcn.org

Roses for Northern California's coastal climate;
heirloom roses found or raised before 1900. An
especially fine collection of ramblers, all organically
raised. Free list of roses and their attributes available.

Mountain Valley Growers, Inc.
38325 Pepperweed Road, Squaw Valley 93675
(559) 338-2775, fax (559) 338-0075
website: www.mountainvalleygrowers.com

Culinary, fragrant, and ornamental herbs (over 400
varieties) and everlastings. Perennials which attract
bees and butterflies. V. J. and Keith Billings have
introduced Buddleia 'Twilight', a cultivar of B. 'Black
Knight' and B. 'Dwarf Purple'. Catalogue available
by mail or on their informational website.

Protea Farm of California
P. O. Box 1806, Fallbrook 92088
(760) 728-4297

Australian and South African shrubs and bulbs,
perennials. Proteaceae, including Protea,
Leucodendron, Leucospermum, Banksia. Roger
Boddaert's Protea Farm has introduced yellow Clivia
'California Sunshine' and Haemanthus katharinae.

Sutton's Green Thumber
16592 Road 208, Porterville 93257
(559) 784-9011, fax (559) 784-6701

35 acres of bearded iris, the result of an uncontrol-
lable hobby. Catalogue $3. Garden is open in April.

HORTICULTURAL INFORMATION

GENERAL RESOURCES

The Bay Area Gardener
301 Windmill Park Lane, Mountain View 94043
(650) 968-4480, e-mail: editor@gardens.com

Carol Moholt has created the first custom website for Bay Area gardeners, www.gardens.com, which includes all gardening and horticulture classes, sales, shows, tours, special events, and a directory of regional public gardens and garden centers.

Bio-Integral Resource Center (BIRC)
P. O. Box 7414, Berkeley 94707
(510) 524-2567, fax (510) 524-1758

This member-supported education and research center is dedicated to encouraging the use of the least toxic, most practical method of pest control. They advocate using all available methods to control pests (biological, physical, mechanical, and cultural) to avoid toxic chemicals. Information about this Integrated Pest Management (IPM) approach is sent to the 2,000 members via two publications: *Common Sense Pest Control Quarterly* for homeowners and *IPM Practitioner* for professionals.

John E. Bryan Gardening Newsletter
300 Valley Street, #206, Sausalito 94965
(415) 331-7848

This monthly newsletter contains important cultural information for Northern California gardeners, but is broadly subscribed to because of John Bryan's wealth of gardening insights based on a lifetime of experience both here and abroad. Book reviews and information about tours he leads to Europe and South Africa.

California Exotic Pest Plant Council (CalEPPC)
c/o Sally Davis, 32912 Calle del Tesoro,
San Juan Capistrano 92675
(949) 487-5427, e-mail: sallydavis@aol.com

This group is the front flank of California's effort to rid itself of invasive exotic plants, such as pampas grass, tamarisk, French broom, and yellow star thistle, which threaten the state's natural ecosystems. Members receive the quarterly *CalEPPC News*, a discount on registration fees to their annual symposium, and the chance to participate in regional workshops and local working groups.

California Garden
Casa del Prado, Room 105, 2125 Park Boulevard,
San Diego 92101-4792
(619) 232-5762

Since 1907, subscribers to this bimonthly publication have kept informed about local gardening conditions and preferable cultural practices. Descriptive articles about selected plants, book reviews, and local events.

California Garden and Landscape History Society
P. O. Box 1338, Sebastopol 95473

This newly formed membership group is devoted to the study and enjoyment of California's historical landscapes and gardens. It publishes a biannual newsletter, *Eden,* and organizes statewide meetings which explore the landscape heritage of the host area. Members also go on garden tours and help preserve important sites and documents.

California Garden Clubs, Inc.
224 Montair Drive, Danville 94526-3726
(925) 837-7614 Virginia Bennetts
website: www.enweb.com/cgci

This nonprofit association of more than 300 clubs
(20,000 members) in California is part of the
National Council of State Garden Clubs, Inc.
Individual clubs have informational programs at
their monthly meetings, pursue projects in horticulture, conservation, and garden therapy and fund
scholarships. Members may receive the bimonthly
Golden Gardens.

California Horticultural Society
1847 34th Avenue, San Francisco 94122-4109
(415) 566-5222

Founded in 1933, this is the granddaddy of all
horticultural societies in California. Now 700
members strong, they have meetings on third
Mondays at 7:30 pm at the California Academy of
Sciences. Meetings consist of a slide program and an
informative show-and-tell by members about their
plants. Unusual plants are often available at these
meetings and at a big plant sale in March. Members
have access to an annual seed exchange, field trips,
monthly bulletin, and subscription to *Pacific
Horticulture.*

California Oak Foundation
1212 Broadway, Suite 810, Oakland 94612
(510) 763-0282

This educational organization is hustling to conserve
California's oak woodlands, threatened by increasing population. Their semiannual newsletter,
California Oaks, is a benefit of membership; their
other publications are available for purchase. Local
groups organize restoration projects such as oak
acorn gathering, planting, and mulching.

The Center for Agroecology and Sustainable Food Systems

UC Santa Cruz, 1156 High Street, Santa Cruz 95064
(831) 459-4140, fax (831) 459-2799
website: http://zzyx.ucsc.edu/casfs

The center manages a 25-acre farm and a 4-acre garden and offers six-month internships, graduate and undergraduate programs in sustainable agriculture, and the biointensive gardening methods advocated by Alan Chadwick. Plants are sold from the new propagation facility at the garden. A membership friends group hosts events and tours, puts on a harvest festival, and publishes the semiannual *Cultivar.*

Committee for Sustainable Agriculture

406 Main Street, #313, Watsonville 95076
(831) 763-2111

Among their many virtues is this group's ability to define that very elusive concept of sustainability—"producing food and useful forest and fiber products in a way that is economically viable, environmentally sound, and socially just." They help spread the word about the benefits of organic gardening via their Eco Farm Conference and a series of workshops on topics like Landscape and Gardening and Strawberries and Vegetables.

Common Ground Organic Garden Supply/ Ecology Action of the Mid-Peninsula

2225 El Camino Real, Palo Alto 94306 (call to verify)
(650) 328-6752

This is a nonprofit research group dedicated to biointensive agricultural practices—showing that a small plot of land or mini-farm can be, when properly tended, highly productive and sustainable. There are weekend gardening classes and a library at their retail store and education center, Common Ground, in Palo Alto, where they also sell seeds, books, gardening supplies, and fine-gardening tools. Their research and training garden in Willits is not open to the public, although tours are given in the summer. They also run Bountiful Gardens, a mail-order seed and book business.

Community Environmental Council
Gildea Resource Center, 930 Miramonte Drive,
Santa Barbara 93109
(805) 963-0583

The nonprofit council operates a demonstration organic urban farm as part of its effort to demonstrate how all parts of any community are environmentally linked. The farm features greenhouses, orchards, composting activities, and herbal workshops. The council also administers three community gardens, recycling centers, household hazardous waste collections and programs; runs Earth Day celebrations; and does research on sustainable agriculture. Open weekdays, 9:00 am–5:00 pm.

East Bay Urban Gardeners (EBUG)
1801 Adeline Street, #208, Oakland 94607
(510) 834-5342

The headquarters for community gardening activities in the East Bay, working to "green up" urban open spaces while providing opportunities and rehabilitation for residents. Memberships.

Toni Fauver Wildflower Walks
559 Miner Road, Orinda 94563
(925) 254-3953

Toni Fauver will organize a walk for groups up to about 17 people anywhere in California north of Bakersfield and has also led tours to Switzerland. In the past 20 years she has covered a lot of ground.

She enjoys leading day or overnight walks on private ranches, public trails, or wherever you want to go. Her slide shows will delight interested groups.

Foothill Horticultural Society
P. O. Box 7, Grass Valley 95945
(530) 639-1226

Everyone should get the chance to join up with the more than 50 stalwart members of the horticultural nexus of the foothills. It is said they can identify most every plant and pest around. Monthly meetings with guest speakers, information sharing, and plant raffle are held on third Wednesdays at 7:00 pm, at the Nevada County Library community room, 980 Helling Way in Nevada City. Guests are welcome. Membership dues go to regional projects such as the restoration of Mathes Lake. Monthly newsletter.

Garden Literature Press
398 Columbus Avenue, Suite 181, Boston, MA 02116
(617) 424-1784, fax (617) 424-1712 Sally Williams
e-mail: gardenlit@bigpond.com

Garden Literature is an author and subject index of articles about plants and gardens. The short version, *Sprout*, covers a dozen or so of the leading magazines published in the US and UK and is published annually. The grand version, which covers 150 publications, is available only for the years 1992, 1993, and 1994.

The Gardeners of America
(formerly Men's Garden Clubs of America, Inc.)
P. O. Box 241, Johnston, IA 50131
(515) 278-0295, fax (515) 278-6245

This national organization is a collection of many local clubs who get together to further the cause of gardening through information sharing and community service programs. Started in 1932 as a gardening association for men, today it offers members a bi-monthly magazine and newsletters, slide contest, national award, lending library, and annual meeting.

Growing Native Research Institute
P. O. Box 489, Berkeley 94701
(510) 232-9865   Louise Lacey

Joining this organization gets you a bimonthly newsletter on the basics of gardening with natives— for pleasure, water conservation, wildlife habitat.

Hardy Plant Society of Oregon (HPSO)
1930 NW Lovejoy Street, Portland, OR 97209
(503) 244-5718

Semiannual bulletin, monthly newsletter, lectures and slide presentations on horticultural topics, and plant sales twice a year. Patterned after the Hardy Plant Society of Great Britain, this group is allied with other Hardy Plant groups around the US. HPSO has a number of California members, and has much information pertinent to Northern California gardens.

Harmony Farm Supply and Nursery
3244 Gravenstein Highway North, Sebastopol 95472
P. O. Box 460, Graton 95444 (mailing address)
(707) 823-9125, fax (707) 823-1734

A headquarters of biointensive and organic garden-ing, offering advice and selling seeds and supplies. The full-service retail nursery specializes in drought-tolerant and edible landscape plants and grows their own CCOF-certified organically grown vegetable starts.

Hobby Greenhouse Association
8 Glen Terrace, Bedford, MA 01730-2048
(617) 275-0377, fax (617) 275-5693
e-mail: jhale@world.std.com

Since 1980 the HGA has been encouraging and informing greenhouse, indoor, porch, and window gardeners. Members receive the quarterly *Hobby Greenhouse* magazine, a newsletter, chatty round robins, a seed exchange, and discounted books. Their unique and up-to-date *Directory of Manufacturers—Hobby Greenhouses, Solariums, Sunrooms and Window Greenhouses* is available for $2.50. Internet discussion group.

Horticultural Consortium of Santa Barbara
P. O. Box 1990, Santa Barbara 93102
(805) 564-5437   Jeff Cope

A network of individuals and groups who get together to promote horticulture and coordinate all horticultural activities in the area. Twice a year this group publishes *Santa Barbara Seasons*, a guide to horticultural sights and events. Anyone can join; meetings are on the third Thursday of every other month.

Mountain Gypsy Wildflower Seminars
14582 Alderwood Way, Nevada City 95959
(530) 265-4741

For more than 15 years, Julie Carville has been leading wildflower tours all over California for an afternoon, a week, or anything in between. More than just plant identification, her tours delve into the herbal and Native-American uses of wildflowers, botany, and eco-psychology. Her slide show will take you into the depth of the backcountry.

Marshall Olbrich Plant Club
P. O. Box 1338, Sebastopol 95473

A committed cluster of Bay Area plantspeople meet every other month to share information and hear knowledgeable speakers.

Pacific Horticulture
P. O. Box 485, Berkeley 94701
(510) 849-1627

Described in the *Royal Horticultural Society Gardener's Yearbook* (1996) as "the best of the American Gardening Magazines," *Pacific Horticulture* has earned a reputation worldwide for intelligent writing about Western gardening, broad coverage, and superb photography. Now with a 20-year cumulative index, it is a mine of relevant information for gardeners in this extraordinary climate. Articles by leading plantspeople provide a good read for those who know and for those who are just starting to know about the plants, people, places, challenges, and events which have shaped California's landscape. This quarterly magazine also serves as a valuable guide to horticultural resources and events.

San Diego Horticultural Society
1781 Sunrise Drive, Vista 92084
(760) 630-7307

The start-up energy is still flying around this society founded in 1994 to further the knowledge of horticulture. Four hundred members strong and growing, this group meets on second Mondays at 6:30 pm at Del Mar Fairgrounds to share information, hear speakers, and take advantage of specialty plant and book sales and raffle. Both professionals and amateurs will enjoy the opportunity to meet like-minded individuals. Garden tours twice a year. *The Plant Forum Compilation* is available for $10.

San Francisco League of Urban Gardeners
2088 Oakdale Avenue, San Francisco 94124
(415) 285-7584

San Francisco's nonprofit advocate for community greening and gardening programs, SLUG assists over 50 local gardens, maintains a demonstration garden (see Garden for the Environment), has a youth intern program, and offers weekend composting workshops and classes. Its line of vinegars and jams for sale, Urban Herbals, helps develop business skills for its gardener members, as well as some needed revenue. Call their Rotline for fast-breaking news about composting, (415) 285-7584.

Santa Barbara Horticultural Society
P. O. Box 4094, Santa Barbara 93140
(805) 965-1035

This society has been a focal point for plant lovers since its founding in 1880. Meetings on the first Wednesday of the month feature top-notch speakers from around the world and a plant raffle. Membership also brings you a monthly bulletin detailing plants discussed at the previous meeting, monthly garden tours, and the chance to help restore Franceschi Park. Their annual plant sale is usually held the last week of September.

Society for Ecological Restoration (Sercal)
915 L Street, #C-104, Sacramento 95814
(805) 634-9228 (memb. info.), fax (805) 634-9540

Dedicated to restoring damaged sites in order to establish historically correct ecosystems, Sercal offers members a chance to network with others interested in the subject, keep up-to-date with current scientific strategies, and develop ethical standards for restoration. Their quarterly newsletter, *Ecesis,* provides a calendar of related events and workshops.

The Southern California Gardener
P. O. Box 8072, Van Nuys 91409-8072
(310) 396-3083, fax (310) 396-7934

A bimonthly newsletter covering most everything you would ever want to know about gardening in Southern California. It can put you in touch with new resources, introductions, and ideas appropriate to your area.

Southern California Horticultural Society
P. O. Box 41080, Los Angeles 90041-0080
(818) 567-1496

The hub of horticultural interest in Southern California since 1935, the society offers something of value for every level of plant devotee. University professors and amateur photographers share information at evening meetings on second Thursdays which include a speaker, plant raffle, plant forum, plant sale, and occasional book sale.

Western Horticultural Society
P. O. Box 60507, Palo Alto 94306
(650) 856-6454

Well-known nurseryman William Schmidt got this group together in 1963 as an offshoot of the California Horticultural Society, at a time when more folks were moving down the Peninsula and the evening commute back to San Francisco for meetings proved increasingly daunting. Monthly meetings including a speaker, information sharing, plant displays, and a raffle and are held on second Wednesdays, September through May. Western Hort has published *Successful Perennials for the Peninsula* and, in 1996, *Successful Vines*.

PLANT GROUPS

The following national societies can put you in touch with local chapters, but are themselves worth joining for their publications, plant sources, and wealth of information about your specific interest. Local chapters usually hold plant sales at the informative monthly meetings and give members access to energetic, like-minded people.

African Violet Society of America
2375 North Street, Beaumont, Texas 77702
(800) 770-AVSA, fax (409) 839-4329

Benefits: Bimonthly magazine, national convention, entry into all shows, judges' training, use of library. Thirty-five California chapters hold monthly meetings and put on local shows and plant sales.

American Begonia Society
157 Monument Road, Rio Dell 95562
(707) 764-5407

Benefits: Bimonthly *Begonian,* national show, round robin letter-writing for those with no local chapters, bookstore, seed fund for members only. About 20 California chapters sell plants at their monthly meetings and local shows.

American Bonsai Society
P. O. Box 1136, Puyallup, WA 98371-1136
website: www.absbonsai.org

Benefits: Quarterly *Bonsai Journal,* price reductions on selected books, national symposium, small lending library. The ABS is an organization of individuals and has no affiliated chapters, however they can direct you to local clubs and sources.

American Camellia Society
One Massee Lane, Fort Valley, GA 31030
(912) 967-2358, fax (912) 967-2083
website: www.acs.home.ml.org

Benefits: Quarterly *Camellia Journal,* yearbook,
culture booklet to new members, books for sale, and
slide sets for use in programs. Thirteen California
chapters hold meetings and sales of members' plants.

American Clematis Society
P. O. Box 17085, Irvine 92623-7085
(949) 224-9885, e-mail: clematissc@aol.com
website: www.clematis.org

Benefits: Bimonthly newsletter, tours, discounts,
plant sales. The very first (and only) US clematis
society, started in 1996.

American Conifer Society
P. O. Box 360, Keswick, VA 22947-0360
(804) 984-3660, fax same

Benefits: Quarterly bulletin, book discounts, seed
exchanges, plant sales, and auctions at meetings.
This national organization is divided into four
regions offering various activities, including workshops and visits to gardens and nurseries. All
inquiries receive *A Brief Look at Garden Conifers*
for SASE, which includes a listing of gardens with
extensive conifer collections. Sample bulletins
available for $5. No local chapters.

American Daffodil Society
4126 Winfield Road, Columbus, OH 43220-4606
(614) 451-4747, fax (614) 451-2177
e-mail: NLiggett@compuserve.com

Benefits: Quarterly *Daffodil Journal*—64-page
magazine about growing, showing, and what's new
in daffodils. Annual convention, lending library, round

robin letters among members. Northern California has a chapter which holds bulb sales.

American Dahlia Society
One Rock Falls Court, Rockville, MD 20854
(202) 326-3516, (301) 424-6641, fax (202) 326-3516
e-mail: AFisher@ftc.gov

Benefits: Quarterly bulletin (400+ pages, includes color photos, articles, and ads for commercial growers), annual classification handbook, *Growing Guide*, $3 or complimentary to new members. Seven California chapters hold tuber sales, shows, and meetings.

American Fern Society
website: www.visuallink.net/fern/#intro

Benefits: Newsletter *Fiddlehead Forum*. Also fern forays into woods each August.

American Fuchsia Society
San Francisco County Fair Building
Ninth Avenue and Lincoln Way, San Francisco 94122
(408) 257-0752, e-mail: sydnor@ix.netcom.com
website: http://members.aol.com/amfuchsias

Benefits: Bimonthly bulletin (individual issues devoted to newsletters from around the world, yearly introductions, commercial sources of fuchsias), culture book, bookstore, lending library, biannual convention in California, cuttings exchange in April. Twenty-one California chapters offer local activities.

American Hemerocallis Society
P. O. Box 10, Dexter, GA 31019
(912) 875-4110
website: www.daylilies.org/daylilies.html

Benefits: Quarterly *Daylily Journal*, round robin letter campaign for those with specific interests in daylilies (doubles, miniatures, spiders, etc.), and regional meetings and national convention which include tours and lectures. For a small fee there is a slide and video library, specialty booklets including *The AHS Good Humor Book,* and 80-page *Beginner's Handbook.*

American Hibiscus Society
P. O. Box 321540, Cocoa Beach, FL 32932-1540
(407) 783-2576, fax same

Benefits: Quarterly *Seed Pod,* seed bank of hand-pollinated seeds solicited from members for distribution, national convention, bookstore, training of judges. *Hibiscus Handbook* available for a fee. No California chapters.

American Iris Society
c/o Ruth Simmons, Route 1, Box 67, Walters, OK 73572
(580) 875-2271, fax same
e-mail: ruth@sonetcom.com

Benefits: Quarterly bulletin, which contains a commercial sources directory; access to various round robin letters on different topics; 32-page booklet, *Basic Iris Culture.* There are 25 local "affiliates" in California and seven nationwide "sections" devoted to a particular type of iris (such as Japanese, Spuria, Pacific Coast native, etc.). All national society members are assigned to regions (California has two) from which they get regional information, which includes a description of the activities of local affiliates and their plant sales and shows.

American Ivy Society
P. O. Box 2123, Naples, FL 34106-2123
(937) 862-4700, or (941) 261-0785

Benefits: *Between the Vines* published three times a year, newsletter, annual ivy journal.

American Penstemon Society
1569 South Holland Court, Lakewood, CO 80232
(303) 986-8096

Benefits: Semiannual bulletin, beginner's manual, annual meeting, field trips (often with the Rock Garden Society), source list, seed exchange. The APS has no local chapters.

American Rhododendron Society
11 Pinecrest Drive, Fortuna 95540
(707) 725-3043, fax (707) 725-1217
website: www.rhododendron.org

Benefits: Quarterly journal (full color), annual meeting in spring, book discounts, seed exchange, pollen bank. Six California chapters offer programs, cuttings exchanges, plant sales, and local growing information.

American Rose Society
P. O. Box 30000, Shreveport, LA 71130-0030
(318) 938-5402, fax (318) 938-5405

Benefits: Monthly *American Rose Magazine,* (December issue is *American Rose Annual)*, lending library, brochures issued quarterly, listing of rose sources, rose testing program and judges' training. A whopping 49 chapters and affiliated societies in California give everyone a chance to get local information.

Bromeliad Society International
P. O. Box 12981, Gainsville, FL 32604-0981
(352) 372-6589, fax (352) 372-8823
website: www.bsi.org

Benefits: Bimonthly journal, world conference, *Hybrid Checklist.*

Cactus and Succulent Society of America
1535 Reeves Street, Los Angeles 90035
(310) 556-1923, fax (310) 286-9629
e-mail: u4bia@aol.com

Benefits: Bimonthly *Cactus and Succulent Journal,*
containing information about plant sources, Seed
Depot, chance to join round robins (circulating
letters on all segments of hobby), biennial national
convention. Twenty-one California chapters.

California Native Grass Association
P. O. Box 72405, Davis 95617
website: www.mbay.net/~cnga/

Benefits: Quarterly newsletters with information
about native grass vendors, the practicalities of
planting and articles about the success stories of
native grass reintroductions. Grass ID Day and a
Field Day held yearly. This network of agronomists,
growers of native grasses, county planners, environmental consultants, ranchers, and interested individuals are working to promote the use of and
restore native grasses in California.

California Native Plant Society
1722 J Street, #17, Sacramento 95814
(916) 447-2677, fax (916) 447-2727
website: www.calpoly.edu/~dchippin/cnps_main.html

There are 30 chapters of this venerable organization
dedicated to the preservation of native flora, increasing public knowledge about native plants, and
monitoring rare and endangered species. All chapters have informative meetings, field trips, and sales
of hard-to-find native plants. Groups within the
chapters focus on subjects such as photography,
gardening with natives, rare and endangered plants,
and removal of invasive exotics. The Society publishes a bulletin and *Fremontia,* a quarterly magazine. Some local chapters have monthly newsletters.

California Rare Fruit Growers

P. O. Box 6850, Fullerton 92834-6850
(714) 278-3579
e-mail: info@CRFG.org, website: www.CRFG.org

Benefits: Bimonthly *Fruit Gardener,* January scion
exchange. If you are interested in weird and wonderful tropical and subtropical (some temperate) fruits
and vegetables, it pays to join; plants offered here
are available nowhere else. Headquartered at Cal State
Fullerton, CRFG has 16 California chapters offering
informational meetings, plant raffle, and special tours.

Calochortus Society

P. O. Box 1306, Sebastopol 95473
(707) 829-2729

Benefits: Quarterly newsletter, each concentrating on
one species (with color photo) and containing general
information on the genus' biology, habitat, and cultural
requirements. Free seeds distributed to members in
October. Started in 1989 to spread the word that
Calochortus could grow in cultivated gardens.

Gardenia Society of America

P. O. Box 879, Atwater 95301
(209) 358-2231

Benefits: Quarterly *Growing Gardenias*, newsletters,
commercial plant source listing. National organization only; no local chapters.

Heritage Rose Foundation

1512 Gorman Street, Raleigh, NC 27606
(919) 834-2591

Benefits: Quarterly *Heritage Rose Foundation News,*
commercial sources listing, information sheets, annual
conference. This nonprofit corporation emphasizes
the preservation and study of old roses and will help
you identify those in your community. No chapters.

Heritage Roses Group
c/o Beverly Dobson
1034 Taylor Avenue, Alameda 94501

Benefits: Quarterly newsletter, round robin letter
service. Less of a national organization and more of
a federation of regional groups, Heritage Roses
Group can help you find local help.

International Bulb Society
P. O. Box 92136, Pasadena 91109-2136
website: www.bulbsociety.com

Benefits: Annual publication *Herbertia*, biannual
newsletter, seed exchange and e-mail, Blue Forum.

International Carnivorous Plant Society, Inc.
3310 East Yorba Linda Boulevard #330, Fullerton 92831
e-mail: icps@carnivorousplants.org
website: www.carnivorousplants.org

Benefits: Quarterly newsletter (28 pages, color
photographs), access to seed bank, plant resources
listing. Searchable taxonomic database:
www.hpl.hp/com/bot/cp_home. To join their very
active listserv, send a message containing the single
line "SUB CP (your name)" to
listserv@opus.hpl.hp.com. Two California chapters.

International Geranium Society
P. O. Box 92734, Pasadena 91109-2734
(760) 727-0309

Benefits: Quarterly *Geraniums Around the World*,
seed center including seeds not in commercial catalogues. Seven California chapters do shows and events.

International Oleander Society

P. O. Box 3431, Galveston, TX 77552-0431
(409) 762-9334

Benefits: Quarterly *Nerium News,* informational
brochures, culture book, seed and cuttings exchange
(for small handling fee). No chapters.

Monterey Bay International Fern Society

Chaparral Road, Carmel Valley 93924
(831) 659-4104

Benefits: Bimonthly *Fern Journal,* bookstore, lending
library, annual show, monthly meetings, access to
Spore Store.

National Chrysanthemum Society

10107 Homar Pond Drive, Fairfax Station, VA 22039
(703) 978-7981

Benefits: Quarterly *Chrysanthemum,* annual show
and symposia, pamphlets on specific topics such as
bonsai, rooting, and propagating. A primer, *The
Beginner's Handbook,* is given to all new members.
California has three local chapters which put on shows,
do group plant orders, and hold plant swaps and sales.

North American Fruit Explorers

Route One, Chapin, IL 62628
(217) 245-7589

Benefits: Quarterly *Pomona* which includes an
exchange page identifying suppliers of rare fruit,
lending library via the mail. Nafex promotes interest
in rare, antique, or very new fruits for temperate
climates, such as mulberries, pawpaws, native fruits,
unusual pears and apples. No California chapters.

North American Heather Society
11 Pinecrest, Fortuna 95540
(707) 725-3452

Benefits: Quarterly *Heather News,* pamphlets and
growing guides sent to all inquiries. The NAHS is
developing a program to provide technical support
to improve heather plantings in public gardens.
There are two chapters in California, one of which
holds the largest sale of heathers in America each
September in Eureka.

North American Lily Society
P. O. Box 272, Owatonna, MN 55060
(507) 451-2170
website: www.lilies.org/aboutnal/aboutnal.htm

Benefits: Quarterly bulletin, annual meeting, yearbook directory of members and activities. Website
includes information and a subscription listserv.

North American Rock Garden Society
P. O. Box 67, Millwood, NY 10546
(914) 762-2948

Benefits: Quarterly magazine, annual summer
meeting, regional winter study meeting (Western
chapter: 2699 Shasta Road, Berkeley 94708), seed
exchange, sponsorship of trips and international
speakers. Chapters hold plant sales at meetings.

Perennial Plant Club of Sacramento
668 Hancock Drive, Folsom 95630
(916) 985-4262

Started in 1988, this membership group offers
lectures, information sharing, garden tours, and
symposia. Monthly meetings are on the fourth
Thursday of the month at 7:30 pm, September
through March, at the Sacramento Art and Garden
Center.

SCHOOLS AND COLLEGES

The following California schools and colleges offer certificate programs and/or degrees in the following fields related to horticulture and landscaping.

COMMUNITY COLLEGES

American River College
4700 College Oak Drive
Sacramento 95841
(916) 484-8011
Ornamental Horticulture
Forestry

Antelope Valley College
3041 West Avenue K
Lancaster 93536
(805) 722-6300
Ornamental Horticulture

Bakersfield College
1801 Panorama Drive
Bakersfield 93304
(805) 395-4511
Ornamental Horticulture

Butte College
3536 Butte Campus Drive
Oroville 95965
(530) 895-2381
Ornamental Horticulture

Cabrillo College
6500 Soquel Drive
Aptos 95003
(831) 479-6100
Greenhouse Management
Ornamental Horticulture
Landscape Design & Installation

Cerritos Community College
11110 Alondra Blvd.
Norwalk 90650
(562) 860-2451
Landscape Maintenance
Ornamental Horticulture

City College of San Francisco
50 Phelan Avenue
San Francisco 94112
(415) 239-3000
Environmental Horticulture
Floristry

College of Marin
Kentfield 94904
(415) 457-8811
Landscape Construction
& Management
Nursery Management
Landscape Management

College of San Mateo
1700 West Hillsdale Blvd.
San Mateo 94402
(650) 574-6161
Ornamental Horticulture
Floristry

College of the Desert
43-500 Monterey Avenue
Palm Desert 92260
(760) 346-8041
Ornamental Horticulture
Plant Science
Turfgrass Management

College of the Redwoods
Thompkins Hill Road
Eureka 95501
(707) 445-6700
Forestry
Plant Science

College of the Sequoias
2245 South Linwood
Visalia 93277
(209) 730-3700
Floral Technology & Design
Landscape Technology
Nursery Technology
Ornamental Horticulture
Plant Science

College of the Siskiyous
800 College Avenue
Weed 96094
(530) 938-4463
Landscape Design
Landscape Maintenance

Cosumnes River College
8401 Center Parkway
Sacramento 95823
(916) 688-7451
Environmental Design
Landscape Maintenance
Nursery Operations

Cuyamaca College
2950 Jamacha Road
El Cajon 92019
(619) 670-1980
Landscape Technology
Nursery Technology
Floristry

Diablo Valley College
321 Golf Club Road
Pleasant Hill 94523
(925) 685-1230
Ornamental Horticulture

El Camino College
16007 Crenshaw Blvd.
Via Torrance 90506
(310) 532-3670
Ornamental Horticulture

Foothill College
12345 El Monte Road
Los Altos Hills 94022
(650) 949-7777
Landscape Horticulture
Nursery Management

Fullerton Community College
321 East Chapman Avenue
Fullerton 92832
(714) 992-7000
Landscape Design
Landscape Management
Greenhouse/Nursery Production
Pest Management

Kings River Community College
995 North Reed Avenue
Reedley 93654
(209) 638-3641
Ornamental Horticulture
Landscape Horticulture

Las Positas College
3033 Collier Canyon Road
Livermore 94550
(925) 373-5800
Ornamental Horticulture

Long Beach City College
1305 East Pacific Coast Highway
Long Beach 90806
(562) 938-3086
Ornamental Horticulture
Landscape Maintenance
Landscape Design
Landscape Construction
Integrated Pest Management

Los Angeles Pierce College
6201 Winnetka Avenue
Woodlands Hills 91371
(818) 719-6400
Ornamental Horticulture
Floral Design

Mendocino College
P. O. Box 3000
Ukiah 95482
(707) 468-3100
Ornamental Horticulture

Merced College
3600 M Street
Merced 95348
(209) 384-6000
Landscape Horticulture

Merritt College
12500 Campus Drive
Oakland 94619
(510) 531-4911
Landscape Horticulture

Mira Costa College
One Barnard Drive
Oceanside 92056
(760) 757-2121
Ornamental Horticulture
Nursery Production
Landscape Management
Plant Pest

Modesto Junior College
435 College Avenue
Modesto 95350
(209) 575-6498
Landscape Architecture
Ornamental Horticulture
Commercial Floristry

Monterey Peninsula College
980 Fremont Street
Monterey 93940
(831) 646-4000
Ornamental Horticulture
Floral Design

Mt. San Antonio College
1100 North Grand Avenue
Walnut 91789
(909) 594-5611
Ornamental Horticulture
Landscape Irrigation

Ohlone College
43600 Mission Blvd.
Fremont 94939
(510) 659-6000
Landscape Horticulture

Orange Coast College
2701 Fairview Road
Costa Mesa 92628
(949) 432-0202
Ornamental Horticulture

Palo Verde College
811 West Chanslorway
Blythe 92225
(760) 922-6168
Plants of the Desert

Saddleback Community College
28000 Marguerite Parkway
Mission Viejo 92692
(949) 582-4500
Ornamental Horticulture
Landscape Design

San Diego Mesa College
7250 Mesa College Drive
San Diego 92111
(619) 627-2600
Nursery Landscape Technology
Landscape Architecture

San Joaquin Delta College
5151 Pacific Avenue
Stockton 95207
(209) 954-5151
Ornamental Horticulture
Plant Science

Santa Barbara City College
721 Cliff Drive
Santa Barbara 93109
(805) 965-0581
Environmental Landscape Design
Horticulture Maintenance
Nursery/Greenhouse
　　Technologies
Regenerative & Restoration
　　Horticulture
Horticulture Science
Environmental Horticulture

Santa Rosa Junior College
1501 Mendocino Avenue
Santa Rosa 95401
(707) 527-4011
Landscape Management
Nursery Production
Plant Science

Shasta College
P. O. Box 496006
Redding 96049
(530) 225-4827
Ornamental Horticulture
Floral Design

Sierra College
5000 Rocklin Road
Rocklin 95677
(916) 624-3333
Ornamental Horticulture

Solano Community College
4000 Suisun Valley Road
Suisun 94585
(707) 864-7000
Ornamental Horticulture

Southwestern College
900 Otay Lake Road
Chula Vista 91910
(619) 421-6700
Landscape Design
Landscape Architecture
Landscape Occupations
Nursery Occupations
Floral Design

Ventura College
4667 Telegraph Road
Ventura 93003
(805) 642-3211
Environmental Horticulture
Plant Science

Victor Valley College
18422 Bear Valley Road
Victorville 92392
(760) 245-4271 ext 2238
Ornamental Horticulture
Floral Design
Irrigation
Landscape Installation
Nursery Technology

Yuba College
41605 Gibson Road
Woodland 95776
(530) 661-5700
Plant Science
Environmental Horticulture

STATE COLLEGES

California Polytechnic State University
3801 West Temple Avenue
Pomona 91768
(909) 869-7659
Landscape Architecture
Ornamental Horticulture, specializing in:
Horticultural Science
Landscape Management
Nursery Management

California Polytechnic State University
San Luis Obispo 93407
(805) 756-1111
Environmental Horticultural Sciences
Landscape Architecture

California State University
Plant Sciences Department
2415 East San Ramon, AS 72
Fresno 93740
(559) 278-2861
Ornamental Horticulture

UNIVERSITY PROGRAMS

University of California at Berkeley
Department of Landscape Architecture
Wurster Hall
Berkeley 94720
(510) 642-4022

University of California at Berkeley Extension
1995 University Avenue
Berkeley 94720
(510) 642-4111
Certificate programs in Garden Design and Landscape Architecture

University of California at Davis
1 Shields Avenue
Davis 95616
Department of Environmental Horticulture (530) 752-0130
Department of Landscape Architecture (530) 752-3907

University of California at Irvine Extension
P. O. Box 6050
Irvine 92616
(949) 824-1010
Certificate program in Landscape Architecture

University of California at Santa Cruz
Santa Cruz 95064
Center for Agroecology, (831) 459-4140
Six months intensive hands-on study of ecological horticulture
Board of Environmental Studies, (831) 459-3718
Undergraduate programs

UNIVERSITY OF CALIFORNIA COOPERATIVE EXTENSION

This statewide network of county offices is a public service program funded by the state of California making the wisdom of University of California faculty accessible to the public. Cooperative Extension was set up to offer expertise in agriculture, environmental horticulture, home ecomonics, marine sciences, nutrition, and youth development (4-H), though programs vary from county to county. Very decentralized, there is no main number to call for an overview. Each county office is staffed by university faculty and a cadre of volunteers. Many offer a Master Gardener program, training volunteers about good gardening practices so that they may pass along their knowledge and set up community gardening and clean-up projects. Here is where you can find out what is eating your dahlia or your tomato and what to do about it. E-mail addresses follow this pattern: ealameda@ucdavis.edu, ceamador@ucdavis.edu

Alameda County
Hayward, (510) 885-3605

Amador County
Jackson, (209) 223-6482

Butte County
Oroville, (530) 538-7201

Calaveras County
San Andreas, (209) 754-6477

Colusa County
Colusa, (530) 458-0570

Contra Costa County
Pleasant Hill, (925) 646-6540

Del Norte County
Crescent City, (707) 464-4711

El Dorado County
Placerville, (530) 621-5502

Fresno County
Fresno, (209) 456-7285

Glenn County
Orland, (530) 865-1107

Humboldt County
Eureka, (707) 445-7351

Imperial County
Holtville, (760) 352-9474

Inyo-Mono Counties
Bishop, (760) 873-7854

Kern County
Bakersfield, (805) 868-6200

Kings County
Hanford, (209) 582-3211, ext.
2730

Lake County
Lakeport, (707) 263-2281

Lassen County
Susanville, (530) 257-6363

Los Angeles County
Lancaster, (805) 723-4477
Los Angeles, (323) 223-3955

Madera County
Madera, (209) 675-7879

Mariposa County
Mariposa, (209) 966-2417

Mendocino County
Ukiah, (707) 463-4495

Merced County
Merced, (209) 385-7403

Modoc County
Alturas, (530) 233-6400

Monterey County
King City, (408) 385-3618
Salinas, (408) 759-7350

Napa County
Napa, (707) 253-4221

Orange County
Costa Mesa, (714) 708-1606

Placer-Nevada Counties
Auburn, (530) 889-7385

Nevada County
Grass Valley, (530) 273-4563

Plumas-Sierra Counties
Quincy, (530) 283-6270

Riverside County
Morena Valley, (909) 683-6491

Sacramento County
Sacramento, (916) 278-6011

San Benito County
Hollister, (408) 637-5346

San Bernardino County
San Bernardino, (909) 387-2171

San Diego County
San Diego, (619) 694-2845

San Joaquin County
Stockton, (209) 468-2085

San Luis Obispo County
San Luis Obispo, (805) 781-5940

San Mateo-San Francisco Counties
Half Moon Bay, (650) 726-9059

Santa Barbara County
Santa Maria, (805) 934-6240

Santa Clara County
San Jose, (408) 299-2635

Santa Cruz County
Watsonville, (408) 763-8040

Shasta-Trinity Counties
Redding, (530) 224-4900

Siskiyou County
Yreka, (530) 842-2711

Solano County
Fairfield, (707) 421-6790

Sonoma County
Santa Rosa, (707) 527-2621

Stanislaus County
Modesto, (209) 525-6800

Sutter Yuba Counties
Yuba City, (530) 822-7515

Tehama County
Red Bluff, (530) 527-3101

Tulare County
Visalia, (209) 733-6363

Tuolumne County
Sonora, (209) 533-5695

Ventura County
Ventura, (805) 645-1451

Yolo County
Woodland, (530) 666-8143

PLANT INDEX

The nurseries cross-referenced here are those with significant collections or introductions of the mentioned plant genus. Other nurseries, not so indicated, may also carry the genus. It may be helpful when looking for a specific plant also to look under a broader category for that plant. For example, to find other vendors of madrone, look under California native plants or drought-tolerant plants.

GENERAL INDEX

Horticultural attractions are set in italics.

NOTES

NOTES

NOTES